CHUVALO

GEORGE CHUVALO

WITH MURRAY GREIG

CHUVALO

A FIGHTER'S LIFE

THE STORY OF
BOXING'S LAST GLADIATOR

HarperCollins*Publishers*Ltd

HarperCollins Publishers Ltd
2 Bloor Street East, 20th Floor
Toronto, Ontario, Canada
M4W 1A8

www.harpercollins.ca

Library and Archives Canada Cataloguing in Publication
information is available upon request

ISBN 978-1-44341-734-1

Printed and bound in the United States of America
RRD 9 8 7 6 5 4 3 2

This is dedicated to my sons who are gone; to Lynne; to my beautiful grandchildren; and to the memory of my loving granddaughter Rachel—she was the beloved daughter of my late son Steven and his wife, Jacqueline; step-daughter of Tim Rowley; loving sister of Jesse; niece of Mitchell and Vanessa and my late sons Jessie and Georgie Lee; and cousin of Aaron, Elijah, Michaella and Adelayde. Rachel was a high-school teacher who spoke three languages, English, French and Spanish. In high school she received the Governor General's Award for Academic Excellence, and school principals commended her efforts in tutoring and helping other kids who weren't doing as well. She loved Zumba dancing and was an instructor and also taught school for a year in Veracruz, Mexico, and Pine Lake, Saskatchewan. Rachel passed away as we were completing this book on February 28, 2013. She had set aside money in her will for a Métis child to attend university or college. Joanne and I miss her deeply.

WEIGHING

IN

PART
ONE

BITING INTO A BIG, FAT CHOCOLATE EASTER EGG. That's my first conscious memory of life. And today, nearly 75 years later, I can close my eyes and still recall the sticky sweetness and intoxicating aroma as I contentedly munched that sumptuous treat, which was a gift from my godfather.

The momentous occasion took place in the spring of 1939 at my uncle Tony's house, not far from my childhood home on Hook Avenue in the heart of the Junction, an ethnic working-class neighborhood on the west side of Toronto.

Fast-forward four decades and a few miles east, to St. Lawrence Market at the corner of Jarvis and Front streets. It's December 11, 1978. That night I climbed through the ropes for the 93rd time as a professional fighter, aiming to do what I'd done 63 times previously: make the other guy see the black lights. That's how old-timers described what it feels like to drift into unconsciousness.

On this occasion, the "other guy" was George Jerome, a plodding, nondescript logging-camp cook from Vancouver

with a record of 11–11–5. That he was ranked the No. 1 challenger for the Canadian heavyweight title that I'd owned,
almost continuously, since 1958 only underscored how low the
sport had sunk in a country that has produced some of boxing's all-time greats—guys like George Dixon, Sam Langford,
Tommy Burns and Johnny Coulon.

The 2,000 fans jamming the joint couldn't have cared less
who was in the opposite corner; they were there for the blood
sacrifice. That crowd was a far cry from the 15,000-plus who
once routinely watched me headline at Madison Square Garden,
and the $7,500 payday was a fraction of what I'd gotten to slug
it out with the likes of Muhammad Ali, Joe Frazier and George
Foreman just a few years earlier, but I was too keyed up to think
about the past. I was 41 years old and doing the only thing I
ever wanted to do, the one thing I was born to do. I didn't care
who was standing in front of me; I just wanted to whack him
hard enough to make him see those black lights.

That was my rush. That's what I lived for.

It was even better than that chocolate Easter egg.

Jerome didn't put up much of a fight. Midway through the
second round I hurt him against the ropes with a three-punch
combination, then backed him up with a left hook to the ribs.
As he dropped his hands in anticipation of another body shot, I
ripped another left upstairs that split his forehead like a melon,
slicing open a two-inch gash above his right eye. Within seconds his face was a mask of blood, and the crowd went nuts. At
the end of the round, the ring doctor examined the wound and
ordered the fight stopped.

Jerome's corner didn't complain. If he had come out again,
he might have needed a blood transfusion.

Did I feel bad for the guy? Not a bit. It was just another night at the office. The only thing I was concerned about was that my beautiful 11-year-old daughter, Vanessa, was in the crowd. She'd never seen her daddy "work" before, and she looked a little scared. I could only imagine what was going through her head.

I didn't know it at the time, but that would be my last fight.

Jerome was the 35th opponent I dispatched in three rounds or less and my 64th knockout in 73 pro victories—a KO-per-win ratio of 87.6 per cent. It wasn't until 1997, when I was inducted into the World Boxing Hall of Fame in Los Angeles, that my buddy, *Edmonton Sun* columnist Murray Greig, pointed out that Bob Fitzsimmons (89.5), George Foreman (89.4) and Mike Tyson (88.1) were the only lineal world heavyweight champions up to that time with a higher ratio.

But nobody talked about my punching. I got far more ink during my career for having a great chin and for never being knocked down, but for a long time I thought those were negative accolades. Until my first fight with Ali in 1966, nobody mentioned my chin, but afterward it was big news. After I retired, some writers declared I had the best chin in boxing history. If that's true, I chalk it up to three things: being born with a short neck, training to absorb punishment (like a linebacker in football), and chewing a lot of bubble gum to strengthen my jaw muscles.

I'm prouder of the fact that, on the way to compiling a record of 73–18–2, I had more knockouts than both Jack Dempsey (47) and Joe Louis (51), and my 64 KOs are more than Rocky Marciano, Ali, Frazier or Tyson had total fights.

Never kissing the canvas will undoubtedly be my lasting legacy in boxing, but there was a lot more to my career than that. Today, most people think I was a tough guy who took a good rap, which is fine. But I was a much better defensive fighter than I ever got credit for. I didn't get hit with half the punches people think I did. If that were true, I'd be walking around on my heels today. Nobody's that tough.

I'll be remembered as a guy who fought the best of his time, beat a lot of them and lost to some others. I was a world-ranked contender for the better part of two decades, during the reigns of some of the greatest heavyweight champions in history. I knocked on their door a few times, but was I satisfied with that? Hell, no! If you've never been champion of the world, you can never be 100 per cent satisfied.

A fighter always thinks he could've done better than he did, and I'm no different. There's always a gnawing feeling that I might have become a world champ; there's a piece of me that always feels kind of incomplete. Still, I did better than most guys. I won the Canadian amateur title at 17, then held the national professional championship for almost 20 years. I was ranked No. 2 in the world at one time; not many can say that.

Was it worth all the blood and the sweat and heartaches?

Absolutely. Besides, what else could I have become? With education and the right breaks, anyone can aspire to become a doctor or a lawyer—but you have to know real poverty to want to earn your living as a fighter. During much of my career, poverty was a constant companion.

If I could go back and change anything, I would've had better management right from the start and I'd have forced myself to become a southpaw, too. Left-handers are the worst guys to fight because they do everything ass-backwards—but that's a big advantage if you're the guy doing the punching.

I also should have fought out of a crouch more; I stood too straight a lot of times. When people see film of some of my early fights, they're always surprised that I started out as a boxer, a stick-and-move guy. It wasn't until I moved to Detroit that I really learned to use my strength and became more of a brawler. But even when they see it, a lot of folks don't believe it. In their eyes I was always just a "catcher" who never threw anything back.

Maybe they should check with those 64 guys I knocked out.

Throughout my career, a lot of members of the press were just as ignorant. I always found it curious that writers in New York and Detroit and Miami were more knowledgeable about me than their counterparts in Toronto. The media in my hometown was always very negative, even when I won. A lot of the hacks writing about boxing in those days weren't qualified to be writing grocery lists. They didn't know the first thing about the game, so they all jumped on the same bandwagon. They'd write that I was "punch drunk" or that I should quit before I got brain damage. To them, I was a freak of nature, a human shock absorber. Reading the old clippings, you'd think I never did anything except get hit.

I wasn't contemplating retirement after I knocked out Jerome on that December night in '78. I was still in love with the sport, in love with its culture and atmosphere. And more than anything, I wanted a crack at the British Commonwealth title—something I'd been chasing for more than two decades. But the pipsqueaks in the Canadian Professional Boxing Federation never lifted a finger to help make that happen, even though in the world rankings I was ahead of Commonwealth champions like Henry Cooper, Jack Bodell and Danny McAlinden for the better part of two decades. Not once did the faint-hearted Canadian authorities pressure the British Boxing

Board to get me a title shot. Neither did my so-called manager, Irving Ungerman. He was too busy with the movers and shakers in New York, so advancing my career in that direction was little more than an afterthought. Irving never considered the Commonwealth title worth pursuing.

The CPBF took away my Canadian title for what they called "inactivity," but it was really just bullshit politics. At 75, I could come back and win it tomorrow. Or 10 years after I'm dead.

In early 1979, I accepted an offer to defend against Trevor Berbick in Edmonton for $38,000, but the Federation turned around and dictated that the fight had to be in Halifax—Berbick's adopted hometown—because they said the Edmonton promoter, my buddy Nick Zubray, "wasn't qualified." He'd only done 14 of my previous fights, including three Canadian title defenses, and with Murray Pezim he co-promoted my 1972 bout with Muhammad Ali in Vancouver. On top of that, I'd only get $25,000 in Halifax. I started a lawsuit to set things right, but my lawyers told me even if I won, there was no money in it. So I thought, "Screw you, you gutless bastards." And I quit.

It wasn't the best way to go out, but I did it on my own terms. A lot of fighters have their careers aborted early, so they're always saying, "I wish I could have done this or that." Not me. I fought six world champions, I headlined nine times in the Mecca of boxing, Madison Square Garden, and I fought in the golden era of heavyweights against some of the best ever.

I had a good shot at it all, and I enjoyed every single minute. But I digress.

To me, boxing has always represented the purest and truest form of athletic competition. It's much more natural to fight than it is to play football or hockey. A caveman or an alien from another planet would understand boxing, but he sure as hell wouldn't understand golf or tennis.

It's all about respect for power—and no other sport more clearly demonstrates one man's superiority over another. When a guy goes down for the 10 count and can't get back on his feet, everybody knows who won. I guess I was lucky, because I never had to deal with getting back on my feet. Not in the ring, anyway.

Outside the ropes has been a different story.

What's happened to my family and me since I left boxing has been a personal holocaust. If you added up every punch I ever took and then multiplied the total by 10,000, it wouldn't begin to equal the pain of losing three sons and a wife to drugs and suicide.

It started in the spring of 1984 when my youngest son, Jesse, tore off his left kneecap in a dirt bike accident just a few weeks after his 20th birthday. Complex surgery repaired the damage but left him in constant pain. Not long after the surgery, Jesse went to a party, where he complained to someone about the pain in his knee. That someone replied he had something that would help—and that was my son's introduction to heroin. Unable to live with what quickly became a full-blown addiction, on February 18, 1985, Jesse went into his bedroom, put the barrel of a .22-caliber rifle in his mouth and pulled the trigger.

When you have one heroin addict in the family, it's almost a guarantee there will be more. Son number three, Georgie Lee, was next. He died on Halloween night, 1993, in a seedy Toronto hotel room. He was still seated in a chair, wearing only a pair of undershorts, with a syringe sticking out of his left arm.

Four days after Georgie Lee died, my wife, Lynne, scrawled out a short suicide note and gulped down a handful of Fiorinal.

Haunted by the special pain that only a mother can feel, she simply couldn't bear it any longer. First Jesse, then Georgie Lee. It was too much for her.

By 1996 I'd remarried and was looking forward to embarking on a cross-Canada tour with son number two, Steven, after his release from prison for drugstore robberies. Like Jesse and Georgie Lee, Stevie was a heroin addict, but he was determined to beat it. *The Fifth Estate*, a Canadian Broadcasting Corporation television program, even featured us in a documentary. Stevie and I were going to tour the country together to tell the story of how drugs destroyed our family. But it was not to be.

On August 17, 1996—11 days after his release—Steven was found dead in his sister Vanessa's apartment. She had gone to visit friends out of town but had told him she'd be back the following afternoon. Stevie was found slumped over a desk, clad in a pair of undershorts. There was a syringe sticking out of his left arm and an unlit cigarette between the first two fingers of his right hand. After he shot the heroin into his vein, before he could light the cigarette, he was gone.

When people ask me how I cope, it's tough to find an answer. It never goes away. But I'm trying. When you're awake and fully conscious, your mind kind of shields and protects you. But once I stop, once things slow down and the TV is off, the lights are out and I'm alone in the dark with my own thoughts, I have a hard time. A very hard time. Always. It's like an anxiety attack that takes your breath away. I think, "How can you even live after all that? How the hell did it all happen?"

On his 2002 album *Raised by Wolves*, Canadian recording artist Colin Linden included a song about me that contains the line "Gladiators cry alone." I couldn't have said it better myself.

I know in my heart that I'm not solely guilty for what happened to my family, but rather than absolving myself of guilt, I've tried to teach myself to live with certain things. You can never absolve yourself; that's like jiving yourself. You just can't do it. There are plenty of things I feel guilty about, that I second-guess or wish I had done differently. But at the end of the day, all I can do is continue to roll with the punches and live my life the best way I know how.

That's why I wanted to set the record straight by writing it all down. It's all here: the good, the bad and the ugly. And more tears and heartache than any man needs.

In 93 pro fights, I never pulled a punch. Still can't. And even if I wanted to, the truth won't let me.

So here's my story, warts and all . . .

PART
TWO

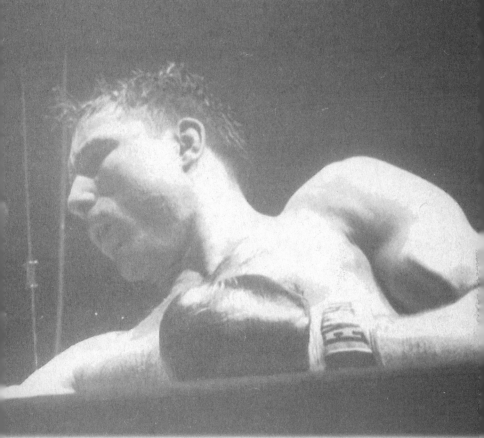

PRELIMS

MY PARENTS, STIPAN (STEVE) CHUVALO AND Kata Kordic, were married on February 2, 1926, in Bosnia-Herzegovina, which at the time was a republic of what used to be Yugoslavia. Seven months later to the day, my father arrived in Canada, looking for the Promised Land. He got off the boat in Quebec City and was supposed to take a train out west to Alberta or Saskatchewan, where the government had assigned him to work on a farm. But he jumped off the train and headed the other way, for the East Coast, finally ending up as a road builder in the Antigonish-Truro area of Nova Scotia. Later he worked in the bush in northern Ontario.

My dad's dream was to work in the mines in Noranda, Quebec, because of the relatively high pay, but they wouldn't let him because of his handicapped arm, which was broken when he fell off a donkey at age 10. Before he could get the arm fixed, my dad's uncle said to my grandfather, "Keep Steve a cripple; that way he won't get drafted into the army." So it never got fixed. As a result, for the rest of his life my dad could never fully straighten his arm. It looked like it was in an invisible sling, hanging at about a 45-degree angle, with this huge elbow sticking out. Because of that, he couldn't work in the mines. Ironically, his older brother George, who was the first Chuvalo to come to Canada and the guy I was named after, died of pneumonia after he was crushed by an ore car in a Noranda mine. The car slipped off the track and slammed into him. His injuries weren't life-threatening, but in the hospital he got pneumonia and died 14 days later.

My mother didn't come to Canada until 1936, but that was only because my father didn't send for her! On the two-week boat trip across the Atlantic from Le Havre, France, all she had to eat was oranges. Not being able to speak French or English, she didn't know how to ask for any other food, so she just kept pointing at "*naranja*" (oranges). That's all she ate for breakfast, lunch and dinner.

As happy as my mother was to finally be joining her husband in Canada, that boat trip must have been sad and terrifying, knowing she'd probably never again see her parents or her eight sisters and one brother. She was 30 years old and had never gone to school, so I can only imagine her awful sense of loss.

My old man was a different kind of guy. I guess he wrote the odd letter to my mother, but that was it. There was a stretch of three years where he didn't communicate with her even once. She used to tend sheep at her father-in-law's farm back in the old country, and her whole life revolved around waiting for letters from Canada. She lived and worked on the farm, and in all that time she never ventured more than a few hundred yards in any given direction and only made the 14-mile trip by donkey to neighboring Mostar, the capital of Herzegovina, once in 30 years. Can you imagine? It wasn't much of a life.

Why my father never contacted her over those three years is anybody's guess; that's just the way he was. In fact, he brought his younger brother Tony over to Canada first, because Tony was the seventh and youngest child in the family. By the time he finally sent for my mother, my old man had been living and working in Canada for a full decade.

My parents' respective family trees kind of illustrate how they were polar opposites. My great uncle on my mother's side, a priest named Petar Barbaric, is revered to this day in the former Yugoslavia—and in the Catholic faith—as a beatified "Servant of God" (sort of a saint-in-waiting) for his pious devotion and service to the church. He was only 23 years old when he died of consumption in 1897, but when his body was exhumed five years later, it looked like he'd only been buried five minutes before.

When word got around that Uncle Petar's corpse was perfectly preserved, his grave became a site of pilgrimage, which led to his beatification. In fact, in 1997 at the Cathedral of Sarajevo, Pope John Paul II cited my great uncle's devotion during an address commemorating the 100th anniversary of his death. He'd become a priest at the age of 21 and spent the last couple of years of his life writing letters in an effort to repair the rift between the Roman Catholic Church in the Vatican and the Christian Orthodox Church in Istanbul, Turkey.

My father's family, on the other hand, wasn't quite so celebrated. In 1952, my dad's cousin, Luka (Louis) Krivic, was kicked out of the U.S. for racketeering!

Shortly after my mother arrived in Toronto, she became pregnant. She thought the fact that King George VI had recently taken the throne was a good omen, so she decided that if her baby was a boy she'd name him after both my father's older brother and the King of England. Not a bad lineage, eh? My middle name, Louis, is what my parents thought was the English derivative of Luka (it's really Luke), which was my grandfather's name on my father's side.

I arrived on the scene on September 12, 1937, at St. Joseph's Hospital. My parents never agreed on what time I was born; my mother said it was 11 a.m., while my father insisted the big event was two hours later. When I was very young, my mother used to take me to my aunt Eileen's place. She was an Irish-Canadian girl who was only 17 when she got married—12 years younger than my uncle Tony. I remember my dad telling me how he and some other guys threw a big stag party before the wedding and everybody was crying because they figured poor Tony would never again enjoy good Croatian cooking. That sounds so innocent today, but back then, contemplating life without Croatian food was a major consideration.

Aunt Eileen took care of me while my mother went to work as a chicken plucker at Royce Poultry Packers on Dupont Street, which was owned by the father of my future manager, Irving Ungerman. Every morning we'd walk a mile to Aunt Eileen's house, and then my mother would walk another three miles to work. Most of the chicken pluckers were Eastern European women, and they all wore the same basic outfit: hair tied in a kerchief, full-length black burlap smock and a pair of rubber boots. Their days were long and the pay was brutal: half a cent per bird.

The guy who killed the chickens would slash their throats, then dunk them in hot water and toss them in a wide, rotating tank lined with rubber studs, which removed most of the feathers. When that was done, the chickens were tossed onto a long table, where my mother and the other pluckers would hang them from strings and remove whatever feathers were left. At half a cent a bird, you had to be fast to make it worthwhile, but my mom did that job for 15 years.

When I was older, I remember reading a letter that my grandmother sent from Bosnia-Herzegovina in 1940, profoundly thanking my mother for the $2 she had sent as a gift. My mother had to pluck 400 chickens to earn that $2!

My father was a cattle skinner at Canada Packers. Today, they have machines that rip the hide from the cow flesh, but in those days they just used knives. If you want to know about my father and his work, there's one story that illustrates it perfectly.

One day, long after my boxing career was over, I was soaking in a steam bath at a Toronto health club when an older gentleman with a very heavy Scottish brogue came in and sat down opposite me. I thought that was a bit odd since we were the only ones in there, but he said, "Hey Geordie, d'ya remember me from Canada Packers?" I'd briefly worked at the plant during the spring and summer of 1953 after I quit school, but I had no clue who this guy was.

"D'ya remember when your old man took his holidays?" he asked. That didn't ring a bell, either. I knew my father had a two-week vacation every year, but I couldn't recall him ever being at home during those times. Then the guy told me why I couldn't remember. He said my father spent his annual vacation sitting with his lunch pail for nine hours a day on a chair down at the Canada Packers slaughterhouse. He was so paranoid about losing his job that every year, for 40 years, he spent his vacation watching not one guy, but two guys, perform his job.

When I heard that, and I thought about my poor father, who never verbalized many things, and how he must have been frustrated and frightened about losing his job, it brought tears to my eyes. He did the job of two men, and he did it with a malformed arm. If he did half the work of one man, that's what you might expect. But he did the work of two men—with half an arm. And all the guys at Canada Packers knew that.

I can't tell you how many times over the years people came up to me, guys who worked with him, and said, "You know what, George? Your old man was a legend. He was an honest-to-God legend." And I'd think to myself, "Why are they calling my old man a legend?" I didn't realize what it was about him until I heard that story from the guy in the steam bath.

My old man was tough as nails, too. I remember one time one of his co-workers accidentally splashed some water on him, which he didn't like too much. He gave the guy a boot in the head and broke his jaw. He got fired for it but was back on the line the next day, thanks to the union.

He was a cut above most guys, my dad. And I never once heard him whine or complain about anything. He had no use for the immigrants who came to Canada in the 1930s and '40s and then griped about how the old country was better. He'd say, "If the old country is better, maybe you should go back there." If anybody ever questioned his lot in life, all he would say was, "Canada good country; give me job."

My father only had a Grade 2 education. When he was eight years old, his parents took him out of school and put him to work in the tobacco fields that were all over that part of Bosnia-Herzegovina. It was rich, moist Turkish tobacco, and he would spend all day chopping and cutting it. The day after he broke his arm at age 10, he was right back in the fields, chopping and cutting. The ironic thing about not getting that broken arm fixed in order to stay out of the army was that he was eventually drafted into the Yugoslavian army in his late teens and was assigned to the nursing corps for a couple of years. Apparently, in those days, a permanently broken arm was not considered much of an impediment to the working duties of a Yugoslav soldier.

My parents met at my uncle's wedding. My dad's older brother married my mother's older sister Janja, so I have cousins with basically the same DNA who are related to me on both sides—and not one of them looks like me!

The first time I visited Yugoslavia, in 1969, I met a lot of relatives at a reception in Zagreb. A guy with curly red hair and light-green eyes walked right up to me and gave me a kiss on both sides of my cheeks. I asked him in Croatian what his name was, and he introduced himself as my cousin Kreso. I thought to myself, "How the hell can I be related to this guy?" I was sure there must've been a little detour somewhere down the old bloodline. He explained that his father was my father's brother, and his mother was my mother's sister. Whoa! When I asked him where the curly red hair and green eyes came from, he told me it was the result of a little R&R by Richard the Lionhearted and his crew on the way to the Crusades in Palestine. That must've been one hot weekend!

The Croatians, of course, were all mixed up with Mongols and a dozen other bloodlines: Kurds, Armenians, Albanians, Hungarians, Turks . . . a veritable ethnic smorgasbord. They also used to have a thing called *primus noctus*, or "first night," back when my ancestors were part of the Ottoman Empire, for 450 years. In those days, when a Croatian girl got married to her Croatian fiancé, the poor guy wouldn't even get the first crack at his new bride. The Turkish landlord reserved that right—and he could continue to exercise it over the course of the marriage. That way, when the girl got pregnant, there would always be some doubt as to who the actual father was. Over the course of so many generations, it's no wonder the bloodlines got all mixed up.

(By the way, if I'm ever in Tampa, Florida, again one of these days, I might go to a certain restaurant there where they can check your DNA via saliva test, and if it proves that you're a direct descendent of Genghis Khan you will score a free dinner. I think that would be pretty cool. Experts realize that ol' Genghis was more than somewhat prolific in the baby-making business and that a very high percentage of Eastern Europeans can trace a lineage back to the Mongol hordes—even to boss man Genghis himself. As a matter of fact, if you have type-B blood flowing through your veins, as I do, then apparently at least one of your ancestors came from the Siberian tundra.)

When I was five years old, I went to a public-school kindergarten for exactly one day. Once they found out I was a Catholic kid, they kicked me out. That was a long day, though. I remember the other kids on my street at the time laughing at me because I had such a heavy accent. Other than a very few words, my mother spoke no English at all—and my father wasn't much better—so at home every conversation was in Croatian. English was the language of the other kids, so the accent made me a target.

The funny thing is that after I was kicked out and ordered to go to a Catholic school, we found out the Catholics didn't have a kindergarten in those years, so I spent my days roaming around the Junction. I always had my ears open, and I learned to speak English by listening to the shopkeepers and snippets of conversations on the street. Years later, my first wife, Lynne, taught my mother conversational English by regularly accompanying her on trips to Toronto's Kensington Market district.

As a kid, I didn't know anything about World War II or about how hard my parents were struggling just to survive and to keep me and my sister Zora, who was a year younger, fed and clothed. In 1943, I started Grade 1 at St. Rita's parochial school, and it was then that I began to realize that my family was a bit different from the rest of the neighborhood.

There was strong ethnic mix in the Junction and everybody was poor, but in my family there was only me and Zora and our parents. A lot of the other kids had six, seven, even eight siblings, so when they saw my mother bringing me a sandwich or a snack, they'd really give it to me. Our mother was very loving, and her kids were her whole world. Every day at recess she would run the quarter of a mile from the poultry plant to my school, and I'd meet her at the fence. She'd have blood and guts and bits of feathers stuck to her smock, and terrible raw sores between her fingers from handling the hot, wet chicken carcasses. But she was always smiling, and she'd flip a pomegranate or a bag of chips over the fence, then give me a kiss through the chain-link fence. After I walked home on cold winter days,

A FIGHTER'S LIFE [23]

she would gently take off my rubber boots and wet socks and rub and kiss my feet. No wonder I was a mama's boy!

I remember exactly what I was eating one day in front of my house: a sandwich on pumpernickel bread with a big piece of flank steak and a dill pickle. It tasted scrumptious! Immediately, a bunch of other kids surrounded me and started yelling, "You bastard! You fuckin' Jew-boy!" I didn't understand—but there was no way they were getting any part of that sandwich.

Our family was as poor as any of theirs, but my parents always made sure we had plenty of good food to eat. Of course, it wasn't always steak. Most of the time it was stuff like tendons, as well as beef tripe, cow brains, kidneys and other organ meats. In those days, all of those things got thrown in the garbage at Canada Packers, so my father would wrap them up in brown waxed paper and bring them home for the family.

Sometimes my mother brought home pigeons that she and the other ladies used to trap and kill in the lofts at the poultry plant. My mother could make a feast out of nothing: collard greens (*rastika*), headcheese, pig's feet. In the mornings she would cook Zora and me a pan full of *maza*—yellow corn meal that looked like grits. That was my favorite—even better than the Kellogg's All-Wheat cereal I used to scarf down in order to get the trading cards depicting Joe Louis and other sporting champions. On the back of the cards were little write-ups by Canadian fitness guru Lloyd Percival, and they were my first real introduction to boxing. I studied each one until I could duplicate the moves it depicted.

I was a pretty good student in elementary school; in fact, I skipped Grade 4. My English was good by then, but I still had problems fitting in. Kids used to throw rocks through the windows of our house almost every week. My old man would go out to chase them away and they'd yell stuff like "Go home, you goddamned hunkies!" It was wartime and there was a lot of animosity, but I didn't understand it at the time. I just kind of sucked it up.

The only time I remember being affected by that kind of thing was when a bigger kid I didn't know called me a "fucking foreigner" on the street one day. I couldn't understand that, because I'd been born right there in the Junction. I went home and cried myself to sleep.

One afternoon when I was eight years old, a kid named Richie Lucas threw a rock through our front window. Richie lived in the house diagonally across the street from ours, and I found out that he had told the other kids he could beat me up.

A couple of days later, peeping through a hole in the wooden fence, I saw him walking at the end of the alley behind our house. I picked up a brick, which I hid behind my back, then waited patiently. When he got close enough, I yelled, "Hey, Richie!" When he looked up, I cracked him right over the head with the brick.

Richie didn't go down, but there was blood spurting out all over the place. His hair was so blond that it was almost white, so you can imagine what it looked like with all that blood streaming down his head and soaking into his shirt. He kind of staggered backwards and ran howling down the alley, while I just stood there and laughed like hell. I felt so proud of myself! Looking back, that might have been the first indication that I had what boxing trainers call the killer instinct.

After that little episode with Richie, I became one of the regular guys around the neighborhood. When we weren't in school, we hung out in the streets, playing wallball or hopscotch or building scooters out of orange crates and roller skates that we raced down a bridge right around the corner from our house.

We had to make our own fun. There was no TV in the neighborhood until an Irish guy named Mr. Davies got one in the late '40s, which was a real big deal at the time. I remember Mr. Davies because he died of a heart attack watching the rematch between Billy Conn and Joe Louis. He bet a bundle on Conn because Billy had given Joe such a hard time in their first fight. That was the end of poor Mr. Davies.

Most of the other kids were scared to death of my father, so we didn't hang around the house much. Like my son Mitchell used to say, my old man looked like he just stepped out of Dracula's castle in Transylvania, so he intimidated anybody who came to the house. He was only about 5 foot 9 and a half and 200 pounds—a tad smaller than my mom, who was a big woman at 5-11 and 215—but my father was the disciplinarian, no question. There was never any conversation or negotiation with him, just terse directives: "Shut up." "Do this." "Do that." He was Sergeant Bilko with attitude.

There was never any warning before my dad lowered the boom—he'd just whack you. If I stepped out of line, he'd wrap his hand around my fingers and thumb and whip them with a pussy-willow branch. That was the punishment for minor infractions, and it hurt like hell. If I did something serious— like the time I busted Zora's baby carriage by loading it up with rocks—he'd spread cinders from the furnace on the basement floor and make me kneel on them while I begged God for forgiveness. That particular penance could last for hours, depending on the crime, so for the most part I was pretty well behaved.

My dad took us to church every week, and I was an altar boy for a couple of years. My mother never went to church because she thought it was too exclusive. Her philosophy was simply to be a good person all the time, not just on Sunday. To her, being a good Catholic meant you didn't lie, cheat or steal, and you didn't have to go to church to learn those things. The old man saw things differently. To him, church was where you went to repent for all the bad things you'd done in the previous six days—even though he had his own ideas about penance.

Was it abuse? I didn't see it that way; it was normal to me. As tough as he was on the outside, my father had a good heart, and I knew he loved me. He could be surprisingly sensitive, too. He loved western movies, and on Saturdays he'd often take me to a show or a concert or to the museum. We lived in a tight-knit community and there was always a Croatian wedding or somebody's birthday party, so we did a lot of stuff as a family.

Like most big brothers, I had kind of a love-hate relationship with Zora. It was a pain when she wanted to tag along when I was doing stuff with my buddies, but I was protective of her. One time when I was eight and she was seven, we were walking through High Park near the Junction when a guy drove up alongside us and offered Zora some candy to get into his car. She was all set to do it, but I knew something was awry and started screaming at the top of my lungs for her not to get into his car, so the guy took off.

One morning, not long after that day in the park, I walked across Dundas Street, right in the heart of the Junction, and wandered into Morgan's cigar store to buy some candy. On my way to the counter I happened to stop and look at the big rack of magazines—all those colorful covers and exotic titles. As I took in the whole display, my eye was drawn to a copy of *The Ring* ("The Bible of Boxing"), which was just about at eye level for a little guy.

I was instantly mesmerized. I took the magazine off the rack and carefully opened it up. Inside were pictures of big, muscular guys punching each other. It was a whole different world from anything I'd ever seen. After browsing for a couple of minutes, I carefully put the magazine back on the rack. I didn't even buy any candy, because I couldn't wait to run home and tell my parents I wanted to be a fighter.

As it happened, around that time we had a little Italian woman and her son and daughter subletting the upstairs of our house, and the kid was an amateur boxer. His name was Rollie Mignacca, and he looked like Gabe from the old Dead End Kids movie serials: tall and lanky, maybe 16 or 17 years old.

Rollie went out one night to fight a guy named Gus Rubicini. I don't know why I didn't ask to go to the fight, or if kids were even allowed to go to the fights; it seemed so very adult to me. But I stayed up until he came home, and I could hear his mother asking him about the fight, which he lost. I can still hear that woman's voice: "Rollie, how coulda you loosa da fight? How coulda you loosa, after I'm a feeda you da porka chops?"

Poor Mrs. Mignacca was crestfallen. She just couldn't fathom how her boy could lose a fight after she fed him meat. By the way, Gus Rubicini, the guy who beat Rollie that night, went on to have a very respectable professional career, highlighted by a win over Joey Giardello in 1951. A few months later, Giardello became middleweight champion of the world.

I took Rollie's loss almost as hard as his mother did. He was a big kid I looked up to. In fact, all the big kids in our neighborhood—who were mostly the older brothers of my buddies—were sort of role models for the rest of us. Most of them belonged to what was known as the Junction Gang, which was the toughest group in the city's west end. They used to have street rumbles with the Beanery Gang, who ruled the east end. Zip guns, bicycle chains, baseball bats . . . name any weapon, and they used it.

Most of them were real tough kids, but the leader of the Junction Gang, who lived on our street, was a little twerp named Johnny O'Hearn. He was five foot nothing, but like all the rest of the gang members, he used to wear what was called a zoot suit, with shoulder pads to make him look bigger. Another integral part of the uniform, if you wanted to look really cool, was a vest chain hanging from your waistband to about halfway down your thigh, which the guys used to twirl when they were walking down the street. After I got my first pair of dress pants at age nine or 10, the first thing I did was run out and buy a chain to twirl like the big guys. Very cool!

It was right around that time that I got my first set of boxing gloves, too. After weeks of listening to me beg, my mother finally purchased them at Eaton's department store. There were four gloves in the set, and five minutes after she brought them home, I ran across the street to round up some pals to break them in. We went to what we called the macaroni field, which was an unpaved parking lot—just a beat-up patch of grass, really—at the pasta plant down the street. We took turns punching each other, and it became our daily ritual.

I'd already learned a couple of tricks from studying those Kellogg's trading cards, including how to get a guy out of position by feinting a left to the body and then shooting a left hook to the head, just like Joe Louis (or so I thought). Even something as simple as that can really boost the confidence of a

10-year-old kid, and I quickly found out that nobody in our little group could lay a glove on me. This went on for a few weeks until one day an older guy on the street—he was probably 18 or 19—stopped to watch. After we finished, he came up to me and said, "Hey George, you're pretty good with your dukes. Why don't you go to the gym?"

When I asked him where that might be, he said it was about a mile away, at St. Mary's Roman Catholic Church, where there was boxing training Monday to Friday evenings and weekend afternoons, and dances for teenagers on Saturday night. That's all I needed to hear.

I showed up at the church the next day. In the basement they had a heavy bag, a floor-to-ceiling punching ball, a couple of medicine balls and an exercise table. There was an old guy who kind of kept an eye on things. He had fought pro and also shared the same name, Mickey McDonald, with a bank robber operating and still at large. But for the most part the kids just fooled around with the bags and then paired off for sparring.

I was one of the smaller ones there, so it took a while before I really got involved. I spent most of my time doing push-ups and sit-ups, learning how to hold my hands up and twist my body when I threw a punch. I watched all the bigger kids and tried to emulate anything that looked useful.

I had my first real fight at the age of 10 at Stanley Barracks, which was part of the armed forces complex down by the Canadian National Exhibition grounds. I was 85 pounds and pretty edgy. I was in awe of the crowd and of the way the whole room was dark except for the lights illuminating the ring. My mother and father were there, along with my sister, my aunt Sofie and my uncle Sam.

My enduring memory of that night is of my trainer, Mickey McDonald, greasing my face with Vaseline in the corner. It was the first time that boxing seemed so serious, but it made me feel like a real fighter. I can't remember the name of the east-end kid I fought in an exhibition, but when it was over they called it a draw.

A couple of years (and four fights) later, the St. Mary's boxing program came to an abrupt end with the arrival of a new priest, Father Paderski, from Winnipeg, who immediately decreed that "Catholics don't box and Catholics don't dance." That was a par-ticularly perplexing turn of events, because my family had just moved into a house right next door to the church.

In order to continue my training, I joined the Diamond Boxing Club, which was a couple of miles away. It was run by Vic and Joey Bagnato, two of the seven brothers who to this day are revered as Toronto's all-time best boxing benefactors. Originally there were 24 Bagnato kids, but only 12 survived. Mrs. Bagnato received an award and some cash from the federal government for having given birth to so many children. There were seven boys, and all but one were fighters. The best of the brood was Joey, a former Canadian lightweight champ who floored world featherweight champion Willie Pep before los-ing to him in 1942. The only Bagnato brother who didn't fight was Vince; he became a successful promoter and pioneered the concept of "So You Think You're Tough" tournaments back in the early '70s. Vince also played a fight manager opposite Tony Curtis in the 1979 movie *Title Shot* and contributed some of the film's cheesy dialog, including such nuggets as "You're a piece of garbage wrapped up in a $300 suit!" and "The first time he gets hit on the button, you'll hear crystal cracking all over town."

If St. Mary's got me smitten with the sport, the Diamond Boxing Club made me fall head-over-heels in love with it. Walking in there the first time as a skinny 12-year-old, I couldn't believe what I saw. The rows of heavy bags and speed bags, the noise . . . even the smell. It was intoxicating.

For me, the most impressive thing was the regulation-sized ring, right in the middle of the gym. I spent hours watching every guy that climbed through the ropes of that ring, whether he was a flyweight or a heavyweight. One of the "old" fighters who caught my eye during those sparring sessions was a 20-year-old banger named James J. Parker—the guy I would knock out in one round to win the Canadian heavyweight championship just nine years later.

One spring morning in 1950 I walked into the gym and saw Vic Bagnato talking to a fighter named Les Irwin, a future mobster who got shot to death in Vancouver several years later. I asked Vic if he could spare a ticket to the upcoming fight between Li'l Arthur King, Toronto's world-ranked lightweight contender, and Johnny Rowe, a tough customer from Rochester, New York. Vic was a little reluctant about handing out a free ducat, but then Les started ragging on him—"Come on, give the kid a ticket, you cheap bastard"—and it worked.

I rode the streetcar to the fight at the CNE Coliseum all by myself, and it was a huge thrill—the first pro card I ever attended. I watched Les lose his prelim to a guy named Eddie Zastre, but then King knocked out Rowe in the third round, so it was a memorable night. The ring introductions and the noisy crowd made it all seem so big-time through the eyes of a 12-year-old. I've never forgotten what it felt like to be there that night, or that it was a future mobster who helped a wide-eyed kid get a ticket to soak it all up. I was always thankful to Les, and I was very sorry when he got shot, but I guess he must've done some pretty bad stuff to end up like that.

By the way, the first "big-time" heavyweight fight I saw in person was in 1954, when world-ranked Canadian champion Earl 'The Hooded Terror" Walls fought Tommy Harrison at Maple Leaf Gardens. Little did I realize that I would become Walls's successor just a few years later.

By age 14 I'd moved over to the Earlscourt Boxing Club, which was part of a recreational complex in the park at St. Clair and Lansdowne avenues. They had tennis courts, and later they added a skating rink. I was fighting regularly and earning a bit of a reputation as a kid who was pretty good with his mitts.

I also started building up my body. One day in Latin class I happened to swing my arm over the back of a chair to talk to the kid behind me, and he made a comment about how skinny my bicep was. When I got back to the gym, I started lifting weights, a passion that's still with me today. Over the next year I put on 75 pounds of solid muscle—and I've never heard a crack about my biceps since.

When I was 12 years old, I also used to do push-ups on chairs. I'd place three chairs in a triangular position, put my feet on the back one and dip my body between the other two just ahead of me. When I started, I could only do four push-ups on the floor. Nine months later, I could do 400 on the chairs. Of course, I made all kinds of noises while doing this, grunting and groaning. Hey, it was a tough workout! My old man would be trying to sleep because he had to get up at 4:30 a.m. to go to Canada Packers, and I'd be up in my room in the dead of night, doing all these push-ups. He didn't take too kindly to it. My mother would get upset and holler, "George, what are you doing up there?" And I would yell back, "I'm trying to get somewhere!"

In 1952, the Canadian Broadcasting Corporation began televising the weekly amateur boxing program from the East York Arena, and later from the Palace Pier. The bouts were shown live in the Toronto market, and the following week a film of the show would air on a dozen CBC affiliate stations across the country. I thought it was pretty cool to see myself on TV, and the shows were run very professionally. A sportscaster by the name of Steve Douglas did the blow-by-blow commentary and conducted post-fight interviews with the winners, which really made us feel important.

By age 15, I was a full-fledged 198-pound heavyweight, and thanks to a dismissive comment from my father—and a sneaky jab from a guy named Glen Mowat—I made the conscious decision to become a professional fighter.

The comment from my dad came one day when we were walking to the pool hall on St. Clair Avenue, where he used to meet his pals to shoot a few games. I can't even remember what we were talking about, except that it had nothing to do with boxing. Then, out of the blue, he blurted out in his thick Croatian accent, "When your nose start bleeding, you quit!"

I couldn't figure out what he was getting at. But today, 60 years later, I think I know. I mentioned earlier that Papa Steve took care of business when I misbehaved. He was most definitely old school, from the old country. Whenever I received the all-too-familiar pussy-willow lashing (my father's favorite form of corporal punishment) on my fingertips, knuckles, or bare buttocks, I would yelp and howl like a natural-born sissy.

My baby sister, on the other hand, would simply grit her teeth and let out nary a whimper. She was tougher than I was.

It was plain to see that my dad figured my kid sister was more resilient than I was in the take-a-beating department. How the heck could I ever make it in the fight game? Still, I was shocked and hurt, because I'd already had a few amateur fights and would never quit. Of course, I would never disrespect my father by talking back to him or challenging anything he said, but that comment really stung me. I was hurt, and I got mad. I said to myself, "All right, old man. I'll show you!"

Before I could show my dad just how tough I was, however, I was expected to at least finish my education. But when it came to choosing between boxing and school, there really was no choice.

In 1950, I enrolled in Grade 9 at the brand new St. Michael's College high school, but by that time I was so passionate about pursuing a career in the ring that I didn't really care if I attended classes or not.

St. Mike's had great sports programs, and I had a lot of fun there. I played fullback on a house league football team and for a while I was a sprinter on the track team, but neither of those things came close to giving me the rush that I felt in the ring.

In Grades 10 and 11, my classmates included future National Hockey League stars Dick Duff and Charlie Burns, and a kid named Tony Roman, who went on to play for the Ottawa Rough Riders in the Canadian Football League. Duff, who won six Stanley Cups with the Toronto Maple Leafs and Montreal Canadiens, was voted into the Hockey Hall of Fame in 2006. During his induction speech, when he said that he taught me how to fight, I blurted out, "Yeah, and I taught you how to skate!"

By Grade 11, I'd had enough. I quit St. Mike's in early 1953, and when I wasn't training I worked in construction and other odd jobs, including a stint at Canada Packers. In the fall I decided to give school another shot, so I enrolled at Central Tech with the idea of studying electronics. That lasted all of three weeks, because I didn't have the prerequisite courses. I moved on to Humberside Collegiate but got the boot for cutting too many classes. Just before I was expelled, my English teacher, Mr. Green, told me, "George, you'll never amount to anything more than a pick-and-shovel guy."

For the next few months, it looked like Mr. Green was right. I went back to construction work and then took a job moving furniture for 90 cents an hour. After one particularly brutal stint of hauling pianos and sofas for 36 straight hours, the thought of doing any more of that kind of labor was all the incentive I needed to start seriously planning to become a professional boxer.

It was also around this time that I gave up smoking, a bad habit I'd picked up a few months earlier. I don't even know why I started—except that I thought it looked very adult. The first cigarette I ever smoked was at Burt's Turkey Palace, a big park on the outskirts of Toronto where the Croatian community used to have picnics. One day my buddy Johnny Milkovich asked if I wanted to smoke a Black Cat cigarette. I had no idea at the time how harmful tobacco was, and it didn't take long before I was hooked, even though I knew it was no good for my wind. I've got to be honest, though; I really liked the taste of tobacco, and I developed a neat little trick where I could exhale the smoke three or four inches in front of my face and then suck it back in. I thought it was pretty cool.

As much as I enjoyed smoking, I quit cold turkey on August 11, 1954, the same night Archie Moore retained his light heavyweight championship by knocking out Harold Johnson in New York. I really admired Archie as a fighter, so I quit as kind of a tribute to him. And I've never smoked since.

A few weeks later I packed it in as a furniture mover, and thanks to a sparring session with Glen Mowat, I knew I'd chosen the right career path. Mowat was 24 and the Ontario amateur heavyweight champion. We hooked up in the gym on a Wednesday afternoon because he was fighting the following Monday on the TV card and wanted some last-minute work.

Halfway through the first round, he caught me with a good left hand and busted my nose. I knew it was broken right away, because there was blood all over the place, and when I went back to the corner my trainer could kind of slide my nose from side to side—not the greatest feeling in the world. Anyway, I finished the session and went home. My mother nearly fainted when she saw my face, but I didn't think it was such a big deal—certainly not worth a trip to the doctor's office.

The next day I showed up at the gym as usual, and my trainer, Sonny Thomson, told me I had to spar some more because Glen Mowat had a fight coming up the next week and needed the work to get sharp. Sure, why not? Well, Mowat started whacking me on my schnozz right away—and, of course, it started pouring blood again. But I stayed in there with him for the full session.

Looking back, you could say that was my rite of passage. I said to myself, "I don't think most guys would even get back in the ring with a freshly broken nose, never mind risk getting punched on the honker again." It made me feel a little special. I thought about my father, and what he'd said to me that day on the street, and I knew I was tough enough. I knew I'd be okay.

By the way, three months later I owned Mowat in the ring. I could toy with him. I figured out how to slip his jab and nail him with a right uppercut to the body, followed by a hook to the head. Before the year was out, we ended up boxing in an exhibition at the Palace Pier and I beat the hell out of him.

✧   ✧   ✧

My first fight for Earlscourt Boxing Club was at East York Arena against a guy exactly twice my age: a 30-year-old Newfoundlander named Andy Humber, who was also a member of the Earlscourt club. The fight was televised, and even though I wanted to go for a knockout, my corner wanted me to go easy on him because we were from the same gym. Andy was a nice guy and I felt a little bad about laying a beating on him. I won an easy decision.

Amateur boxing in those days wasn't nearly as well organized as it is today; there weren't as many clubs, and competitive cards were few and far between. It was especially tough finding heavyweights to fight. I had a total of just 19 amateur bouts, plus a few exhibitions. Compare that to today, when most guys on the national team have more than 100 fights.

My only loss came in my very first appearance at Maple Leaf Gardens. It was to a guy named Eddie Smith. He was from Buffalo and had defeated Floyd Patterson in the amateur ranks a couple of years earlier. In my next appearance at the Gardens I beat the Michigan state champ, and before the year was out I beat the crap out of a French-Canadian guy from Sudbury to win the Ontario title.

On May 7, 1955, I knocked out Peter Piper in Regina to win the Canadian amateur championship. That was a very big deal, especially traveling all the way to Saskatchewan on the train. For most of the fighters representing Ontario it was our first trip out west, and we couldn't believe that there was still snow on the ground in May.

My title fight was scheduled for 10 p.m. on the last night of the tournament, so at about three o'clock that afternoon I and another Toronto fighter named Willie Barboie went looking for something to eat. Willie was one-quarter black and three-quarters Italian and he talked like a New York street kid. He was fighting Edmonton's Wilfie Greaves for the middleweight championship a couple of bouts before mine.

We walked into a restaurant in downtown Regina, and the waitress took out a little pad and asked us to write down what we wanted to eat. I'd never seen that before. I wrote down a steak with salad, dry whole-wheat toast and a cup of tea with honey and lemon. Willie ordered a big plate of bacon and eggs, a double order of buttered toast, a strawberry milkshake and a slice of strawberry shortcake. I couldn't believe it.

"What the hell are you doing?" I asked him, but he just smiled and in that affected New York twang of his he said, "Don't worry about me, Georgie. This is what I eat before every fight."

Well, you can picture the scene a few hours later, when shortly after the opening bell, Greaves nailed him with a breath-robbing body shot: up came the bacon, the eggs, the greasy toast, the milkshake and the strawberry shortcake. Poor Willie puked his guts out all over the ring just before he got knocked out. The canvas was still wet and slippery from his projectile vomit when I went in to fight Piper, so I made sure to knock him out on one of the dry patches.

Greaves, by the way, went on to become a very good professional middleweight. Twice he gave Sugar Ray Robinson all he could handle, but for some reason he never got the recognition I think he deserved. And Piper became a pretty decent trainer and manager. He was one of the guys who helped put Winnipeg's Donny Lalonde on the path to the world light heavyweight championship in the mid-1980s.

Winning the Canadian title was the highlight of my amateur career and paved the way for my first big-time TV appearance a couple of months later on *The Wayne and Shuster Show*, an enormously popular comedy/variety program that was produced by the CBC in Toronto and hosted by Johnny Wayne and Frank Shuster. I played the role of the referee in a boxing skit, and while I only had a couple of lines, it was a real thrill to be on the set with Canada's most recognized TV stars. I almost didn't make it, though. On the big night, I was stopped by a security guard outside the studio. When I explained that I was going to appear on *Wayne and Shuster*, the guy kind of looked me up and down and said, "What are you, a dancer?"

Another benefit of winning the national title was that I was the first of four fighters picked to represent Canada at the 1956 Olympic Games in Melbourne, Australia, which was quite an honor. Unlike today, however, there was no financial benefit attached to being on the Olympic team. No allowance for training or living expenses, not even a few bucks for traveling to other parts of Canada to defend my title.

There was no doubt in my mind that I'd do well at the Olympics, and it would've been a huge thrill to fight for my country, but it didn't make economic sense, especially since the

Summer Games were being held Down Under in November. With no money coming in, that was too long to wait.

I was being pressured to turn pro by Sonny Thomson and Dave Zuk, the guys who handled me at the Earlscourt Club, so they arranged to enter me in something called the Jack Dempsey New Talent Novice Tournament at Maple Leaf Gardens on April 23, 1956. I figured that was a good omen, because on the Catholic calendar April 23 is St. George's Day—named for the Roman soldier who became a saint for slaying a dragon and refusing to renounce his Christian faith under torture.

The tournament was promoted by Frank Tunney and Jack Allen and was similar to what later became known as "tough man" competitions—except that a lot of the guys who entered had already turned pro. The rule was that you could have up to six pro fights and still qualify as "new" talent.

I didn't care who they put in front of me, just as long as I got paid.

The big draw was that Dempsey himself refereed the final, so that pretty much guaranteed a big crowd and a lot of media attention. I ended up knocking out four guys—Ed McGhee, Ross Gregory, Jim Leonard and Gordon Baldwin—in a total of 12 minutes and 36 seconds, which made me the talk of the tournament. There were lots of sportswriters in attendance, and Dempsey said some nice things about me, how he thought I had a big punch and a lot of potential, that kind of thing. It was all pretty exciting stuff for an 18-year-old kid . . . and the $500 in prize money made me feel like a millionaire.

Any time a heavyweight debuts by knocking out four guys in one night, it's going to attract some attention. But to be honest, I wasn't surprised at my success. In the gym, I'd been more than holding my own sparring with old pros like James J. Parker and Earl Walls, who had been ranked No. 4 in the world just a couple of years earlier. I was pretty precocious in a lot of ways, starting with the fact that I was unusually strong for my age.

Parker was a guy I'd been studying for years. Originally from Saskatchewan, he'd been devastating as an amateur, once knocking out 25 consecutive opponents. He turned pro in early 1950 and won his first six fights by KO. That earned him a date at Madison Square Garden with world-ranked Dan Bucceroni just before Christmas, but Bucceroni, who was 28–1 at the time, stopped Jimmy in the second round.

Parker had mixed success over the next few years, beating guys like Charley Norkus and Jimmy Slade but losing to Nino Valdes and drawing with Walls in their Canadian title fight. In early 1956 he won a 12-round decision over South African champ Johnny Arthur, then KO'd German champ Heinz Neuhaus to earn a crack at Archie Moore, the No. 1 contender for the world title vacated by Rocky Marciano.

Just a week before Parker fought Moore at the Maple Leaf Stadium ballpark on July 25, 1956, I busted him up pretty good during a sparring session. I staggered him with a left hook, but just before I could finish him off, his trainer, Joey Bagnato, jumped into the ring to save him.

From that moment on, I knew I owned Parker. If I could do that at 18, what was I going to be like at 21?

A couple of years later, in just my 18th pro bout, I knocked him down three times in the first 90 seconds of our Canadian title fight. The fourth time he went down—exactly two minutes after the opening bell—he didn't get up.

And Parker never fought again.

PART
THREE

MAIN

EVENT

ROUND 1

THREE WEEKS AFTER THE DEMPSEY TOURNAMENT, with Jack Allen as my new manager, I made my official pro debut against Johnny Arthur, a world-ranked contender who had gone 12 rounds with Parker in January. He had a 30–7 record and had just fought future light heavyweight champ Willie Pastrano on TV's *Gillette Cavalcade of Sports*.

Arthur was a big guy—at 228 he outweighed me by 25 pounds—and very experienced. But Allen, who was pushing 80, didn't want to waste time by having me fight prelims. Nowadays, any manager who threw a raw 18-year-old kid into a debut against a veteran like Arthur would be run out of town, but things were different back then. For me, it was like going from kindergarten straight into high school, with nothing in between. The learning curve was steep, but Allen expected me to just suck it up and take care of business.

Allen wasn't so much a manager as he was a boxing impresario. He was as gay as a plaid rabbit, and everyone called him "Deacon" because of his dour demeanor. He preferred to conduct business only after dark because he claimed to be allergic to sunlight. Another quirk was that he always had a pint-sized mentally challenged guy named Mike Levinsky hanging around him. Mike was always dressed in a striped shirt, wide suspenders and an ever-present oversized bow tie. He also claimed he was Irish (Levinsky?) and that he had swum across the Atlantic to come to Canada. He called himself Allen's social secretary, and any time a stranger wanted to talk to the Deacon, Levinsky would put out his hand and say, "Twenty-five cents, please." I guess he had to make a living.

The Deacon was born in Fresno, California, but grew up in Sacramento, where he was introduced to the fight game as a kid by hanging around a saloon owned by Ancil Hoffman. Hoffman went on to manage Max Baer to the heavyweight championship, and Allen kind of looked up to him as a mentor. Allen later drifted up to Vancouver and opened a saloon of his own, which gave him an opportunity to start dabbling in boxing. He managed Canadian bantamweight and featherweight champ Vic Foley, as well as lightweight Billy Townsend, the "Blond Tiger" from Nanaimo, British Columbia, who was a popular headliner in New York in the early '30s.

Allen's biggest success as a promoter had been a heavyweight fight between Earl Walls and Tommy Harrison in Toronto, which was the first time he hooked up with Frank Tunney. Tunney was the king of Toronto's wrestling promoters, and they put together the Dempsey tournament that became my springboard to the pros.

I remember being nervous climbing through the ropes at Maple Leaf Gardens to fight Arthur. All my buddies were there, and because I'd created such a buzz by knocking out those four guys at the Dempsey tournament, I wanted to put on a good show. Arthur was slick, but after the first round I knew I had him. He had fast hands, but I was walking through his punches. And every time I landed a good shot, I could tell I was doing damage. I didn't knock him out, but I won all eight rounds.

Allen didn't waste any time lining up my next fight, a first-round KO over Joe Evans at the Gardens on September 10. Five weeks later he put me in with another world-ranked contender, Howard "Honeyboy" King, a big Texan who was 31–10–5 and coming off a draw with Archie Moore. King had been in the world's top 10 for some time, but he was the kind of spoiler that everybody avoided. He had a style that made you look bad. I thought I hit him a lot more than he hit me—and harder, too—but he won the split decision over eight rounds. I got my revenge by knocking him out in two in our rematch 14 months later.

In between the two fights with King, I notched KOs over Sid Russell, Walter Hafer, Moses Graham and Emil Brtko at the Gardens, a decision over Bobby Biehler, and a KO of Joe Schmolze (fighting under the alias of Joe Olson) in Fort William, Ontario, and I dropped a decision to Bob Baker.

The Baker fight was my first 10-rounder and my second loss. With a record of 47–11–1, Baker was a top-10 guy whom not even Rocky Marciano would mess with. A few months before we fought, he was ranked No. 4 in the world by *The Ring*. I had him hurt on the ropes early, but I was too inexperienced to know how to finish him. I kind of went nuts after staggering him with a good shot to the head in the eighth, but he was a wily old pro who knew just exactly how to weather the storm. Every time I threw a flurry upstairs, he'd move his head or shoulders just enough to take the steam off my punches. It was like how you move your hand backwards when catching a ball to soften the impact. He did it expertly, and over the last two rounds I ran out of gas.

Baker wasn't a big puncher, but he had a very good jab. That fight was also the first time my eyes really got messed up, and one of the very few times in my entire career that I remember feeling pain. He whacked me pretty good on the nose, and between the swelling of my cheekbones and the nicks around my eyes, I looked pretty messed up when it was over.

After the fight, Baker did a classy thing. He came to my dressing room and told me I had nothing to feel bad about. "George, the only thing that beat you tonight was my experience," he said. "Don't forget, I've had 60 pro fights and you're just starting out. You're going to beat a lot of guys and make a lot of money." That made me feel a little better.

Through my first 14 fights, I was 12–2 against opponents who had a combined record of 179–77. Not a bad showing for a 19-year-old kid with only 49 pro rounds under his belt.

Fight No. 15 was against Cuban champion Julio Medeiros at Maple Leaf Gardens on January 27, 1958. Medeiros was a scary-looking guy: very black, with virtually no white in his eyes. When he looked at you, all you saw were little red bloodshot flecks around his incredibly dark, cold eyes. He was a hot-and-cold kind of fighter who in the previous year had split two decisions with Bob Satterfield, one of the hardest-punching heavyweights ever. And in 1955 Medeiros knocked out Roland LaStarza, a guy who had gone a total of 21 rounds in two tough fights with Marciano.

A week before the fight, I was getting ready for a run in High Park when it started snowing heavily. We had a Croatian boarder named Sigmund Schauer staying at our house, and he offered to drive me and my mother down to the park so they could wait in his car while I did my 45-minute run around frozen Grenadier Pond, a small lake about a mile long. For some reason—probably because it was so damn cold—I decided to run across the pond rather than around it. Just as I started doing so, I noticed a sign that said DANGER: THIN ICE! but I figured if I started to hear a cracking sound I'd just head for the shore.

There was no cracking sound. In fact, there was no sound at all until I suddenly found myself crashing through the ice and into the murky depths of Grenadier Pond. Now, I'd just run about three miles and was bathed in sweat, thanks to the cotton tracksuit I was wearing, along with heavy work boots. My first thought was that I was going to have a heart attack. I'm not the greatest swimmer in the world to begin with, and I was sinking fast.

To this day, I can still smell the stench of the weeds that were all around me. After what seemed like forever, I finally managed to thrash my way back up to the surface, where I broke off three big chunks of ice before finding a spot that would hold my weight. But by the time I dragged myself out of the water, I was almost too weak to stand. After catching my breath for a few seconds, I got up and ran like hell all the way back to the car, which was about half a mile away. I remember collapsing into the back seat and Mr. Schauer and my mother throwing their coats over me to keep me warm.

Amazingly, I never got so much as a sniffle from that little episode. I felt great going in against Medeiros, and I knocked him down twice in the second round. The second time was a whistling left hook that dropped him like a sack of wheat in the middle of the ring, and I thought it was all over. The referee was James J. Braddock, the old heavyweight champ. He started counting over Medeiros and got to nine when the bell rang. In those days you could be saved by the bell, so his guys dragged him back to the corner and brought him around. I should've put him away in the third, but my trainer, Tommy McBeigh, kept telling me to relax and take it easy, not to punch myself out like I did against Baker. The fight ended up going the 10-round distance, but I won it easily.

Three months after beating Medeiros, I got my revenge against Howard King by knocking him out in two rounds. I was now 14–2 and still unranked, but people were starting to notice. My next fight was back at the Gardens on June 20 against South American champion Alex Miteff. Though it turned out to be the fight that got me ranked in the world's top 10 (at No. 8) for the first time, to this day it still leaves a bad taste in my mouth.

Miteff was from Maria Teresa, Argentina, where he'd compiled an incredible amateur record of 126–3–11, with 90 knockouts. With author Budd Schulberg (*The Harder They Fall*) as one of his sponsors, he turned pro after winning the gold medal at the 1955 Pan-Am Games in Mexico City and reeled off 12 straight victories before Mike DeJohn starched him in 77 seconds in Syracuse in 1957.

Miteff rebounded in his next fight to beat No. 5–ranked Nino Valdes in New York, which got him ranked No. 6 by the time we hooked up in Toronto.

Alex was a decent puncher. He tried to work the body, but everything he threw, I caught on my elbows. Because his shots were easy to block, he spent most of the night pounding on my arms and elbows. Meanwhile, I was using my jab and sharp one-twos to keep him on the outside, but apparently that strategy wasn't impressing the judges. Maybe they should've asked the guy who was getting hit with them!

To make a long story short, in the 10th round I nailed Miteff with a big uppercut. You know how Mike Tyson used to twist and throw the uppercut from his hip? Well, that's how I launched the one that cracked Alex flush on the jaw. He staggered backwards into the ropes, and for a second I saw his whole body shiver. He was still wobbly when I moved in and caught him with a hook and right then another left hook and right that knocked him almost completely through the ropes and onto the ring apron. With his left leg suspended over the middle rope, he landed so hard on his back and shoulders that he nearly kicked me in the crotch as he crashed onto the lip of the apron, just above the press table.

By the time referee Billy Burke extricated Miteff's foot from between my legs and directed me to the neutral corner, Alex had been lying there for a good nine or 10 seconds. Burke turned to pick up the count from the timekeeper, an older Irish gentleman named Harry Campbell, whom I knew from the gym, but Harry was so excited and so happy for me that he forgot to start counting, so Burke had to start over again.

While this was going on, I looked over and saw Al Nicholson, a sportswriter for the Toronto *Globe and Mail,* along with a couple of other newspaper guys, and they were helping Miteff back on his feet, pushing him back through the ropes. Well, I went nuts. I started screaming at them: "What the hell are you doing? Leave him alone!" I was livid—but they just kept going, pushing Miteff back over the middle rope until both his feet were touching the canvas.

A good 20 seconds had elapsed since I'd dumped him, and there was no way in hell he would have beaten the count without those guys helping him. But what could I do about it? The final bell sounded half a minute later, and Miteff wobbled back to his corner.

The fight was scored a draw, which was total bullcrap, but in the July rankings I was No. 8 in the world. Nicholson said afterward that he was "only doing the Canadian thing" when he and those other clowns pushed Miteff back into the ring, but that's a load of you know what. As far as I'm concerned, they cost me a knockout—and probably a higher ranking. The Canadian thing, my ass. More like the Benedict Arnold thing.

What really galled me was that Nicholson played it up like he was some kind of hero and couldn't fathom why I was so upset. Did those guys think that Argentinean sportswriters would help me beat the count if the fight had been in Buenos Aires and I was the one getting knocked out of the ring? Forget about it!

About the only good thing to come out of that mess—other than my breaking into the top 10—was that *Toronto Telegram* photographer Lou Turofsky's shot of me blasting Miteff out of the ring ended up being named United Press International's sports photo of the year.

The fight got me some international notice, too. The following week *Sports Illustrated* mentioned it in the "For the Record" section, and the August 1958 issue of *The Ring* ran a feature story by Lew Eskin headlined "Heavyweight Hopefuls." Eskin named me as one of the three best "up-and-coming" heavyweights on the planet, along with Charley Liston of St. Louis and a guy from Nampa, Idaho, named Roque Maravilla. Liston, of course, soon dropped the "Charley" and became known to the world as Sonny (more on him later). As for Maravilla, I never heard of him before or since.

Miteff and I hooked up again at Maple Leaf Gardens on March 27, 1961, and—big surprise—I had to nearly kill him to get a 10-round split decision. It was a memorable outing for two reasons: one, I was sticking and moving and using my jab more than I ever had to that point, and two, it was the first time an opponent spoke to me during a fight, and in retrospect, I felt terrible about it.

When I tell people today that at one time I was a pretty good stick-and-move guy, they either burst out laughing or they think I'm bulljiving, but it's true. Remember, I was pretty much self-taught, so early in my career I relied less on strength and power and more on the kind of boxing skills I picked up from more experienced sparring partners. Besides that, Tommy McBeigh was convinced that the best way for me to fight was at longer range, so at least for a while, I became more of a boxer.

The incident that prompted Miteff to talk to me during our rematch was a direct result of that. From the opening bell I was up on my toes, moving in and out, stabbing with the jab. I hit Alex early and often, and by Round 4 he was badly cut over his right eye. Every time I jabbed him, more blood flowed. But the referee, a guy named Bobby Laurence, refused to stop the fight.

By the eighth round we were both covered in Miteff's blood and I was really frustrated at Laurence for not stopping it, so

I decided to force his hand by getting inside and throwing a head butt to open the cut even wider. It was a rotten thing to do, but I was only thinking about ending the fight.

Late in the round, I got Alex against the ropes and tried to slam my head into his cut, but he slid sideways and I just kind of banged him on the cheek. As we fell into a clinch he sighed and wearily said, "George, you don't have to do that to win this fight." He was so exhausted and so bloody that it made me feel like a piece of crap for even trying.

Alex wound up taking 27 stitches around the eye, but fortunately his face eventually healed up nicely. Later that year he snagged a small part in the movie *Requiem for a Heavyweight*, starring Anthony Quinn and Jackie Gleason, along with a very young Cassius Clay, who appears in the opening scene.

The sting of what happened with Miteff was still fresh in my mind three months later, and on September 15—three days after my 21st birthday—I vented my frustration on James J. Parker, whom I'd first sparred with when I was 16.

I knocked Jimmy down with my first punch just 30 seconds after the opening bell, then dropped him twice more before referee Sammy Luftspring counted him out exactly two minutes into our showdown for the Canadian heavyweight championship. It was Yom Kippur, and I wanted to send Luftspring home early to celebrate.

Parker, who came into the ring that night with a record of 30–6–4 and 25 KOs, never fought again.

The euphoria of becoming the youngest fighter ever to win the Canadian title lasted exactly 32 days. On October 17, I made my New York debut in a 10-rounder against "Irish" Pat McMurtry at Madison Square Garden. And I blew it, big time.

McMurtry was a former Marine sergeant from Tacoma, Washington, who had been ranked No. 5 in the world in 1957. He had a great amateur career, winning 103 of 105 fights, and he was also the first guy I ever heard of who got a boxing scholarship, to Gonzaga University in Spokane.

Pat turned pro in 1954 after serving in the Marine Corps and had only lost two of his 32 fights, scoring 25 knockouts. But like his idol, Gene Tunney, McMurtry was more of a boxer than a puncher. The gamblers made me the 9–5 betting favorite, and I was equally confident about my chances. Too confident, as it turned out.

I wasn't in the kind of shape I should have been in for such an important bout, but that was nobody's fault but my own. To be honest, I think the combination of being the newly crowned Canadian champ and headlining at the Garden for the first time at such a young age made me a little cocky. I'd dreamed of headlining in New York since the first time I listened to Don Dunphy broadcast a fight from the Mecca of boxing, but I probably didn't take it as seriously as I should have. Later on in my career it wasn't such a big deal to fight at MSG, but the first time was something pretty special, and it was a bit overwhelming.

Compared to Toronto, New York seemed very sophisticated. I was like John Boy Walton going to the big city for the first time. Everything was new and different and exciting, from the food vendors in the street to the way the kids hustled newspapers. I remember buying a papaya fruit drink at a little stand just around the corner from the Garden and thinking that I'd never quaffed anything so exotic!

To add to the excitement, the fight was televised on the *Gillette Cavalcade of Sports*, so I knew all my buddies in

Toronto would be watching, along with several million fight fans across North America. Jimmy Powers called the blow-by-blow action, and he made a point of telling everybody out there in TV Land that I was wearing custom-made size 12½ boxing shoes.

In the second round I staggered McMurtry with a good left hook off a jab that pretty much had him ready for the cleaners but, as had been the case in my fight with Bob Baker, I couldn't finish him. Later on in my career I became a much more accomplished finisher, but at that point I just wasn't experienced enough to know how to do it efficiently.

Pat managed to remain vertical, and in the third round he went to work behind his jab. He threw short, quick shots straight up the middle, and because I was looping my hooks, he started to tag me flush on the nose. Every time I threw a hook to the body, he fired back with two, three or four stiff jabs to my face. By Round 5, my schnozz was so banged up I was having a lot of trouble breathing, and when that happens in the ring, you get tired pretty quickly. By the 10th I was bone tired, and when McMurtry was awarded the decision, I could only blame myself.

When you lose a fight—any fight—it's the worst feeling in the world. First of all, you feel like you let down your corner. Then you think about all your friends and relatives that were watching, which only compounds the disappointment. My parents and my sister, Zora, were there at the Garden, along with some of my buddies from Toronto, and I felt like I really let them down. Worst of all is that you start second-guessing yourself, wondering why you did this when you should have done that. You replay the fight over and over in your head, punch by punch, and inevitably you conjure up mental images of how you should have responded rather than how you actually did respond. It's a pretty lonesome feeling, and it can drive you nuts.

I was more embarrassed than disappointed after losing to McMurtry, because in my heart I knew I hadn't prepared properly. Deacon Allen told the newspapers that "maybe George was a bit overmatched. . . . McMurtry has never fought better, and my guy couldn't have been worse."

I was despondent for months afterward. I started lifting weights again and bulked up to 255 pounds, but then Allen got worried about my weight so we spent a couple of weeks at a resort in Hot Springs, Arkansas, to sweat some of it off. That trip was a real eye-opener for me. A lot of mobsters and entertainers went to the resort, but they seemed just like regular people. We stayed at the Arlington Hotel, where I met comedian Henny Youngman, and Allen introduced me to an old-time gangster named Owney "The Killer" Madden, who looked and talked like a Baptist minister.

Madden's connection to boxing stretched back to the early 1930s, when he was partners with the mobsters who managed Italian giant Primo Carnera and arranged all the fixed fights that eventually led to Carnera winning the heavyweight championship. In 1932, Madden was apparently mixed up in the murder of a guy named Vincent "Mad Dog" Coll, who had allegedly been extorting money from Billy Duffy and Jean DeMange, who promoted Carnera's conqueror, Max Baer. Allen knew Madden through his connection to Baer's manager, Ancil Hoffman.

Madden might have had a sordid past, but I found him to be an interesting and thoughtful old gent to talk to. You'd never have guessed he was at the top of the FBI's Most Wanted list just a few years earlier.

If losing my New York debut taught me one thing, it was that I needed better preparation in the gym. Allen was a real cheapskate when it came to paying for good sparring partners—and he'd only bring them in for a week, at most—but they were the only guys who helped me in those days. You can learn a lot on your own, just by watching, but I was young and I needed the benefit of experienced fighters in the gym, something Allen rarely provided. One of the few exceptions was an old pro by the name of King George Moore, who came up from Detroit. He'd fought some name guys, including Cleveland Williams, and he taught me a lot, including how to spin a guy and how to avoid being spun. Little things like that.

Tommy McBeigh, my so-called "trainer," was basically just a yes-man for Allen and absolutely clueless when it came to instructing me. He threw a left hook like Stan Laurel's wife, and his idea of a fighting stance was something out of John L. Sullivan's day: standing straight up with arms extended and fists pumping up and down, like riding a unicycle with your hands. It sounds ludicrous, but that was the way he wanted me to fight.

Lousy training aside, another reason why my head wasn't where it should have been against McMurtry was because I was in love—and my girlfriend was pregnant.

The first time I spoke to Lynne Sheppard was in front of the Toronto-Dominion Bank on the corner of Keele and Dundas streets a year or so after I turned pro. A buddy named Bill Lehman and I were on our way to the gym, and he introduced us. Bill knew Lynne from the neighborhood, and she seemed like a nice kid. The Sheppard family roots went back to the *Mayflower;* they were United Empire Loyalists who moved up to eastern Ontario during the American Revolution. What Bill didn't tell me—and you sure couldn't tell by looking at Lynne—was that she was only 14 years old. She had a steady boyfriend at the time, but he was history once we started dating.

It was pretty casual at first. Lynne worked after school at a hair salon not far from the gym, so when I finished my workout we'd meet for a walk around the Junction. I liked her a lot, but as much as we enjoyed each other's company, we always seemed to end up arguing about some little thing.

Lynne was very pretty, with a great smile. She reminded me of Sandra Dee, the cute actress who lit up the big screen as the star of *Gidget* a couple of years later. Lynne's hair was blonde at the time because she dyed it. That's one reason I thought she was older; working in a salon after school seemed kind of sophisticated. She was also smart and quick-witted, which I found very attractive. She could size things up in a second and a half, and she was usually bang-on. Our favorite song was "Could This Be Magic" by The Dubs, which we used to sing to each other.

Once in a while I brought Lynne down to the gym to watch me train, but Deacon Allen and Tommy McBeigh got upset because they thought it was a distraction, so eventually she stopped coming. (Incidentally, when I first met Lynne on the northeast corner of Keele and Dundas, I had no idea the woman who would become my second wife, Joanne, was living a block and a half away. I guess I like girls from the same neighborhood!)

Lynne was very headstrong, which I wasn't used to, and she wasn't shy about expressing her opinions. It didn't occurr to me how young she was even though I would pick her up at Western Tech Commerce (where our son Mitchell became a teacher 30 years later). Here I was, a 19-year-old professional fighter, and I was dating this kid who was in Grade 9! If I had known how old she was, I would've felt like Jerry Lee Lewis, the cradle-robbing rock 'n' roller.

Love is kind of a double-edged sword when you're that young, and neither one of us was ready to deal with the consequences. When Lynne got pregnant at 15, I almost had a stroke. To begin with, I couldn't believe how ignorant I was. We'd been going together for about a year and half and I was crazy about her, but that didn't change the fact that this wasn't exactly the most ideal situation for either of us. The fact was that her father had to go to city hall to sign permission for Lynne to marry me; that's when I found out she was only 15. I thought she was 17. But in the end it didn't make any difference. We ended up tying the knot on March 31, 1959, and Mitchell Aaron was born four months later on July 25—four days after Lynne's 16th birthday.

I was proud and thrilled when Lynne delivered the son I'd been rooting for. Mitchell was Lynne's mother's maiden name, and we both liked the name Aaron. That was Moses's brother in the Bible . . . and also Elvis's middle name!

Becoming a father for the first time and being responsible for another life was a bit overwhelming. All of a sudden I found myself thinking about his health, his education, all that stuff . . . and he was still a brand new baby! I just wanted to protect him and do my best to guide him. What's a bigger responsibility than that?

Mitchell was a happy little guy, but he had a serious side, too. From an early age he was very inquisitive, and he went on to become an excellent student. He skipped a grade in elementary school (just like me), and after high school he was awarded a full-ride football scholarship to play fullback at Florida State. After injuring his knee, he transferred to the University of Guelph back in Ontario, where he earned his degree.

Mitchell later taught and coached at Toronto's Western Tech—the same high school Lynne was attending when she became pregnant with him—and in 2000 he won the NFL and CFL's Youth Coach of the Year award, which recognizes volunteer coaches across Canada who dedicate themselves to the development of young players both on and off the field. Today he's a teacher and wrestling coach at University of Toronto Schools, an independent secondary institution for academically gifted students, affiliated with the University of Toronto.

Getting married and then almost immediately becoming parents took our lives in directions that neither of us was prepared for, but to be honest, Lynne handled it with much more strength and maturity than I did. To put it bluntly, I wasn't ready or willing to make the adjustments that necessarily go along with being a new husband and father.

It's not that I didn't love my wife; it was more a case of me loving her on my own terms. In our rush to do what in those days was called "the right thing," I felt pressured—to the point where I resisted making those adjustments and instead made some stupid, terrible mistakes.

For starters, I was disrespectful to my wife. That sounds trite, but in retrospect it was a horrible, selfish way to start our life together. Of course, I never thought anything about it at the time because my buddies and I were all cut from the same bolt of cloth, and I honestly didn't think that being a married man should change any of that. That's how ignorant and disrespectful I was. And the fact I didn't want to change only made matters worse.

Did I mess around? Yes, I did. Was it right? No, not in any way, shape or form. But in some small corner of my brain, that herd mentality took over and I convinced myself that nothing had changed, that I could continue doing the things my pals and I had always done before a wife and baby came into my life. And that's exactly what it was, a herd mentality. When everybody's doing it, that kind of life doesn't seem so immoral. But it was, and I got into some bad trouble because of it.

Three weeks after I took my marriage vows, I was arrested for rape.

ROUND 2

THE RAPE CHARGE WASN'T MY FIRST RUN-IN WITH THE law. As a kid, I was arrested for fighting on the street and spent two and a half days in Toronto's Don Jail, which was more than enough to convince me I never wanted to return. I was put in what was known as "Gunsell's Alley," the under-21 area with a bunch of other young guys. You'd get handed somebody's comic book, passed from cell to cell, to use as toilet paper. The toilet was just a wide-mouthed spittoon. That was most unpleasant especially when you consider that in those days the used spittoons in the cells weren't changed until the next morning—but nothing compared to what I was about to face.

Instead of being at home with my pregnant wife on that April night in 1959, I was out with a buddy named Jack, cruising around Chinatown in my car, when we spotted a girl walking down the street. It sounds crude and ridiculous today, but I'd picked up so many girls in bars and on the street just by talking to them that it had almost become second nature, and the fact that I was now a married man didn't even enter into the equation.

Anyway, we pulled up beside this girl and Jack rolled down the window and started making small talk—"Hi beautiful, how ya doin'? Need a lift?" Pretty standard stuff. She didn't hesitate about getting into the car, and to make a long story short, before very long I was having sex with her in the back seat at a drive-in restaurant, of all places. When we finished, I asked her, "How about taking care of my buddy, too?" She kind of balked at first, so I didn't press her on it, but a couple of minutes later she agreed. Jack hopped in the back seat with her, finished his business (we both used condoms), and that was that. I drove back to where Jack had parked his car, and we all got out.

Jack went to his car, and the girl and I started walking to the Premium restaurant, our regular hangout, which was just down the street. She said she had to make a phone call, which I thought was odd, but then I remembered she'd mentioned having a kid, so I assumed she was calling her babysitter. I went into the restaurant, sat down and ordered something to eat. When the girl didn't come back from the phone booth after a few minutes, I just assumed she'd decided to go home. No big deal in my mind.

I should have gone home too, but I didn't. By now it was about four in the morning, so I went to another restaurant, a place called the Brazil on the corner of St. Clair and Lansdowne. After a little while I went back to the Premium. Just as I was getting comfortable, I looked up and saw the girl coming through the front door with a police officer. They walked right up to my booth and the cop said to me, "You're under arrest. Come outside." I was too shocked to even ask what the charge was, but when we got to the police station, the sergeant informed me I was being booked for rape.

I was dumbfounded and horrified at the same time. A cop hustled me into a little room, where I was ordered to take off my pants and underwear for an examination. After they checked out the rest of my body for scratches, I was fingerprinted and photographed, then taken to a holding cell. A few hours later, after a paddy-wagon ride to court, I was released after promising to appear in the same court the following week, but by the time I got back home, the story—along with my picture—had already hit the front page of the morning paper.

Looking back, I would rather have been charged with murder. Except for being an accused pedophile, nothing is worse than a rape charge. Once the story gets out, regardless of what the truth is, the public naturally assumes you're guilty. I remember being in a store the following day and the clerk looking at me like I was the lowest piece of shit on the planet. Everywhere I went, strangers stared at me with a disgusted look that told me their minds were already made up. I was supposed to be the best man at the wedding of my buddy, Johnny Milkovich, but the priest phoned him to say I wouldn't be welcome at the church. That hurt a lot.

The lawyer I retained to fight the charge was a guy named Arthur Maloney, who years later became the Provincial Ombudsman of Ontario. I told him exactly what happened from the moment we saw the girl on the street, making it very clear that she hadn't been raped or otherwise forced to do anything against her will. I wasn't sure Maloney believed me, but at some point during our initial conversation he asked if the girl knew I was a fighter. I told him that shortly after we picked her up, she asked what I did for a living. As stupid as it sounds in hindsight, I told her I was a pro golfer. Don't ask me where that came from. I told Maloney that before going to the drive-in we stopped to buy some gas, and when I took the money out of my wallet to pay the bill, my New York State boxing license fell out on the floor. I didn't see that happen, but the girl scooped it up and handed it back to me a few minutes later, which gave her plenty of time to see what it was.

The way the whole thing unfolded became clear a couple of weeks later when I was at a party at my cousin Marie's house. I got called to the phone, and on the other end of the line was a voice that said, "George, you don't know me, but I'm a cab driver and I've been trying to reach you because something happened to me this week that I think you should know about." When I asked him what he was talking about, he said, "I picked up a fare, and when she got in the back seat of my cab she said, 'Do you know who you look like? George Chuvalo, the fighter.' I kind of laughed and said, 'Oh yeah?' And then, out of the blue, she said, 'I've got him on a rape charge.' Then she told me that you didn't really rape her, but that she'd make a bundle of money out of it."

I was so stunned that I nearly dropped the phone. I got the guy's name and number, and the next day he met with Mr. Maloney and repeated the exact same story. The following week, the cabbie was sitting in the back row of the courtroom at my preliminary hearing.

When it came time for Maloney to question the girl on the stand, he asked her, "Do you recognize this gentleman?" When the cabbie stood up, the girl froze like a statue. She didn't say a word, just sat there dumbfounded. Maloney repeated the question two more times, but she gave no response. Five minutes later, after being informed about the cabbie's pending testimony, the judge ordered the charge dropped and the case was dismissed.

Remember how my arrest was plastered all over the front page of the papers? The day after I was exonerated, a two-paragraph story about the charge being dropped was buried on the comics page. As for the little Italian cab driver who saved my butt all those years ago, I'm embarrassed to say that I can't recall his name—but I'm eternally grateful to him.

Even though my name was cleared, the rape charge haunted me for a long time. As hellish as it had been for me, it was even worse for Lynne. It's a horrible, horrible thing to face a pregnant wife of three weeks and tell her that you've been charged with rape, but in an odd way it really showed how strong she was. Lynne knew how embarrassed and humiliated I felt, because she was going through exactly the same thing. And as awful as it was for me, it must've been 100 times worse for her. I wouldn't have blamed her if she'd just packed up and left without a word, but on that day I came home from the police station, after she'd seen the headlines and faced the humiliation of people phoning her and telling her what an asshole I was, the first thing she said to me was, "George, I'm really angry and I'm really hurt . . . but I know in my heart that you could never rape anybody."

Lynne didn't forgive me (and I don't blame her), but she let me off the hook. And her belief in me made it a whole lot easier to face up to what was ahead. She was made of sterner stuff, which showed me how special she was.

You don't realize how crazy you can be sometimes. If I'd been respectful towards my wife, the whole episode would never have happened. And I couldn't even imagine what my poor mother, father and sister must have felt. Same with Lynne's parents. They believed in me, thank God, but we still had to talk about it. I remember telling them, "I'm in a lot of trouble because I did something very wrong. I was with another woman, but I didn't rape her."

I was so overcome with shame and humiliation, and when it becomes public knowledge, you can't take it back. I had disgraced them all—even my unborn son. And who would want their brand new son-in-law charged like that? But my in-laws didn't start pointing fingers or berating me, and to their credit, they didn't turn their backs on me. Their thoughts were with Lynne, and they didn't want to make a bad situation worse.

It took a couple of years for the rape charge to be completely behind me. Once in a while it came up in a newspaper story, but how could it not? Even now, 54 years later, how could I ignore it or gloss over it? It was on TV and the radio and in the papers, so it's not like I could just pretend it would go away. I couldn't take two steps without feeling like shrinking into a hole. I was stupid and I paid a price for that monumental stupidity. I just thank God there were no tabloids back then.

As for the girl, I never saw her again.

Five months later I returned to the ring and knocked out California's Frankie Daniels in seven rounds at Maple Leaf Gardens. I thought all my troubles were behind me—but they were only just beginning.

By the time I knocked out Daniels—two days after my 22nd birthday—I'd been a pro for nearly three and a half years. I was 16–3–1, world-ranked . . . and stuck in neutral. After blowing my New York debut against McMurtry, it didn't look like I was headed back to the Big Apple anytime soon, and nobody was stepping up to challenge for my Canadian title, so I went into a bit of a tailspin.

With a wife and new baby to take care of, my heart wasn't much into training and I began to ponder how I could end my association with Jack Allen and Tommy McBeigh, the two guys who were supposedly overseeing my development.

McBeigh handled all of Allen's fighters. Sonny Thomson was the No. 2 guy, even though he knew a lot more about the game than Tommy. McBeigh was almost totally clueless. In the gym, all he ever did was smear Vaseline on my face and shout "Be first!" during sparring sessions—not exactly inspiring or instructive. He knew nothing about how to slip the jab or how to pivot, stuff like that. Everything I learned about the mechanics of boxing I picked up from the sparring partners that Allen brought up from Detroit (and those All-Wheat cards I collected as a kid!).

For me, as a student of boxing, studying the different styles and skills of my sparring partners became a deliberate process. If you pay close attention you can learn a lot. And no matter how good you get, there's always something new to learn.

Boxing is very much a game of inches and angles, and it's often the tiniest, most innocuous detail that makes the difference between winning and losing. Take a guy like Roberto Duran, one of the best pound-for-pound fighters in history. An opponent would be standing right in front of him with his hands raised in a perfect defensive posture, but Roberto, simply by sliding his right foot six or eight inches to the side, could shoot a left uppercut through the guard and a right hand over the top. Little things like foot movement make all the difference in the world, but McBeigh had no clue about stuff like that.

The same goes for something as simple as blocking a hook. Just like when you slip a punch, you want to be moving closer to the other guy—not leaning back—when you block a hook to the head. That way, after catching the punch on your right hand, you're in position to land one of your own. Obviously, anybody with a decent left hook is going to throw it to the body too, but McBeigh couldn't comprehend the logic of keeping my elbows tucked in to absorb punches with my arms. He was always insisting that my arms should be extended way out in front.

Working with old-school sparring partners like King George Moore and Billy Hunter, I discovered I could make a guy drop his hands just by quickly slamming the front of his shoulder with an open glove, then I'd nail him with a right hand or hook. Moore was the guy who showed me how to relax my arms in a clinch so I couldn't be spun.

It was also in sparring sessions with those guys that I first hatched the idea of stepping on an opponent's toes so he couldn't get away—which I later used with great success against Doug Jones. There's nothing in the Marquess of Queensberry rules that says you can't do that, so I worked on making it part of my repertoire. I'd plant my left foot on top of the other guy's left foot so he couldn't get away, then shoot a right to the body or head. It worked like a charm against taller guys, and to this day I regret not trying it with Ernie Terrell and Muhammad Ali.

Even more frustrating than the fact McBeigh and Thomson couldn't teach me any of the technical aspects of boxing was that Allen insisted I follow their instructions to the letter, even though most of those instructions were unbelievably stupid.

But he was the manager, right? For example, they were so concerned about me not having sex for three or four weeks before a fight that they came up with a way of preventing wet dreams, which they thought weakened you.

I'd always thought having a wet dream was Mother Nature's way of kind of taking care of things if you're not getting lucky, but then again I was only 18 years old, so what the hell could I know? For the first year of my career I acquiesced to McBeigh's "solution," which was for me to tightly knot a rubber band around the head of my penis before going to sleep—the idea being that getting an erection would be painful enough to wake me up.

That theory crumbled when I had three wet dreams the night before I KO'd Joe Evans in the very first round. Still, a stubborn McBeigh ordered me to use a piece of thread next time, which was as painful as it sounds. The first time I woke up with blood all over the sheets was the last time I went with the thread.

I've never bought into the idea that abstaining from sex makes a fighter meaner or sharper. You'd hear old trainers say, "His legs is gone!"—meaning their guy had sex and couldn't possibly be ready to fight, but I always thought that was a load of crap. Sex is normal, and I think for guys who are very edgy before a big fight, it's probably the best and most natural way to relieve tension. It depends on the individual, of course. I didn't have to have it because I think I was a pretty cool customer going into a fight.

I was never edgy or fidgety or what you'd call unnerved going into the ring. If anything, I just got real quiet. Some guys get very outgoing, very gregarious on the day of a fight, but that was never my style. If I was in Toronto, I liked to have a few friends around to listen to music or just sit around and kibitz with each other and have a few laughs. Anything was better than hanging with my trainer and manager, neither of whom was any good at keeping things light. Most trainers are naturally kind of somber, and managers are too wound up to know how to help you relax.

Even later in my career, when Teddy McWhorter was my trainer and Irving Ungerman was managing me, they weren't the best guys to hang with on the day of a fight. Far from it. Ungerman would get so keyed up that he couldn't even speak intelligently; he'd just kind of babble about whatever popped into his head. It was as annoying as it was ludicrous. He had no clue about how to help me relax, and he'd even shoo away anybody who dropped by the dressing room to lighten things up.

When you're getting ready for battle, you don't want to look at a couple of sad sacks with long faces that remind you of what you're going to be doing in a few hours; you want to keep the atmosphere upbeat. You want a guy like Angelo Dundee, who was a master at creating a calm, serene environment, even in the circus atmosphere surrounding champions like Ali and Sugar Ray Leonard. I never had that.

On the road, I liked to get away by myself and watch an afternoon movie. I found that getting absorbed in a good story up on the big screen was the perfect way for me to relax because it would take my mind off what I was going to do a few hours later. The films I recall most vividly are *The Arrangement* (when I fought Jerry Quarry), *Joe* (George Foreman) and *Dirty Harry* (my second fight with Ali).

An incident that happened during training for my title defense against Yvon Durelle marked the beginning of the end of my association with Allen and McBeigh. It was my first defense—November 17, 1959, at Maple Leaf Gardens—and there was a lot of pre-fight hype.

Durelle, the "Fighting Fisherman" from Baie-Sainte-Anne, New Brunswick, was a wild, powerful puncher and the reigning British Commonwealth light heavyweight champ. Half of his 85 wins had been by KO, and the previous December, in one of the greatest title bouts in history, he floored the great Archie Moore four times before the champ finally stopped him in Round 11. Still, I figured it would be like shooting fish in a barrel. I wouldn't have to look for Yvon; with his wild style I was confident that he'd be right in front of me for the taking.

Four days before the fight, during my final sparring session, a left hook thrown by Dave Shoulders, a pretty good banger we'd brought up from Detroit, punctured my right eardrum. It was a freak thing, caused by the impact of the air being driven into my ear. I knew what happened right away, because I suddenly couldn't hear anything out of that ear. But when I told Allen and McBeigh that something was seriously wrong and I needed to get it checked out, McBeigh just laughed and said, "I never spend a biscuit on a doctor." That was in the days before Canadians had free medical coverage, so I knew there was no way my manager was shelling out for an examination. Then McBeigh chimed in with some rather sage advice: "Just pour some hydrogen peroxide in your ear and it'll be as good as new." I had never heard of that particular remedy, which in my ignorance sounded completely logical.

I went home to Lynne and told her to administer McBeigh's "treatment," but she said I was crazy and refused to do it. It never dawned on me that, having worked as a hairstylist, my teenage bride was very familiar with hydrogen peroxide. Instead, like a jerk, I got mad and yelled at her to shut up and just do what she was told. I lay down on the bed and she poured the stuff directly into my ear.

Well, I never felt that kind of physical pain in my life—before or since. It was like having a hot poker shoved into my ear. I was certain the hydrogen peroxide was frying my brain. I'm sure my screams could be heard a block away, and all I could hope for was that the river of tears streaming down my face would somehow find their way into my ear canal.

No such luck.

After what seemed like an eternity, the pain dissipated somewhat. But the following day—a Sunday—infection and swelling set in, and I knew I needed professional help. On Monday morning I went to see a doctor, who took one look at my ear and said that McBeigh should be horsewhipped for dispensing such stupid advice.

The doc gave me some penicillin and strongly suggested that we call off the fight, which was scheduled for the following night. He told me that if I got whacked on the ear, I'd probably go deaf—permanently. I should have heeded his warning, but I really needed the $6,000 payday.

Durelle was a street brawler who threw wide punches from every angle, but I figured I could take him out early, before he got a chance to land one on my ear. As it turned out, I dropped him with a left hook in the first round, then six more times before he was finally counted out in the 12th. Yvon was a very tough customer, strong and relentless, but I kind of let him off the hook. After every knockdown, instead of moving in to finish him off, I held back because I was worried about getting whacked in the ear. When he went down the last time, he was out cold and one of his legs was twitching, like when you shoot a horse. That was scary.

After the fight, Durelle was quoted in the papers as saying he could have beaten me if he were younger (he said he was 30, but he was really 29) and if he'd trained harder, but to me it just sounded like sour grapes.

Durelle fought only six more times after that, retiring in 1963 with a terrific record of 90–23–2. We hooked up again for an exhibition bout a couple of years later in Halifax to raise money for former Canadian lightweight champ Richie "Kid" Howard, whose young daughter had been killed in a traffic accident. I was still pissed off about some of the things Yvon had said after our title bout, and I'm ashamed to say that I slapped him around pretty good in that exhibition as payback.

Years later we met again at a sportsmen's dinner, and without really saying anything or rehashing old grudges, we hugged and eventually became pretty good friends. I once visited his house in Baie-Sainte-Anne, and whenever we were in the same city we'd get together and talk about the old days. When Yvon died in 2007 I felt terrible about not being able to attend his funeral, but I was en route to Tanzania to cheer on my second wife, Joanne, who was climbing Mount Kilimanjaro to raise money for the Canadian Liver Foundation.

That punctured eardrum resulted in some long-term damage that persists to this day, but it wasn't bothering me in my next outing eight months later, when I lost a 10-round decision to 1956 Olympic gold medalist Pete Rademacher. I wish it had been, because that bout was the worst one of my career.

I'd actually signed to fight Cuban veteran Nino Valdes in the interim, but that was canceled when a routine medical examination by the Ontario Athletic Commission revealed that Valdes, who was coming off a KO of England's Brian London, was almost blind in his left eye. He never fought again.

The fact of the matter is that I was young and arrogant, and I didn't train worth a damn for Rademacher. It was kind of ironic, because if I'd delayed turning pro and gone to the 1956 Olympics in Melbourne, I probably would've ended up fighting him for a medal. As it turned out, he KO'd a Czech, a South African and a Russian to win gold for the U.S., and a year later he became the first guy ever to fight for the world heavyweight championship in his pro debut.

Still, there's no way in hell Rademacher should have beaten me in our outdoor fight at Maple Leaf Stadium in Toronto. Floyd Patterson knocked him out in six rounds in their 1957 title bout in Seattle (which overshadowed the fact that Floyd was decked in the opening round) but Pete wasn't much of a banger. He looked like an accountant and punched like a florist. He piled up points because I just stood there like a dummy and let him hit me, without ever firing back more than one punch at a time. I knew I wasn't in shape, and maybe I was a little cocky because at 7–3–1 he was only the third opponent who'd had fewer fights than me (the others were Sid Russell and Moses Graham, both of whom I KO'd in one round in '57), but that's still no excuse.

Rademacher outboxed me and he won, fair and square. As the next day's headline in the *Toronto Star* put it,

"Chuvalo's stock hits rock bottom after inept showing against Rademacher."

It's the only one of my 18 defeats that still makes me wince with embarrassment more than 50 years later.

The loss to Rademacher spiraled me into a long period of soul searching. Sure, I still had the Canadian title, but I wasn't making any real dough and I was feeling more and more like a guinea pig running around in one of those little wheels. The harder I worked at it, the less I felt like I was accomplishing anything. I was definitely unhappy with my management and with what I perceived as a lack of progress.

The five-year contract I'd signed with Allen when I turned pro in 1956 still had a year to go (I didn't find out until later that five-year deals were illegal in Ontario; the maximum allowed was four), and even though my end of each purse was two-thirds of the total (with the 10 per cent trainer's fee and all other expenses taken off the top), I was constantly broke.

Twenty-eight days after the debacle against Rademacher, I went to Montreal to defend my Canadian title against Bob Cleroux. Bob was strong and awkward and fought out of a low crouch. A week after my fight with Rademacher, Cleroux jumped ahead of me in the rankings by knocking out Roy Harris, the pride of Cut 'n' Shoot, Texas. That was the first (and last) time that two Canadian-born heavyweights were ranked among the world's top 10, so there was a tremendous amount of buildup for our fight, especially in Quebec's French-language press.

All the publicity really took me by surprise. Sometimes there were seven or eight photos of me in the French papers in a single day, and twice as many of Bob. There'd be pictures of me running, eating breakfast, lighting candles at church. The pre-fight hype was unbelievable, but I loved it.

When we met on August 17, Jersey Joe Walcott was the third man in the ring and Cleroux ended up being awarded a split decision (notice I don't say "winning"), which was a joke. Walcott indicated he was going to stop the fight after the 10th round, but Cleroux's corner convinced him to let it continue. I don't think I lost a single round, but in his hometown I would've had to kill him to get the win. Al Bachman, who was Cleroux's manager, admitted as much when he was interviewed for a cover story about me in the January 1964 edition of *Boxing Illustrated:* "There was a natural indignation among French-Canadians about the way George had clobbered Durelle, and I knew they'd be banking on Cleroux to avenge their honor," said Bachman. "It was my finest hour. Not only did we make more money than we would have in Toronto, we had the advantage of a Quebec ring and Quebec officials. Chuvalo should have got the decision, but he didn't. We had the home advantage."

Cleroux wouldn't come to Toronto for a rematch, so we squared off again in Montreal on November 23, and this time I got the nod and regained the title. Before the bout, a guy who knew my manager told me if I bet $1,000 on myself and won, I'd pocket three grand. He said he could get those odds, but when he came back after the fight, he told me he hadn't found anyone to take the bet. I knew he was bullshitting and had just pocketed the profit himself. Live and learn.

Still, getting my title back was more important than the money, especially since it was only three weeks after Lynne gave birth to our second son on November 2. I was in Montreal when he was born, and I couldn't wait to get home.

Unlike Mitchell, who looked more like his papa (me), our new son looked like Lynne . . . and my mother. We picked Steven as his first name in honor of my father, but when Lynne said she wanted his middle name to be Fredrick (after her father), I quickly vetoed the idea. I really liked Lynne's dad, but there was no way I was naming any kid of mine Fredrick, with all due respect to the Fredricks out there. Not a chance. Well, Lynne got mad, but I stood my ground. On the birth registration I wrote in "Steven Louis" (my middle name), and she reluctantly signed it.

With another mouth to feed in the Chuvalo household, I was looking forward to keeping busy and moving up the rankings.

I was supposed to fight British contender Brian London at Maple Leaf Gardens in early 1961, but a few days before the bout I got hit with the flu bug and lost eight pounds overnight. We asked for a one-week postponement, but London didn't want to stick around. He claimed that the church bells across the street from his room at the King Edward Hotel were driving him nuts, so he hightailed it back to Britain.

In March, I won my rematch with Alex Miteff at the Gardens, then knocked out German champ Willie Besmanoff in four rounds in June. Besmanoff was a tough, durable guy with 44 wins, including decisions over Bob Baker and Pat McMurtry, two guys I'd lost to. He'd been cut up and stopped in seven rounds by Sonny Liston a couple of years earlier, but Liston couldn't knock him down.

I dropped Willie seven times in a little over 12 minutes before his corner threw in the towel. That was the worst beating I ever gave anybody, capped by what I think is the hardest punch I ever threw. It came off a classic shoeshine: six shots to the body, then a left hook I threw from the hip. The punch exploded off his jaw. Poor Willie was out cold, but his legs were twitching like he'd been electrocuted. I felt pretty good about it, because not even Liston had been able to put him away like that.

On August 8, six weeks after starching Besmanoff, I fought Cleroux again in a rubber match for the Canadian title at Delorimier Stadium in Montreal. It was the only one of our three fights that was close. They gave it to him, and I couldn't argue. Early on he whacked me with a right hand, and my ear swelled up to a couple of inches thick. It was painful, but losing the title hurt more. I'd been around long enough to appreciate that being introduced by ring announcers as the Canadian heavyweight champion was a lot better than just being another schmuck from Palookaville, and while it would be another couple of years before I got the title back, enough things were happening in my life to keep that goal on the back burner for the time being.

It wasn't until after my last fight of 1961—a disqualification loss to former British Commonwealth champ Joe Erskine at Maple Leaf Gardens on October 2—that I finally concluded that my only shot at becoming world champion was to get out of Toronto. My climb up the rankings had been temporarily derailed, but I knew I hadn't come close to realizing my full potential. I figured I could still get back on track if I just had the right people in my corner.

The disqualification against Erskine, a Welshman, was entirely my fault. We were wearing Frager gloves, which had the thumb overlapping the meaty part of the glove, so it was easy to poke a guy in the eye with the thumb, even if you weren't trying to do so.

Erskine was probably the lightest puncher I ever fought, but in the first couple of rounds he thumbed me twice in the eye, and I got hot. Not being slick enough to headbutt properly, after Joe thumbed me the second time, I just reared back and smacked him with my forehead. It was stupid and immature—but then I did it a couple more times for good measure. It was a classic example of how *not* to butt an opponent. (Two-Ton Tony Galento later taught me how to follow a butt with a short right hand, making it look like the punch caused the damage.)

Unfortunately, Joe's thumbing wasn't as obvious as my retaliation, and after a couple of warnings, referee Sammy Luftspring finally disqualified me in the fifth round. I was mad at Sammy, but I should've been mad at myself. Erskine had a good record—he was 38–5–1 at the time, including a couple of wins over Henry Cooper and a decision over Willie Pastrano—but he wasn't giving me any trouble. If I hadn't lost my cool, I would've beaten him easily.

What ticked me off the most was that I had a verbal agreement to fight Floyd Patterson for the world championship on December 4 at Maple Leaf Gardens if I beat Erskine. Patterson had regained the title by knocking out Ingemar Johansson in March, and he wanted me for his first defense. Instead, Floyd ended up knocking out No. 7–ranked Tom McNeeley in four rounds.

Despite the back-to-back losses to Cleroux and Erskine, in early 1962 the World Boxing Association ranked me No. 2 on the planet, which only reinforced my decision to buy out my contract with Allen, dump McBeigh as my trainer and get the hell out of Toronto. I knew I could hold my own with anyone in the world, but I needed better training and better direction than I felt I was ever going to get with those guys.

What I didn't count on was not fighting for 17 months while I scrambled to take my career in a new direction.

ROUND 3

MY FIRST MOVE AFTER CUTTING TIES WITH Allen and McBeigh was to switch gyms. I went from training at the Toronto Athletic Club to training at a smaller place run by the Bagnato brothers, but with no fights lined up for the foreseeable future and less than $200 in the bank, my top priority was to find an alternative source of income.

That's when I got a call from a friend who was a janitor at a luxury apartment building. One of the tenants, a well-known Toronto stockbroker, had recently imported a brand new Aston Martin sports car as a gift for his wife. She didn't like it, and finally, in disgust, the broker told my buddy that if he could sell it, he could keep anything over $2,000. My pal asked me to partner up on the deal, on the understanding that we'd split the profit if either of us sold the car. I put a small ad in the paper, and a day or two later I unloaded it for $3,000.

I couldn't believe it was so easy to make $500—especially since I knew less about Aston Martins than I knew about astrophysics. If we'd been a little more on the ball we could have gotten five or six thousand, easily. One guy who came over to look at the car ran his hand over its flank like it was a horse or a slave girl, and he nearly cried when I told him it was already sold.

Still, I was pretty happy to make $500. For the next several months, when I wasn't training at the gym, I learned the used car business. I wasn't particularly successful at it, but I made enough money to keep the wolf from the door.

It was through my auto connections that I met a gentleman named Murray Schwartz. He was a well-known car dealer and a big boxing fan who occasionally dropped by the gym to watch the sparring. One afternoon, he said he'd drive me down to Detroit to meet somebody who might be interested in becoming my new trainer.

I was still contractually bound to Allen and McBeigh, so I begged and borrowed the $3,000 I needed from friends and relatives to buy my freedom.

On November 7, 1962, I walked into the Big D Gym in Detroit for the first time and Murray introduced me to a skinny little black guy who was doing the glove beat with Irish Billy Collins, a world-ranked welterweight from Nashville. The little guy's name was Teddy McWhorter, and I liked him right away.

Teddy looked like he'd just stepped out of a cartoon. He had a pencil-thin mustache, all but three of his teeth were missing, and he was wearing a stitched floppy brown leather hat, oversized boxing shoes, blue denim work pants and a purple bowling shirt with "Sammy" stitched in red lettering on a white patch above the breast pocket.

But looks can be deceiving. Born in Alabama, McWhorter was an old-time fight guy who years earlier had befriended another ex-Alabamian who relocated to Detroit: Joe Louis.

They'd trained together at Brewster's Gym and remained close all through Joe's career. Teddy had been a passable amateur fighter, but he never went pro. His real talent was in the corner. In addition to Collins, he'd trained guys like Chuck Davey, Yvon Durelle and Johnny Summerlin, a world-ranked heavyweight who lost back-to-back decisions to Sonny Liston in 1954.

Within five minutes, McWhorter agreed to work with me. I didn't know anybody in Detroit, I was on my own as far as management was concerned and I was almost totally broke—but I couldn't have been more pleased.

To me, the Big D was like the Garden of Eden. It represented the land of opportunity . . . the kind of environment I knew I needed in order to take that next step, and I was filled with a tremendous sense of anticipation.

For the next three years, I was one of the very few white guys training there, but that was never an issue with anybody. Right away, I was sparring with top-notch fighters like Sonny Banks, Cody Jones and Lucky Little. Earlier that year, Banks had dropped Cassius Clay (he wasn't yet known as Muhammad Ali) before being stopped in the fourth round, and Jones would go on to become one of Ali's favorite sparring partners.

Two of the young fighters who immediately caught my eye at the Big D were Hedgemon Lewis and Ronnie Harris. They were just 16-year-old kids, but I remember thinking that both of them were budding boxing geniuses. Lewis went on to become welterweight champion of the world, while Harris won lightweight gold for the U.S. at the 1968 Mexico City Olympics before launching a very respectable pro career.

Another young face around the Big D belonged to a quiet 18-year-old kid who was always willing to help out in the corner, run out for tea or coffee for the fighters or take care of any of the thousand and one little chores that come with helping pros prepare for battle. His name was Emanuel Steward. Years later he became the kingpin of the Kronk Gym stable and trained or managed more than a dozen world champions, including Thomas Hearns, Michael Moorer and Lennox Lewis. It was a huge loss for boxing when Manny died after a long illness in 2012. He was 68.

After watching me work at the Big D for a couple of weeks, a guy named Burns Stanley, who co-managed Banks with his partner, Ted Ewald, was impressed enough to offer to pay off the $3,000 debt I still owed for buying my freedom from Jack Allen. Stanley was a lawyer for the Ford Motor Company and a real Southern gentleman. Although there were no strings attached to his offer, he made it clear that he wanted to add me to his stable. We talked it over, but after what I'd just gone through with Allen, I wasn't in the market for a new manager. Still, thanks to Mr. Stanley's generosity, I essentially became a free agent. I figured that with McWhorter training me, I could handle all the rest of the stuff myself.

I moved into a seedy hotel called the Berkshire, which was right in the heart of downtown Detroit on Winder Street, not far from the gym. It was a black neighborhood, but there were a few other white guys living there. For the grand sum of $11.25 a week, I got a tiny room on the ground floor. There was a shared bathroom down the hall and the walls were paper thin, but it was home for the next couple of weeks until Lynne came down from Toronto. She was eight months pregnant and wanted to be with me when the baby was born, so I really had to watch my nickels and dimes.

Most of the time I was too broke to eat more than a piece

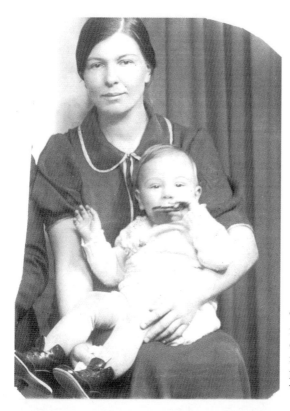

The greatest feeling in the world: being cuddled by my mother, for a studio portrait in 1938. I was a year old.

The first two members of the Chuvalo clan to move to Canada: my uncle George (whom I was named after), on the left, and my father.

Donning my Sunday best for First Communion, 1943.

I could look downright studious with a book in front of me. This is in Grade 7, when I was 11.

Posing in the backyard of our house on Gillespie Avenue. I was 15 years old and a lean, mean 198 pounds.

That's me on the left, sparring with St. Mike's classmate Myron Blozowski in 1951.

A slice of cake and a hug from my mother was the perfect way to celebrate my 21st birthday, in 1958.

On September 15, 1958—just three days after my 21st birthday—I KO'd James J. Parker in the first round to win the Canadian heavyweight title. That's my trainer Sonny Thomson raising my arm in victory.

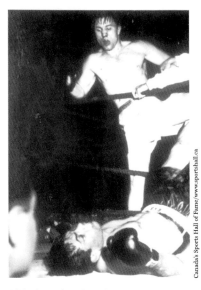

This shot of me knocking Argentina's Alex Miteff out of the ring was voted 1958's Canadian sports photo of year by United Press International.

After training at Kutsher's Resort in Monticello, New York, I was razor-sharp for my 1965 title elimination bout with Floyd Patterson.

Looping a right to Ernie Terrell's midsection in our title bout at Maple Leaf Gardens on November 1, 1965.

Versions of this shot of my right fist distorting Floyd Patterson's face have been used on a couple of album covers, including the Rolling Stones' *Exile on Main St.* Our 12-round war was named 1965's Fight of the Year by *The Ring*.

Muhammad Ali complained loud and long about my hitting him low in our first fight, at Maple Leaf Gardens on March 29, 1966—and judging by this photo, he had a case. But I swear it wasn't deliberate!

People always say to me, "Hey George, you were the first guy to go 15 rounds with Ali!" but I prefer to think Muhammad went 15 with me. That's referee Jackie Silvers looking on.

This shot of me blasting Italian champ Dante Cane at Maple Leaf Gardens in 1968 is the one that Rocky Balboa pulls out of his wallet in the first Rocky movie.

Joe Louis stands between me and Joe Frazier outside Madison Square Garden the day before our fight on July 19, 1967. The eye injury I sustained, courtesy of Frazier's trademark left hook, kept me out of the ring for 11 months

Although Ali wasn't nearly as fast in our second fight—which was 12 rounds—the result was the same. He got the decision, but I thought it should have been a lot closer.

Knocking out No. 4–ranked Manuel Ramos at Madison Square Garden on September 26, 1968, was one of the most satisfying wins of my career.

The punch that knocked out Jerry Quarry on December 12, 1969, at Madison Square Garden. Good thing I got him when I did—the ring doctor was going to stop the fight because of my swollen eye.

Irving Ungerman joins the celebration after I KO'd Quarry. If you look real close, you can see the M (for manager) on Ungerman's left sleeve.

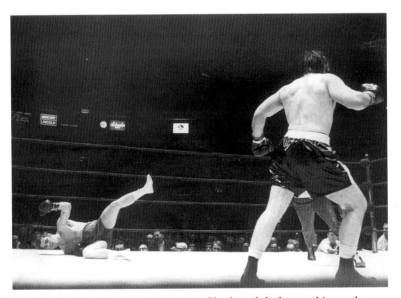

This angle shows how far Quarry staggered backwards before crashing to the canvas after I nailed him on the temple.

of fruit or some toast and coffee for breakfast, and I never ate lunch, but every day after training, Teddy and I would go for tea at the lunch counter at Glen's Pharmacy. One of us would plunk a dime in the jukebox to play "Our Day Will Come" by Ruby and the Romantics, and Teddy would snap his fingers as we sang the chorus together. Besides being a great tune, it kind of became our theme song because it embodied the dreams both of us had about winning the world championship.

In the evenings, I'd cook hamburgers on a hot plate in my room or munch on a big bag of Brazil nuts. That was a real treat! When I could afford it, I'd spend $1.25 to feast at one of the great soul food joints in the neighborhood. Fried chicken, collard greens, pinto beans, sweet potatoes, corn bread, black-eyed peas. *Mmmmm!* I'd scarf down as much as my meager budget would allow, then wash it all down with a bottle of Faygo strawberry diet soda.

When Lynne arrived, we moved into a little apartment block in Ferndale, on the southeast edge of Detroit, where it seemed like all the other tenants were black hookers. Our third son was born on November 21, and when Lynne brought him back from the hospital, all the working girls made a big fuss over him. I was stumped for a name until Lynne suggested the obvious—"Why not George?"—and since he was born in the U.S., we picked a middle name that sounded distinctly American: Lee, as in Robert E.

By the way, Georgie Lee was the recipient of the fastest circumcision I've ever heard of—he got clipped mere moments after making his way into the world. Lynne didn't believe in wasting any time! A week later, my wife and our new son were back home in Toronto.

Meanwhile, I had to downsize to another fleabag hotel on East Euclid because I still had to come up with the monthly mortgage back home. More than once I had to sneak out of these dives in the dead of night to avoid paying the bill—which is how I became acquainted with how deft some of Detroit's inner-city residents were at breaking into cars.

One night I parked in front of my apartment building, grabbed a bundle of stuff and locked the car door before heading inside. Unbeknownst to me, somebody on the street was watching and timing how long I was away from the vehicle—which wasn't more than a few minutes. They waited for just the right moment to smack the top of the driver's-side door with a karate chop—which made the window fall down—then helped themselves to my clothes and whatever else was lying around. This happened a few more times over the next couple of months (I had to keep buying new clothes) before it dawned on me to never leave anything in the car.

After living and training in Detroit for four months, I finally made my first foray as a self-managed fighter . . . and it was a disaster.

The date was March 15, 1963, the venue was the Graystone Ballroom and the opponent was a guy named Rico Brooks, who hailed from Arizona. It was my first fight since being disqualified against Joe Erskine 17 months earlier, and I was in the best shape of my life. Problem was, on the day of the fight, I had no boxing boots to wear. Mine were so worn out from all that work in the gym that they couldn't be repaired, so I borrowed a pair from one of my sparring partners, Sam Poe.

The other—and far more acute—problem was that I was starving. I'd been unable to afford a real meal for a couple of days, so on the morning of the fight I took the two complimentary tickets the promoter had given me and sold them to a guy at Arturo's Bar, which was next door to the gym.

A few hours (and one nice soul food dinner) later, I painfully discovered that Poe's feet were a tad smaller than mine, but I managed to squeeze into his boots long enough to knock out Brooks in the second round for a princely purse of $200. Right after the fight, some cops showed up in my dressing room and arrested me for working in the U.S. without the proper papers. I hadn't even given that a second thought when I came down from Toronto, but they were quite adamant that it was a serious charge. It took a few phone calls to get things straightened out, after which I was right back where I started: broke and hungry.

Over the next few months in Detroit all I did was train, eat and sleep while looking forward to sporadic (and minuscule) paydays. My daily gym routine consisted of a lot of work on the heavy bag, sparring with two or three different guys and working with McWhorter on little things like refining my footwork and mixing up my punches.

Teddy realized from the start that I was a brawler, not a boxer, so he never tried to change my natural style, God bless him. Another thing I liked about him was that he wasn't a "do this, don't do that" type of taskmaster. Teddy knew his stuff and he knew how to make a point, but a lot of what he taught me was just kind of passed along in our conversations over a cup of tea.

The more I got to know Teddy, the more I liked him and respected the way he did things. McWhorter trained all of his fighters in the same style—straight ahead, not much lateral movement, try to stay close and work the body. That was probably an error on his part, but it was great for me. Unlike anyone else I'd ever worked with, Teddy realized right away that my best weapon was my strength, so he concentrated on showing me how to muscle the other guy, get him against the ropes and pound to the body. That became kind of my personal trademark for the rest of my career. I could muscle anybody, as long as I could catch them. I ended up fighting some very strong guys—George Foreman and Jerry Quarry are at the top of the list—but I never felt that anybody was stronger than I was. Foreman was able to push me off a couple of times, but he had really long arms. I just couldn't get in tight on him like I wanted to.

When I was training to fight Floyd Patterson, Teddy talked about our relationship in an interview with *Sports Illustrated* writer Gilbert Rogin: "When George came here he had all the qualifications; he just needed someone to bring them out. What he did he did as well as he knew how. For a kid to come through the fights he come through, they had to teach him something. But he had no confidence in his handlers. They had him moving around like a lightweight. Didn't seem right, a big guy like him moving around like that. He has too much weight on him to run around. Big guy can do that just so long. Big guy like him, he'll come to you. He's willing to go forward all night, that's the thing."

Five weeks after stopping Brooks, I knocked out James Wakefield in six rounds across the border in Windsor, Ontario. Wakefield was a big, beefy guy with a fat gut. Every time I nailed him to the body, it felt like I was punching a bag of pudding. This went on for five rounds with no effect, and I was getting a little concerned. In the sixth, I started aiming for his chin, and the first shot I landed knocked him dead.

Seven days later, I KO'd Chico Gardner in four rounds in London, Ontario. A friend of mine who claimed to know something about promoting helped arrange those two fights, but I shouldn't have taken him at his word. I only got a few hundred dollars for Wakefield, and my payday for Gardner (who later became one of my sparring partners) was exactly zero. There was a screw-up in the contract and I knew going in that I wouldn't get paid, but I needed the work. Besides, a lot of people had bought tickets.

My promoter friend assured me he'd make up for it in my next fight—a two-round KO of Lloyd Washington in Battle Creek, Michigan, on May 18—and although it was still only $500, it was enough to get back home to Toronto to be with Lynne and the kids for the summer.

It was wonderful spending June, July and August with my wife and sons. I worked out regularly, but it's not the same as when you have a fight coming up. When I wasn't at the gym, I mostly just hung around the house, reacquainting myself with all the little domestic chores and savoring every moment with my wife and our three beautiful sons. Money was tight (the Chuvalo clan ate a lot of hot dogs and hamburgers that summer), but I wasn't too worried. I was a world-ranked contender, and I figured that sooner or later a real promoter would come calling.

It finally happened on September 12, my 26th birthday.

I was back in Detroit, sparring at the Big D, when my buddy Ed Trotter called from the gym in Toronto and said he'd just gotten off the phone with Teddy Brenner, the matchmaker at Madison Square Garden. Brenner had an offer for me but didn't know where I was. Playing middleman, Trotter told

Brenner he'd put us in touch—for a piece of the action. To make a long story short, a few minutes later I was talking to Brenner in New York and he offered me $4,000, plus a percentage of the gate, to fight Mike DeJohn on the *Gillette Cavalcade of Sports* two weeks later in Louisville, Kentucky.

It was short notice because Ernie Terrell had pulled out, but all I could think about was that four grand. It was like manna from heaven! By the standards of the day, that was a real nice payday for a TV fight, and it instantly felt like a big weight had been lifted off my shoulders. No more worries about how to feed my growing family—not to mention making the mortgage and car payments for the next six months.

DeJohn was a big man (6 foot 5, 215 pounds), with a big record. A pro since 1951, he'd notched knockouts in 32 of his 47 victories, including first-round KOs of Alex Miteff and Charley Powell and a decision over Bob Cleroux. And he'd lost only 10 fights in 12 years. With just two weeks to get ready, I had my work cut out.

Teddy lined up Sonny Banks, Cody Jones and Chico Gardner for my sparring sessions and instructed me not to hold back anything in the workouts. There was no question that the best strategy against a tall, rangy boxer-puncher like DeJohn was to stay inside and bang to the body, so that's what we worked on. I took McWhorter's instruction so seriously that he eventually had to custom-order a thick rubber wraparound body belt that protected pretty much the entire torso of my sparring partners—none of whom were too thrilled about getting thumped in the belly

Banks and Jones were terrific to have in camp because both of them were fast on their feet, which forced me to swarm in and trap them on the ropes before I could start winging punches. And Gardner was quick and elusive. I had better, harder sparring in the 10 days before we traveled to Kentucky than I'd had in my entire career to that point.

Teddy and I flew to Louisville on a Sunday, four days prior to the fight. After we checked into the Holiday Inn at 4th and Walnut (it's long gone now), we got a call from promoter Bill King telling us to report for the pre-fight medical the following morning.

When we got to his office, King pulled us aside and said, "George, Cassius Clay is here and he's just signed a letter of intent to fight Wednesday's winner. If you beat DeJohn, Cassius has agreed to fight you on November 8 in Miami Beach. If Mike wins, he gets the fight. Is that agreeable to you?" I couldn't hide my glee. "Give me the paper," I said. "I'll sign right now!"

We went into the next room and there was Cassius, holding court with the press. Now, remember, he hadn't yet joined the Nation of Islam or changed his name to Muhammad Ali, but he was already a larger-than-life man-child who'd reeled off 19 straight victories since turning pro after winning the gold medal at the 1960 Rome Olympics. Fifteen of those wins were by KO, and *The Ring* had just ranked him the No. 2 contender (behind Floyd Patterson) for Sonny Liston's title. Thanks to my 17-month hiatus and the two losses to Cleroux, I'd been dropped to No. 12 by *The Ring*, while DeJohn was No. 15.

DeJohn and I were asked to pose for a picture with Cassius. This was the first time I'd met Clay in person, and to be honest with you, I wasn't overly impressed. He was dressed like a preppy white guy, in a very conservative three-piece Ivy League suit over a starched white shirt and a thin, dark tie. He had a cocky air about him, but he was clean-cut and very polite.

The photographers posed him flexing his arms between Mike and me, and they asked us to grab onto his biceps. As the cameramen clicked away, I whispered to Clay, "Hey Popeye, you must have some big forearms, eh?" He pretended not to hear, so I repeated it a little louder: "Hey Popeye, you must have *big* forearms!" This time, he looked at me and said, "Why you callin' me Popeye?" I smiled and replied, "'Cuz you've got awfully small biceps!"

Some of the photographers kind of snickered, but Cassius wasn't amused. "Alex Miteff talked that way . . . Willie Besmanoff talked that way . . . Sonny Banks talked that way . . . and I whupped 'em all!" he shot back. "Yeah, yeah," I replied. "But they're not me. Don't worry about it; you're not witty enough anyway."

He looked startled—but there was no snappy comeback. That might have been the first time in the young career of "The Louisville Lip" that he was at a loss for words.

Another interested observer at that pre-fight medical was Green Bay Packers halfback Paul Hornung, who was a friend of King's. Hornung had Hollywood good looks, thick blond hair and the kind of firm handshake you'd expect from one of the most versatile Hall of Famers in NFL history. He was a Louisville native who'd run into a little trouble earlier that season when a gambling scandal involving him and Alex Karras of the Detroit Lions led to both of them being suspended indefinitely by commissioner Pete Rozelle.

Hornung was one of the most beloved sports figures in all of Kentucky, but in talking to him I got the impression he was a little bit jealous of Cassius, who at 21 was already emerging as a media darling. He kept his distance from Clay and repeatedly referred to him as "that jackass."

I went in against DeJohn at 212—10 pounds heavier than when I KO'd James Wakefield in Windsor five months earlier. I felt very strong at that weight and, thanks to the hard sparring in Detroit, I was razor sharp. And as a good-luck charm, I had a pair of my son Mitchell's little brown socks in the pocket of my ring robe. They were ready for the washing machine but had inadvertently been stuffed into my bag before I left home.

Along with McWhorter, the other two guys in my corner were Freddie Dawson and big Ed Trotter, the "middleman" from Toronto who'd intercepted the phone call from matchmaker Teddy Brenner. Dawson, from Chicago, was one of the best lightweights never to win the world championship. He retired in 1946 with a phenomenal record of 101–13–3 and went on to become one of the most respected trainers in the business.

I was familiar with DeJohn, who hailed from Syracuse but trained in Miami under Angelo Dundee, and I knew he'd be gunning for a quick KO, hoping to catch me cold. Mike was a great puncher (as was his middleweight brother, Joey), and his trademark shot was a stiff, ripping uppercut. It was because of that uppercut that I began incorporating headstands into my training regimen, a little trick Sonny Liston used all the time. I'd stand on my head with my legs up against the wall and rotate my body weight on my neck, sometimes for as long as half an hour.

As expected, when the bell rang DeJohn stormed out of his corner with bad intentions. He moved well for a big man, but I was able to rake him with a couple of good body shots.

Halfway through the first round, he unleashed an uppercut as I tried to move inside. The punch caught me flush on the chin, and looking back at the film, it was probably one of the hardest shots I ever took—including the bombs Joe Frazier and George Foreman landed on my noggin a few years later. Thank God for those headstands! I don't remember being hurt by the punch, but it was the only time in my career that I felt my knees buckle ever so slightly for a split second. Still, I shook it off and won the round on two of the three scorecards.

In the second, Mike was a little more wary and we spent much of the first two minutes banging each other in clinches, which referee Don Asbury was slow to break. With 46 seconds left, I backed DeJohn against the ropes and ripped a left hook to the body that really hurt him. I felt his torso kind of cave in a little, so I followed up with a left hook to the head that dumped him over the top rope. It was like he did a backflip. The force of the punch bent all 6 foot 5 of him almost in half, and the weight of his body pushed the top rope to the waistband of his trunks.

When you get a guy in a position like that, there's nothing in the rule book that says you can't keep punching, so that's exactly what I did. There was no way I was going to let him off the hook, so I just followed my natural instincts and pounded away. I hit him with eight punches that knocked him colder than a Missouri mule before his cornermen, Dundee and Joe Nietro, jumped into the ring screaming, "Foul! Foul!"—at which point Asbury pulled me away. DeJohn's body slithered down the ropes until he was sitting on the canvas, and then he collapsed in a heap.

It was absolute chaos. The crowd was going nuts, Dundee and Nietro were screaming bloody murder and Asbury was frozen in indecision. They dragged DeJohn back into his corner as Asbury conferred with ringside commissioner Bob Evans, a short, fat white guy with a thick Southern drawl. But as far as I was concerned, the fight was over.

I went back to my corner and told Teddy to take my gloves off, which he did. As he was cutting the wraps from my hands, Evans charged over and barked, "George, what y'all doin'?" I told him, "I won the fight fair and square, and I'm not fighting anymore." His response was short and sweet: "George, y'all don't fight, y'all don't get paid."

That's all I had to hear. I told McWhorter to put my gloves back on. My right hand was still wrapped, but there was no time to rewrap the left one. From the time DeJohn collapsed on the canvas to the time the round resumed, more than 15 minutes had elapsed, which was more than enough time for Mike's corner to coax him back from la-la land. After the long delay, the fight continued with just a little time left in the second round. To add insult to injury, the official ruling was that I had committed a foul and therefore lost the round by a 5–3 margin.

I went out for Round 3 figuring we were in a peck of trouble. If they weren't going to count the knockout, what was I going to have to do to win this fight? In the fourth, I caught DeJohn at an awkward angle and slammed a left to his kidney, but as soon as the punch landed, I knew something was wrong. The impact tore my elbow ligament, so now I had something else to worry about. For the rest of the fight there was no pain when I landed a shot, but when I threw a punch that missed, it hurt like hell.

In the meantime, DeJohn had fully recovered his senses and was fighting back hard. In the sixth, he threw a big right that I managed to duck under and counter with a perfectly timed left hook to the chin that dropped him like he'd been shot. I thought he'd be out for a week, but Mike struggled to his feet at the count of seven and Asbury waved me back in.

Another flurry on the inside sent DeJohn tumbling through the ropes and onto his butt on the ring apron, but this time Asbury walked over, picked him up and dusted off his gloves before giving him a standing eight count. I couldn't believe my eyes! I'd never seen a referee pick a guy off the canvas before, never mind help him get ready to keep fighting. It was ridiculous.

Over the last three rounds I stepped up the pressure and threw punches from every angle, not caring where they landed. I really wanted to knock this guy out, but DeJohn was tough— and brave.

The fight ended up going the 10-round distance, and despite my scoring three knockdowns—and what should have been two legitimate knockouts—I didn't have a good feeling standing in my corner as we awaited the decision. It must have shown on my face, because Asbury sidled over and said, "Why do you look so glum, George? You won by a country mile."

A moment later the scores were read. The two ringside judges had me winning by 47–42 and 46–42 . . . and Asbury scored it 49–49! A majority decision.

There was a lot of booing after the scoring was announced and a bunch of ringside fans started chanting "ASS-bury! ASS-bury!" at the ref, but I was too tired to wonder what the hell was going through his mind to score it a draw. I hugged McWhorter and Dawson, and if you look closely at the tape you can see me blowing kisses to my pregnant wife and our sons back home. That felt good.

A couple of hours after the fight, Bill King joined Teddy and me for dinner at a nice restaurant in downtown Louisville. Bill was apologetic because he couldn't pay me right away, but he assured us that if we stuck around we'd get the cash the following night, right after a rock 'n' roll show he was promoting. He also invited us to the show, which was nice.

In the meantime, we were sitting at the table for about half an hour without so much as a glass of water, so I finally called over a waitress and asked for menus. From the look on her face, you would have thought I'd asked for one of her kidneys. "Didn't y'all see the sign?" she hissed. "We can't serve you with *him* in here." She was glaring directly at Teddy. "For coloreds, it's takeout only."

McWhorter was hurt. He didn't say anything, but I could see it in his eyes. He'd been down this road many, many times, but it still stung. "Let's get out of here," I said. We ended up going to a swankier place in Louisville's black quarter, where we enjoyed a sumptuous feast. And those folks didn't have any qualms about serving the only white guy in the joint.

The following morning there was a headline on the front page of the *Louisville Courier* sports section that said, "Cassius refuses to fight Chuvalo." In the accompanying story, Clay threw out a couple of disparaging remarks about Canada, then told the reporter, "I don't like the way Chuvalo fights. He can cut you. He butts and does everything else dirty. He's rough and tough and fights like an old washerwoman."

I thought it was kind of funny, but at the time I didn't know what the hell Cassius was talking about. I thought it was just something that popped into his head while he was talking to the reporter. In fact, it wasn't until 25 years later, when I was producing and hosting a syndicated TV series called *Famous Knockouts,* that I realized where the inspiration for the "washerwoman" handle came from. The show's introduction included a clip of me pounding DeJohn over the top rope—and sure enough, it bore a striking resemblance to somebody using both arms to work an old-fashioned washboard!

Over the next few years Cassius came up with a lot of imaginative nicknames for his opponents—Liston was "The Big Ugly Bear," Patterson "The Rabbit" and Ernie Terrell "The Octopus," to name a few—but I still think "The Washerwoman" was his most creative. To this day a lot of folks think it was mean and uncomplimentary, but I've always thought it was kind of cute.

And though neither of us realized it at the time, we'd soon end up having some fun with it.

ROUND 4

COUPLE OF DAYS AFTER THE WIN OVER DeJohn, I was back at work at the Big D in Detroit, awaiting word on who I'd be fighting on November 8, now that Clay had reneged on his letter of intent.

Ed Trotter, who'd helped set up the bout with DeJohn and traveled to Louisville to work my corner with Teddy, was now serving as sort of an interim manager, which allowed me to concentrate on training. But I was worried about Lynne. She was back home in Toronto with the kids and she was three months pregnant. I missed her and the boys terribly. The only good thing was that, thanks to the DeJohn fight, our finances were solid—at least for the next few months.

In mid-October I got a call from Teddy Brenner, offering Tony Alongi as the substitute for Clay in Miami Beach. It was another TV fight, and my purse would be $4,750, plus a piece of the gate. A few days later, Cassius himself made a surprise visit to Detroit as part of a rock 'n' roll review at the Fox Theatre, the same place where I'd watched the closed-circuit telecast of his KO over Archie Moore the previous November.

A lot of people don't know that Cassius was a talented singer back in the day, even before he started all his "I Am the Greatest!" shtick. He hung around with guys like Miles Davis and Sam Cooke, and in 1964 he recorded a terrific version of Ben E. King's classic, "Stand by Me." Yeah, the cat could sing!

While he was in town, Clay decided to drop by the Big D to do a little sparring with his pal Cody Jones. When word got around that he was coming down to the gym, every hooker, hustler and pimp in Detroit headed over to get in on the action.

When Trotter and I found out that a local sportscaster named Dave Diles was going to do a live TV interview with Cassius after the sparring, we decided to make a "statement" of our own. Trotter found a costume rental place in the Yellow Pages, and when we got to the store I asked the proprietor if there was anything in stock that would be suitable for a 6-foot-1, 215-pound "washerwoman."

Half an hour later, decked out in a full-length flower-print dress, an old bonnet and granny glasses, I was nearly ready for my grand entrance. Trotter painted some red lines on my face to look like wrinkles, and as a final touch we loaded up an old bucket and a shopping bag with rags, a big box of Grandma's Lye Soap and, of course, a mop, a scrub board and a contract. We made it back to the gym just as Clay and Jones were wrapping up their sparring and Diles was preparing to do his interview in the ring.

The joint was packed, a full house, with people standing around the ropes. Stooped over, waving Clay's letter of intent, I shuffled my way to the front of the crowd, chirping in my best Southern falsetto, "Yoo-hoo! Yoo-hoo! Is that Cautious Clay I see up there? Cautious, why are you afraid to fight a little ol' washerwoman?"

When I reached the ring, I swung the mop and bucket through the ropes and then climbed through. Out came the rags. Out came the box of Grandma's Lye Soap. Cassius looked stunned. He was quiet and confused, just like he'd been when I'd chided him about his Popeye arms in Louisville.

I knew full well how ridiculous I looked, but the stunt had the desired effect. Diles quickly instructed his cameraman to swing over to me before he stuck his microphone in my face. Naturally, I stayed in character. "Cautious Cassius backed out of fighting me," I cackled, waving the letter of intent at the camera. "He's chicken. How can he possibly be afraid of fighting someone like little ol' me?"

My stunt was the lead item on all the TV sportscasts later that evening, and in the next day's papers Clay danced around the questions by saying he wasn't going to fight anybody— least of all "that dirty Chuvalo"—before his upcoming title shot against Liston in February.

My appearance in drag wasn't the only excitement at the Big D that afternoon. While all the commotion was going on in the ring, somebody slipped into the dressing room and swiped Clay's wallet. A handful of shady suspects who were hanging around the room were questioned, but the culprit was never found. I later found out that Cassius only had about $80 in his billfold, but he was furious that anyone would have the temerity to rob him. I guess he found out Detroit was a lot less friendly than Louisville.

Shortly after we arrived in Miami for the Alongi fight, I was wrapping up a light workout at the Dundee brothers' famous 5th Street Gym when I bumped into DeJohn, who'd dropped in to do some training. After we exchanged pleasantries, Mike invited me over to his house for a cup of tea. Neither of us knew it at the time, but he would never fight again after the beating I'd laid on him in Louisville just five weeks earlier.

It was kind of an odd feeling, because that was the only time during my whole career that I had a chance to sit down and talk to a guy I'd fought without the press being around. DeJohn was a real gentleman, and we spent an enjoyable hour or so talking about the fight game and some of our common opponents—a list that included Cleroux, Besmanoff and Miteff, among others. Then he surprised me by bringing up our fight. "I don't remember a goddamned thing about it," he said wistfully. "All I know is that they said you fouled me."

He didn't seem angry, just a little confused.

"Mike, when you get a chance to see the film you'll see that I hit you fair and square," I told him. "I had you bent over the ropes, but we both know there's nothing in the rules that says I can't hit you while you're in that position." He nodded in agreement but didn't say anything more about it.

I don't know if Mike knew at that point that he was going to retire (he was only 32), but the fact he couldn't remember anything about our fight was a pretty good indicator that he'd probably sustained a concussion and might want to think about doing something else. I sensed he was a little apprehensive about life after boxing, but we didn't get into it. We wished each other luck and said goodbye. I never saw or spoke to him again.

With a couple of days to kill before my fight with Alongi, we decided to liven things up a little in the Chuvalo camp by staging another pre-emptive strike by The Washerwoman. The target was the 5th Street Gym, where Angelo and Chris

Dundee entertained sportswriters and TV crews almost on a daily basis.

Once again, Trotter arranged for appropriate attire—but this time we had signs made up and mapped out a walking route for several blocks along Collins Avenue, right in the heart of Miami Beach. In addition to Trotter and me, our little raiding party included a very mortified Teddy McWhorter (who tried to hide behind his sign) and my sparring partner Chico Gardner.

Angelo and Chris were genuinely horrified when we showed up at the gym, but once again it had the desired effect. We made the front page of *The Miami Herald* and all the local TV sportscasts, and it probably helped sell a few more tickets for the fight.

Like DeJohn, Alongi was a tall transplanted northerner. Born in Clifton, New Jersey, he was an early protégé of Angelo Dundee and turned pro with him in Miami Beach in 1959. At 6 foot 3 and 205 pounds, he had a record of 31–2 going into our fight, with 19 KOs. The biggest wins on his résumé to that point were a KO of Don Warner two months earlier and a decision over George Logan at Madison Square Garden in 1961. Clay had knocked out both those guys in '62, so I wasn't too worried.

As it turned out, our fight was almost a replay of what happened with me and DeJohn.

The first indication that it might be a long night came right after we were introduced to the full house at the Miami Beach Auditorium. After referee Cy Gottfried finished giving us his final instructions, he asked if there were any questions. Alongi, sounding like a frightened kid in the schoolyard, asked him to "watch out for the rough stuff."

What was this, ballroom dancing? Imagine a world-ranked heavyweight contender saying something like that!

Tony had long arms and he was a decent counterpuncher, but right from the opening bell I was in his face, hammering him to the body. Every time he tried to clinch or push me off, I landed hard to the ribs or head. But Gottfried apparently took Tony's pre-fight plea to heart because he repeatedly warned me about punching on the break—and I didn't want a replay of what had happened in Louisville.

Thirty seconds into Round 3, I staggered Alongi with an overhand right. He kind of sagged into the ropes, and on the tape it looks like his knee touches the canvas, but it wasn't scored a knockdown. No matter. A minute later I floored him with another right to the head, and this time Gottfried started counting. Tony was on his feet at five, but I knew I had him.

Over the last seven rounds Alongi kept looking up at the clock, as if hoping to speed things along through sheer will-power. I was outpunching him by about three to one—an output that prompted blow-by-blow commentator Don Dunphy to gush, "Wow! That man Chuvalo is a real street fighter!"

Alongi was scoring some with his jab, but I was never in trouble. In the last two rounds I really opened up, looking to knock him out. He was staggered again in the ninth, and in the final round I landed three big hooks to the head that sent him reeling across the ring.

Shouldn't even be close, right? That was the consensus in my corner. But a few seconds later, when the ring announcer bellowed, "Judge Jimmy Ruby scores it 95–93 . . . Alongi!" I thought, "Here we go again." The second judge, Bunny Lovett, got it right: 99–92, for me. Obviously nothing wrong with

Bunny's eyes. The deciding vote went to Gottfried, who scored it 95–93—for Alongi!

Apparently Dunphy was as shocked as I was. He told the nationwide TV audience, "The crowd is vehement in disagreeing with this split decision." I looked out into the sea of faces—remember, this was Alongi's own backyard—and everybody was standing and booing. That made me feel a little better, but I was still very upset.

Right after the fight, we filed a protest with the Miami Beach Boxing Commission, and the next day they met to review the scoring. It turned out that an error was made in adding up Gottfried's scorecard, so the official verdict was changed to a draw. That was still highway robbery as far as I was concerned, and I told them so, in no uncertain terms.

When I finished, Morris Klein, the chairman of the commission, made an insulting effort to smooth things over by offering me a "gift" of a used sports jacket. Can you believe that? I told Klein that I might only be a poor, struggling fighter from Canada, but I didn't need clothing handouts from the Salvation Army, thank you very much.

Another post-fight incident brought back memories of what had happened in Louisville a few weeks earlier, but with a different twist. An hour or so after we left the Auditorium, Teddy and I were unwinding at a nightclub in the black section of Miami. It was an upscale jazzy little place, and I was just sitting there, enjoying the music, when a nice-looking girl came over to our table and asked if I wanted to dance. Without giving it a second thought, I accepted and stepped out onto the floor.

The music had only been playing for about 10 seconds when all of a sudden I felt someone tapping on my shoulder.

I turned around, and there was the manager. "Sir, there is no mixed dancing here," he said.

While the guy was admonishing me, he was also glaring at the girl, who I suppose he assumed should have known better. I didn't make a fuss, but I told the young lady I was sorry before walking back to the table.

A minute or two later, who should appear at our table but Luis Rodriguez, the hammer-fisted Cuban who had won and lost the world welterweight championship in two decisions with Emile Griffith earlier that year. He looked like a Havana goodfella, all decked out in a pale blue suit, a frilly baby blue shirt and a snappy bow tie.

"Hey George, what's going on?" he said.

"It's no big deal, Luis. They just told me I can't dance. Black and white don't mix here, I guess."

"Who said that, the manager? The manager won't let you dance?"

I nodded.

That's all Rodriguez needed to know. As Teddy and I watched in amazement, he walked up to the manager, pulled a snub-nosed pistol from his waist, shoved it in the guy's gut and snarled, "My friend Chew-valo can dance with whoever he want to, okay?"

And dance I did. The rest of the evening was most enjoyable, to say the least.

With the two nice paydays for DeJohn and Alongi, I was ending 1963 on a high note. Most of the money was already spoken for, thanks to a growing stack of bills back in Toronto, but I didn't care. Lynne and the boys were coming down to Detroit for a short visit before we all went back home, and all

I could think about was how nice it was going to be to spend Christmas with my family.

Unfortunately, my rattletrap 1954 Ford product didn't want to cooperate.

No sooner had we left the Detroit city limits than the passenger-side window fell down into the door and couldn't be coaxed back up again. Lynne, who was five months pregnant, solved that problem by balancing a suitcase on her shoulder in order to keep the wind and snow off Mitchell, Steven and Georgie Lee in the back seat. Twenty minutes later, the gas pedal broke. I stepped on the cotter pin, but that busted, too.

I pulled over to the side of the highway and broke a branch off a small tree. "You're going to have to get down on your knees and push this stick through the hole to give us gas," I told Lynne. She looked at me like I was nuts, but since I was the only one with a driver's license, she knew there was no other way.

For the next two hours, the Chuvalomobile was transformed into a mini circus. Three little guys keeping up a steady banter when they weren't snoozing or shivering in the back seat, and my pregnant wife on her hands and knees, depressing the gas linkage bar with a busted tree branch. "Okay honey, we're going through a town now," I would tell her. "You gotta slow us down." Or, "We're out on the highway now, dear, so we gotta do 60."

I didn't know if Lynne was cursing or praying down there, but every time I looked at her I thought to myself, "She ought to be on television." At one point Mitchell woke up and peered over the seat to see what his mom was doing on the floor. Very solemnly, he asked, "Papa, when are we going to get a new car?"

Christmas came and went (and no, Santa didn't bring me a new car), and then I was back at the Big D, getting ready for a January 17 TV date with cagey veteran Zora Folley in Cleveland.

Although he only turned pro a year before I did, it seemed like Folley had been around forever. He was born in Texas in 1932 and grew up in Chandler, Arizona, with his sights set on a career in pro baseball before he joined the U.S. Army. It was in the military that he started boxing, and within a couple of years he earned the All-Army and All-Service championships. Zora was awarded five battle stars while serving in the Korean War, and he turned pro shortly after being discharged in 1953.

By the time we hooked up, Folley was 65–7–3 and had tangled with many of the top names in the division. He'd beaten Bob Cleroux and Henry Cooper, KO'd DeJohn and split two fights with top-ranked Doug Jones, but he'd also lost a decision to Ernie Terrell and been on the receiving end of a vicious knockout by Sonny Liston in 1960.

Folley was a very slick, highly skilled stick-and-move guy. In terms of pure boxing ability, he was one of the best I ever faced. That said, he wasn't a big puncher. He only had 23 knockouts in 65 wins going into our fight (I had 19 KOs in 25 wins), but he was known as a guy who could take you out with either hand if the opportunity presented itself. Ranked No. 5 in the world, he was the biggest name on my résumé to that point in my career.

My training for Folley went very well, right up until we arrived in Cleveland two days before the fight.

On the morning of the official weigh-in and pre-fight medicals, I woke up in the hotel with a throbbing pain in my ear and the pillowcase smeared with dark brown pus. And when I went to get up, I noticed a slight change in my equilibrium. I was really worried that the fight might be called off, especially when the doctor told me that I had either a bad infection or boils inside the ear canal. But he assured me that a shot of penicillin and a dose of Demerol would clear it up within 24 hours.

When you watch the fight, it's not hard to tell that the doc's prognosis was a little off, to say the least.

Zora was a hell of a fighter, no question, but it's pretty obvious that I wasn't in any kind of shape to be mixing with the No. 5 heavyweight in the world. From the opening bell, I felt like I was fighting in a vat of toffee. I didn't know what the hell Demerol was, and the powerful painkiller was still coursing through my system. Every time I threw a punch, it seemed to take 10 seconds to reach Folley. In the meantime, he was sticking and moving, dancing and jabbing. Not once during the entire 10 rounds did I hit him with anything close to what I should have been able to land, so the result was never in doubt. I managed to win only two rounds on one scorecard and three on the other two, dropping my record to 25–8–2.

Although I was still ranked No. 9 in the world, I was depressed as hell after the loss to Folley because once again I hadn't been 100 per cent for a TV fight that could have catapulted me right back into the top five. The ear problem persisted for another month, but I didn't have much time to dwell on it because we got a call out of the blue to fight Hugh Mercier for the vacant Canadian championship on March 18 in Regina. The title had become open when Cleroux gave it up after his loss to DeJohn in 1962. Bob wasn't interested in a fourth fight with me, so the championship remained vacant for almost two years.

Mercier, billed as the "heavyweight champ of Saskatchewan," was a big, strong guy from Ponteix, Saskatchewan. He had a linebacker's build but not a lot of boxing skill. It turned out to be the quickest stoppage of my career. The bell rang, he threw one lazy punch and we clinched. Referee Vince Leier moved in to break us, and as I stepped back I could see Mercier had his hands down by his waist. There's a real good reason why the ref's final pre-fight instruction is always "Protect yourself at all times," but Hugh obviously wasn't paying attention when Leier said that. I ripped him with a single left hook that nearly sent him all the way back to Ponteix.

It took less than a minute to get my Canadian championship back.

Between my bouts with Folley and Mercier, another fight took place that would have a profound impact not only on my career but on all of boxing history—and the social history of the 20th century.

On February 24 at the Miami Beach Convention Centre, 22-year-old Cassius Clay entered the ring as a 7–1 underdog to challenge Sonny Liston for the world championship.

Like millions of others watching on closed-circuit television, I figured Clay was going to get his ass handed to him. But before the ring introductions, as I watched him bouncing lightly on his toes in the corner, occasionally executing the quick shuffle step that had become his trademark, I was struck by how cool he looked. Other than saucer-wide eyes, he appeared no more nervous than when I'd watched him knock out Archie Moore a couple of years earlier in the closed-circuit telecast at the Fox Theatre in Detroit.

A few moments later, with the nonchalance of a cat burglar on a routine heist, Liston climbed through the ropes in the opposite corner. As if to underscore his reputation as an executioner, Sonny wore a hooded robe and his dead eyes took in the scene with a look of detached resignation.

What transpired over the next 35 minutes was, I believe, the greatest performance of Clay/Ali's career. He moved like a gazelle, scoring with lightning-quick jabs and lashing hooks before melting like a mirage, just out of range of Liston's retaliatory bombs.

It was a masterful performance by young Cassius, and when Liston refused to come out of his corner for the seventh round, sports history was changed for all time. Clay's ascension to the title provided a platform from which he could step beyond boxing to address the social and political questions of the day, and he became the first world heavyweight champ to make headlines around the globe for verbalizing his views on hot-button issues that transcended sport.

The very next day, Clay announced that in addition to being the new heavyweight champion of the world, he was a member of the Nation of Islam, a radical political sect that advocated racial segregation. A few weeks later he told the world that he was abandoning his "slave name" and would henceforth be known as Muhammad Ali.

Before that historic night in Miami, I'd come close to fighting Liston myself.

In early 1958 my manager, Jack Allen, got a call from Jack Kent Cooke, a business tycoon from Hamilton, Ontario, who'd relocated to Los Angeles. Cooke handled promotions for Liston's management, and he offered Allen $25,000 for me to fight Sonny. That was a lot of money at the time, but Allen didn't think it was enough to risk my 14–2 record against a top-ranked contender who was 23–1.

Five years later, shortly after I beat Mike DeJohn, I got a call from Jack Nilon, a mob-connected industrialist who was also in charge of concessions at Municipal Stadium in Philadelphia. Nilon was Liston's manager of record, and he invited me down to Philly to discuss another offer to fight Sonny, who had just made his first defense by obliterating Floyd Patterson in their title rematch. I was excited at the prospect and figured Nilon's offer would be at least $100,000.

We met in a warehouse, of all places, so maybe that should have been a foreshadowing of the gross disappointment that was to follow.

Nilon came right to the point. "You wanna fight Sonny, George?"

"Absolutely. How much?"

"Twenty-five grand. Take it or leave it."

I was stunned. Twenty-five grand in 1963 didn't have nearly the buying power that it did in '58, when we'd turned down Cooke's offer of the same amount. I countered by saying I'd take the fight for $75,000. When Nilon rejected it, there was nothing left to talk about. I went back to Toronto, thinking Nilon would reconsider and offer me $50,000—which I would have accepted. But he never called again.

Meanwhile, my quick win over Mercier was memorable for more than just regaining the Canadian title. It marked the start of a long association and warm friendship with the inimitable

Nikola Pavolych (Nick) Zubray, a Runyonesque promoter and entertainment impresario from Lethbridge in southern Alberta.

Zubray had originally scheduled me and Mercier for March 17, St. Patrick's Day, but then changed it to the following day. "All the Micks will be too busy getting drunk to come to the fight," he said.

I loved Zube. After immigrating to Canada from Ukraine, he settled in Lethbridge, where he made a living selling pipe for the oilfield industry before he was bitten by the promoting bug. After dabbling in wrestling and live theater productions, he moved to Edmonton and formed Continental Boxing & Wrestling Promotions.

Nick was the kind of throwback who should have been haunting the streets of New York with Tex Rickard and Doc Kearns back in the 1920s. The self-proclaimed "King of the Ankle Express"—that was his quaint way of explaining a lifelong propensity for having to slink out of town, one step ahead of creditors, when his big ideas turned into flops—he exuded the kind of style that could take over a room in a matter of seconds.

Always immaculately dressed in a tailor-made suit with a pink carnation jauntily tucked in the lapel, Zube was also a master negotiator, whether dealing with fighters, hotel managers or one of his many girlfriends. Nick's favorite tactic was to blow into town, check into the best hotel, and then talk the manager into extending him unlimited credit while he put together his fight card.

Working from the command post of his luxury suite—which was always overflowing with fresh flowers, opera music and empty bottles of his trademark pink champagne—no detail was left to chance. Zube would hammer out contracts with the fighters, design the poster, write the program copy, wine and dine the local media, line up TV and radio spots and oversee ticket sales. Money was never an object when he was planning his shows. "Don't worry, it'll flow," he'd bark. "This is gonna be like shooting fish with an ax!"

In between, he'd entertain his girlfriends. No matter where he was, Nick seemed to know a local woman or three, and he had a briefcase filled with 8-by-10 glossies of most of them. When one was coming up to the suite, he'd pop her picture into a cheap frame and put it up on the dresser. Same routine the next night, but with a different lady.

Besides an affinity for wine, women and song, Zube had a photographic memory and a gift for the kind of blunt repartee that made him a sportswriter's dream. He never forgot a face, and his signature expressions became legendary. "I won't go back to Calgary; that town wouldn't spend a nickel to watch Christ wrestle a grizzly bear," he'd huff. Or, "My strategy for this show is simple, George: fart and fall back." On one visit to the house, he peeled $200 off a thick wad of cash, handing a crisp $100 bill to my son Mitchell, who was only about 10, and a trio of fifties to Steven, Georgie Lee and Jesse. They squealed in delight. When I inquired how his own adult sons were doing, he just sighed, shook his head and replied, "They're no fuckin' good, George; too lazy to work and too yellow to steal."

One of Nick's dreams was to open a nudist colony on the outskirts of Edmonton—a city that happens to be on roughly the same latitude as Moscow! The bitter cold didn't faze him. "Sure, the nudist season is kinda short out here, but how can I miss? Show me a kid in today's generation who doesn't wanna run around buck-naked!"

That was Zube. And when his dreams didn't quite pan out, he always had a backup plan. "I've got a great deal for you," he'd purr when a hotel manager inevitably came calling to settle his bill. "You help me put on my next show and I'll guarantee you get all your money back—plus a nice profit!" Of course, there were the inevitable pitfalls—like in the spring of 1972, when he bought the closed-circuit rights for Ali's fight with Mac Foster in Tokyo and planned to pack Vancouver's Pacific Coliseum with fans willing to pay $7 to watch the bout on the big screen. It was only after Nick put the tickets on sale that he discovered the fight was being carried on free TV by a Seattle station that everyone in Vancouver could watch! The irony of it being held on April Fool's Day wasn't lost on him. "Screw it," he said. "You go by limo or you go by boxcar . . . you're still movin'!"

Nick ended up promoting 14 of my fights, from small towns like Lethbridge and Penticton, B.C., to my second bout with Ali at the Pacific Coliseum in 1972. He was fun to be around, always treated me fairly and never lost his zeal for life. He once told the *Edmonton Sun* that his proudest moment was finally getting his Canadian citizenship in 1980, "but after living here for 50 years, it's only natural that some of the thrill has worn off."

That was Zube in a nutshell. When he died in 1983, I lost one of the best friends I ever made in boxing.

The $3,000 I made for starching Mercier couldn't have come at a better time. Still without a manager and with Lynne only weeks away from giving birth to our fourth child, I was once again feeling that old familiar financial pinch.

I knew that if I was ever going to be more than the heavy-weight champion of Canada, I needed a manager—somebody with money and connections. Irving Ungerman, the owner of Royce Dupont Poultry Packers, where my mom worked, had been bugging me for years, and there was no doubt that he had the money. He first broached the subject of managing me when he drove me home after I KO'd Yvon Durelle in 1959. I'll admit I was impressed with the fact he drove a shiny new Cadillac with a crapshooter's license plate (7–11), and I remember Ray Charles was belting out "What'd I Say?" on the radio when Irving pulled up in front of our house and told me he was capable of "taking me places." Still, I thought that was pretty brazen because I already had a manager—and Irving knew it.

Looking back, that little incident should have tipped me off that this was a guy I shouldn't get involved with. Ungerman's only saving grace was that he had money—millions and millions of dollars made off land development and the blood and sweat of piecemeal poultry workers, like my mother. Actually, my mother harbored no resentment toward Irving, and in a crazy kind of way she liked him. But looking back, I'm embarrassed and angry with myself to have been so closely associated with someone like him.

Ungerman loved to be seen and photographed with cops and politicians. I guess it reinforced his sense of power. Later on, I was also turned off by the fact he was such a bullshitter. He looked and talked like a dumpier version of Jack Ruby (the petty criminal who murdered Lee Harvey Oswald on live TV on November 24, 1963), and he tried hard to convince people that he wielded a lot of muscle around town, but that was just his delusional way of thinking.

To put it bluntly, Ungerman had the coin to take my career to the next level, and I appreciated his enthusiasm. I was in dire straits and I needed his backing. What he didn't seem to have was any knowledge of boxing. He told people he had been a for- midable 105-pounder in his youth and had boxed while serving in the Royal Canadian Air Force, but I had my doubts. He never showed me anything to indicate he had a clue about boxing.

In all the years we were together, Irving was never more than a cheerleader in the corner. He could bulljive with the best of them when the media was around, but with very few excep- tions he was always a "me first" pain in the ass in our one-on-one dealings when it came to decisions about my career. I always had the impression he'd take care of himself before he took care of me—and that's not the best way to think of your manager.

But I'm jumping ahead.

My immediate concern in the spring of '64 was the impending birth of our fourth child, but as thrilled as I was about the prospects of bringing another Chuvalo into the world, nothing could have prepared me for Jesse's unortho- dox arrival on April 7.

I remember it like it was yesterday. Lynne smacked me awake from a sound sleep at 3:30 a.m. with the unsettling news that her water had broken. "The contractions are killing me," she said. "I think I'm going to have the baby right here." That scared the hell out of me, but I still reacted like a jerk. With all the patience of a man waiting for his morning toast to pop, I made it clear there was no way she was giving birth in our bedroom. "Hold on," I coolly commanded. "We're going to the hospital."

With no time to even get dressed, my poor wife threw on a bathrobe and waddled out to our rickety old wreck. It was obvious Lynne was in tremendous pain, but she was tough as nails. As I fumbled for the keys, she put her head on my right thigh and calmly exhorted me to get a move on. "No problem, honey," I said. "We'll be at the hospital in 10 minutes."

Fat chance.

I roared up Weston Road, heading for Humber Memorial on Church Street. What I didn't realize as I nudged the speedometer over 70 miles per hour was that a cop car had spotted us and was in hot pursuit. Just as I made the right-hand turn off Weston onto Jane Street, Lynne quietly said, "George, the baby is coming." What could I do? Responding with my usual flawless logic, I barked, "Close your legs, goddamn it!"

That wasn't going to do it. Lynne was writhing in agony, so I reached down to remove her underwear. Meanwhile, I'm still speeding. Just as we started the climb up toward Dominion Bridge, she said, "It's too late."

I looked down and saw the back of a tiny head, moving left to right as if to say, "No, no." I thought, "You're saying no? Not now, kid!"

A second or two later, the baby shot straight out, attached to a long umbilical cord that looked like an inverted U. Staring down like my eyes were on swizzle sticks, I still managed to steer the car while trying to comfort Lynne, who was as cool as a cucumber.

"Put the baby on my stomach," she said. I reached down and lifted the new arrival onto her stomach, where she bundled up her bathrobe. What a trooper! Lynne was great; only 20 years old, but she never flinched. I bragged about her for months afterward. I still do.

As the drama was unfolding in our car, the cops were still chasing me. I turned left onto Church Street, then squealed to a stop in the hospital parking lot. Even though I was panicking about cutting the umbilical cord, my primary concern was the gender of the baby. I lifted it up to take a look and instantly felt a great sense of relief. "Thank God, another son!" What a chauvinist I was! Mama Mia!

Leaving Lynne in the car, I ran into the emergency room, screaming like a crazy man: "My wife just had a baby in the car! Cut the cord, cut the cord!" They told me to relax, because the baby could remain safely "attached" for up to 48 hours.

It took about two minutes to round up a doctor, and when we got back outside, half a dozen embarrassed-looking cops were surrounding the car. They were flabbergasted at the situation, but after being assured everything was all right, they took off.

An hour later, with Lynne safely ensconced in the maternity ward at Humber Memorial, I was feeling high as a kite. Driving home, I pulled up at the light at Keele Street and Rogers Road. When I looked over at the driver in the cab stopped beside me, it was none other than Gus Rubicini, the ex-middleweight who defeated Joey Giardello back in 1951. I rolled down the window and spat out about 1,000 words in 30 seconds, babbling like a maniac about my son being born in a speeding car on the way to the hospital. Gus looked at me like I was nuts before driving away.

Back at the hospital, the baby was placed in isolation because of concerns that he'd been exposed to germs during his unique debut, and it was a full week before he was circumcised. I remember thinking the wait was almost like a religious experience.

As for a name for son number four, we'd run out of possibilities as far as Lynne was concerned. Back at the house, I was going through a list of names in the back of our family bible, running them past my mother. We were speaking Croatian, and as I read out names, she shook her head no. When I came to "Jesse," who was the father of King David of Israel—and which loosely translates to "Where are you?" in Croatian—my mother replied, "Oh, I like that!" So the little guy was named Jesse Miles. Lynne wasn't crazy about it, but back then it was unique.

A few weeks after Jesse's birth, I got a call out of the blue from Rocky Marciano. He'd seen me fight in New York and Miami, and he wanted to discuss becoming my manager. I'd previously had a similar conversation with George Gainford, who managed Sugar Ray Robinson, so I was a little wary. I also knew that Rocky had a reputation for being notoriously cheap, so I wasn't very hopeful.

Marciano cut right to the chase. "Listen to me, George," he said in that thick New England accent. "I can move you like nobody else can. I've got the connections."

When I asked what he had in mind, he said, "We'll go 40 per cent for you, 60 per cent for management. A four-year deal, and management pays all the expenses." I was stunned—and insulted. "Are you nuts?" I said. "Would you sign a deal like that, Rocky? I'd have to be out of my bloody mind." He sounded surprised. "No, it's very fair. Nobody can move you like I can, you know that." I told him where he could stick his 60 per cent.

A couple of weeks later I was relaxing at home when there was a knock at the door. It was our mailman. "Some schmuck sent you a postcard from Florida with a Canadian stamp on it," he said. "You owe me eight cents."

The "schmuck" who sent that card was Marciano. Scrawled on the back was a single line: "Hope you'll reconsider." Fat chance.

By the early summer of '64 I was once again dead broke and out of options, so I phoned Ungerman. I proposed a contract based on a 50–50 split, with him paying all expenses. I didn't want to have to worry about training camps, sparring partners or anything else—those would be his responsibilities. I also wanted to make sure McWhorter got a percentage and that Irving would foot the bill to set Teddy up in a hotel across the street from the gym.

To my great relief, Irving agreed to a four-year deal. He gave me some peanut money up front and then put together a syndicate of investors under the name of Apollo Promotions, which set up an account I could draw on. The syndicate was made up of Irving, his brother Karl and a guy named Moe Wasser—all of whom were in the poultry business—along with Mel Newman, who owned a furniture factory, and Aaron Sokolsky, a restauranteur.

It was a good deal all around, although I was never happy about the way it turned out for Teddy. McWhorter was always worried that Ungerman would let him go as my trainer, even though I controlled that part of the agreement and repeatedly assured Teddy there was nothing to worry about. I never looked at my trainer in the same light after seeing how easily he let Irving dictate the terms of his contract, which, I'm ashamed to say, I signed as a witness.

Although I appreciated Ungerman's enthusiasm, almost from the moment we signed he began acting like an egomaniac. Once or twice a week he'd make a point of summoning Teddy and me to his office, where we'd find him holding court with cops or politicians. Perched behind his big desk, framed in a cloud of cigar smoke, Toronto's potentate of poultry would schmooze for a few minutes before sending his cronies on their merry way with a couple of frozen turkeys or a box of chicken legs.

While I was still getting used to my new manager, things were heating up in the heavyweight division.

On June 19, the World Boxing Association stripped its championship from Ali because of his association with the Nation of Islam and declared that Ernie Terrell, the WBA's No. 1-ranked contender, would fight Eddie Machen for the vacant title the following March. Meanwhile, the rival World Boxing Council and *The Ring* continued to recognize Ali as champ.

My first fight with Ungerman on board was on July 27 against "Chief" Don Prout at a baseball park in New Bedford, Massachusetts. The card was put together by Sad Sam Silverman, who promoted some of Rocky Marciano's early fights. He was an old-school promoter with a reputation for dreaming up ridiculous scenarios to bump ticket sales. My purse was a whopping $600.

With a respectable record of 21-4, Prout was the New England heavyweight champ. A fringe top-10 contender, he fought out of Providence, Rhode Island, and had only been stopped once in 25 fights. A couple of years earlier he'd split a pair of fights with Tom McNeeley, the guy who challenged Floyd Patterson for the world championship in Toronto in 1961.

Prout was nicknamed "Chief" because he was supposed to be Mohican, but when he climbed into the ring I realized he was a light-skinned black guy, not an Indian. No problem. Silverman had solemnly informed the press that this was a "revenge" match, with me cast as an avenging "French-Canadian" looking to settle old scores with Prout's treacherous tribe. On fight night, Silverman had poor Don enter the ring wearing a headdress of eagle feathers, accompanied by "warriors" beating on tom-toms. I laughed like hell when I saw that.

Late in the opening round, Prout nailed me with a good uppercut right on the point of the chin, opening up a nice, clean cut. A slice of any kind always gets a trainer's attention, and in the corner McWhorter pleaded with me not to fool around. Thirty seconds into Round 2 I threw a left hook that dumped the Chief on his ass. He got up at five, so I threw another left and down he went again.

The third round was an instant replay. Prout came charging out at the bell, but before he took three steps I whacked him with the left hook to the chops and he dropped in a heap. He staggered to his feet just as referee Bill Connolly counted six, but instead of turning to face me Prout walked over to the ropes and started to climb out of the ring. Everybody was booing and throwing stuff, so Connolly grabbed his arm and said, "Hey Don, where you going?" Without missing a beat, Prout glared at him and replied, "Fuck you; you fight him!"

Don never fought again. It wasn't the most honorable way for the New England heavyweight champ to wrap up a pretty good career, but what the hell. At least it was a memorable exit. Afterward, I went to the hospital to get my chin stitched up. It was sliced right to the bone, and when the doc held up a mirror I was shocked to see just how white that bone looked. Left a nice scar, too.

Oh, by the way, Irving got stiffed on my $600 purse. Sad Sam came up with some lame excuse about not being able to pay us right after the fight, but Ungerman kept hounding him until we got the dough a couple of months later.

ROUND 5

THE DELAYED PAYMENT FOR BEATING PROUT INTO retirement didn't detract from it being a good win, and I wasn't about to squander the sense of momentum that was starting to build for us. Teddy was adjusting comfortably to the new arrangement and Irving had proven capable of lining up solid sparring partners.

When we got back to Toronto, I told Ungerman to get me a top-10 guy for my next fight. I figured we were only one or two wins away from a shot at the world title, and I was anxious to get them as quickly as possible. When Irving asked if I had anyone in mind, I suggested No. 4–ranked Doug Jones. Madison Square Garden matchmaker Teddy Brenner had made some overtures about me fighting Jones a few months earlier, but nothing had come of it.

"Forget it, George," Ungerman sniffed. "You can't beat that guy. For Christ's sake, he nearly knocked out Cassius Clay last year!"

Hearing my neophyte manager tell me I couldn't win really got my dander up. "Listen, Irving," I told him. "If you don't make the call, I will. And if that happens, you'll be on the outside looking in." Reluctantly, Ungerman made the call, and Brenner quickly agreed to make the match.

The fight was signed for October 2 at Madison Square Garden, so in early August we set up training camp just outside of Bolton, a sleepy little town about half an hour north of Toronto.

The scene was like something out of *Body and Soul*, the old John Garfield movie. We had the ring set up near the bank of the winding Humber River, a couple of heavy bags hanging from tree branches and a beat-up trailer to accommodate me, Teddy and four sparring partners. Just down the road was a little diner, which Irving supplied with steaks and chickens for our meals—although we later found out that the old gal who ran the joint kept the good steaks for herself and served us the "seconds."

The Bolton camp was the most productive of my career to that point. All the sparring partners gave me real good work, and they were fun guys to have around. Cody Jones was a big, strong heavyweight from Detroit. Greatest Crawford and Jimmy Christopher were light heavyweights, but both could punch and they were slick and elusive. Lucky Little, from Steubenville, Ohio, was a quick, powerful middleweight who could mimic the lateral movement Jones had employed so effectively in going the 10-round distance against Clay the previous year. A pretty talented amateur painter, he also loved to debate me about the relative merits of the U.S. versus Canada.

From day one of camp, Teddy had me working on a combination he called "The Doug": a right uppercut, followed by a hook and a right to the head. Recalling the effectiveness of the spin trick I'd worked on with King George Moore when I was still with Jack Allen, I discovered "The Doug" was even better when I planted my left foot on top of the other guy's left foot, which prevented him from backing out of range. It worked like a charm. By the time we broke camp I could stomp on the foot and fire those three punches faster than Teddy could shout, "Do the Doug!"

Despite the fact Jones was a 3–1 betting favorite, we were brimming with confidence when we arrived in New York a few days ahead of the fight. It was my first bout back at the Garden since the loss to Pat McMurtry in '58, and with my parents and my sister coming down for it, I was anxious to put on a good show.

At the weigh-in, my buddy Dave McCauley overheard Jones say to one of his trainers that "Chuvalo can't fight"—a logical assumption on Doug's part since he KO'd Zora Folley and Pete Rademacher, two guys I'd lost to, but it still surprised me that he'd shoot off his mouth like that. I didn't know the guy personally, but in interviews he struck me as kind of shy and quiet. His comment surprised me a little bit but I figured I'd respond to it in the ring.

Jones wasn't big, but he was solid . . . and very slick. We were the same age, but he'd turned pro in 1958, two years after I did, and had run off 18 consecutive wins before dropping a decision to Eddie Machen. By the time we met he was 24–5–1 and had never been stopped. Jones also had never fought a 12-rounder before, and our bout was scheduled to be the Garden's first non-televised Friday-night main event.

I was able to set a good pace from the opening bell, muscling Doug on the inside and landing short, hard hooks. He tried to use every inch of the 20-foot ring to keep the fight at long range, but every time I trapped him against the ropes, I hurt him. His best weapon was a double jab, and he occasionally tried to feint a right in order to double up the left hook, but there wasn't a lot of snap on his punches. Meanwhile, every time Teddy exhorted me to "do the Doug" in close, I stepped on Jones's left foot and fired the three shots, just like we'd worked on in Bolton.

After 10 rounds, two of the three judges had me comfortably ahead on points, while the third had Jones leading by one. When I sat down on the stool between rounds, for the first—and only—time during a fight, I suddenly felt the urge to pee. It's a good thing that Teddy doused my head with water, because as it ran down my body and legs, I just let go and let it flow, so to speak. Fortunately, nobody noticed—I hope!

I felt a lot less sluggish going out for Round 11, and a little over a minute later I saw a golden opportunity when Jones momentarily dropped his hands while we were trading punches in my corner. And this time I didn't have to step on his foot.

I ripped a short left hook to the body and followed up with a big right hand to his chin. As Jones reeled back against the ropes, I shot four more punches up the middle that sent him tumbling to his knees. He rolled over into a sitting position near the middle of the ring but managed to stagger to his feet as referee Arthur Mercante's count reached five.

Mercante signaled for us to continue, but after I pounded four more unanswered rights to Jones's head, he waved me off and stopped the fight at 1:28.

If you watch the film, you'll see that I was so happy to be

the first guy to stop Jones that I even gave Irving a kiss on the cheek. Why not? My end of the $2,560 purse was only $1,280, but I knew the win would put me back in the top 10 for the first time in more than two years—and I could taste a title shot just around the corner.

Before the fight, Irving had ordered a big cake with "It's Only the Beginning" written in icing, and he brought it into the dressing room afterward. When we finally finished celebrating and got back to the hotel, I was totally exhausted—so tired, in fact, that I reluctantly turned down an invitation from entertainer Sammy Davis Jr. to join him at another party. Sammy was playing the lead role of a fighter in a Broadway musical called *The Golden Boy*, and he'd been at ringside to watch the bout. He called my room at four in the morning to say how much he enjoyed it and that he hoped we could "paint the town" together some time. What a guy!

In the aftermath of the win, nobody wrote about me stepping on Jones's foot, but some New York reporters (as well as Doug himself) complained about what they called my "dirty tactics" of punching below the belt.

For the record, I never intentionally punched low—either in that fight or any other—but because my style was built on maintaining inside pressure and going to the body, it's only natural that some punches would land south of the border. Any time you get close to a guy and start winging with both hands, you're not real concerned about where the punches end up. With slick guys like Jones who liked to move backwards, I threw so many body shots that the number of low blows probably seemed a little disproportionate.

I didn't realize what an impression those punches made

until I ran into Jones again more than 30 years later—but first, a little background.

When I was inducted into the World Boxing Hall of Fame in Los Angeles in 1997, another of the fighters being honored was Cleveland Williams, the former No. 2 contender whom I defeated on the undercard of the Ali–Buster Mathis bout in Houston in 1972. I hadn't seen or spoken to Williams since that night, so I walked up to him, extended my hand and asked if he remembered me. With little more than a dismissive glance, big Cleve just nodded and said, "Yup."

That was it. I felt kind of bad . . . but I suppose some guys don't get too excited about renewing acquaintances with a victorious adversary, even if the bout took place some 26 years ago. I vowed that the next time I ran into a guy I'd defeated, the first thing out of my mouth would be a compliment.

A year or so later, at a function in New York, I went to use the restroom and lo and behold, who's relieving himself at the next urinal? None other than Doug Jones. This was a delicate situation: two guys who had fought each other all those years ago now standing side by side, taking a whiz.

As was the case with Williams, I hadn't seen or talked to Jones since the night I knocked him out, but I was determined to say something nice to him.

As we kind of looked sideways at each other, I sensed that he recognized me, so I broke the ice by saying, "You were a hell of a fighter, Doug. I had a bit of a weight advantage on you, but you had a hell of a sharp right hand on the inside." He sighed and nodded before softly replying, "Yeah . . . and you had a great left hook to the balls." Then he zipped up and was gone.

So much for pleasant memories.

✧ ✧ ✧

THE last two months of 1964 were very eventful, both for me and for the heavyweight division.

I kept busy by knocking out former AAU champ Calvin Butler in three rounds at Hull, Quebec, on November 10. Butler was a last-minute replacement for Philadelphia's Don Walker, who failed to show up at the weigh-in. That improved my record to 29–8–2 with 20 KOs and, combined with the win over Jones, vaulted me into the No. 5 spot in the world rankings, just behind the towering Texan, Cleveland Williams. Williams was 65–5, but he'd been KO'd twice by Liston and once by Bob Satterfield. WBA champ Ernie Terrell, who beat Williams on a split decision in '63, was ranked No. 3, with Floyd Patterson at No. 2 and Liston ranked the No. 1 contender for Ali's crown.

Ali was signed to make his first title defense in a rematch with Liston on November 16 in Boston, but four days before the fight he was stricken with a hernia attack that required an emergency operation. There was some speculation that the "emergency" was just an excuse to postpone the fight because of poor ticket sales, but the attending doctors told the Associated Press that if Ali had suffered the attack during the fight he might have died in the ring.

On November 29, two weeks after the Ali–Liston postponement, Williams was shot by a Texas highway patrolman on the outskirts of Tomball, just north of Houston.

According to the newspaper reports, Williams and three friends—two of them female—were pulled over and arrested for drunk driving. Cleve, who claimed to have only consumed a couple of beers, pleaded with the cop to let them go because an arrest would wipe out his upcoming WBA title fight against Terrell. A scuffle ensued, and Williams ended up taking a .38 magnum bullet in the abdomen.

The upshot of all of this activity was the best Christmas present I could have imagined: an offer to meet Floyd Patterson in a title-elimination bout at Madison Square Garden on February 1, 1965.

The fight took on a life of its own from the moment it was announced.

For starters, the January rankings from the World Boxing Association had me at No. 3, Patterson at No. 2 and Liston at No. 1, with Terrell as champion. Even though virtually every other jurisdiction in the world—along with *The Ring*— acknowledged Ali as the undisputed titleholder, the WBA refused to recognize him because of his Nation of Islam affiliation and the fact that he'd signed for a rematch with Liston instead of facing Terrell. The sanctioning body had officially stripped Ali of his title the previous June.

None of that mattered to me, because behind the scenes an agreement was already in place to circumvent the WBA's bureaucratic bullcrap. If Patterson beat me and Ali beat Liston in their rematch, Patterson would be the next name on Ali's dance card. If I beat Floyd and Liston beat Ali, Sonny and I would rumble for the title. It was a done deal.

Either way, I figured to get a shot at the big prize sooner rather than later. That, along with the $50,000 (plus a cut of the closed-circuit TV money) I would pocket for Patterson made February 1 the most important night of my life.

The pre-fight hype was unbelievable, like nothing I had experienced in my entire career. With reporters coming from all over Europe, Asia, Africa and Latin America to join their North American counterparts, the fight set a record for press credential requests at Madison Square Garden.

The deluge of media attention started as soon as we set up training camp at Huntington Golf and Country Club, near Woodside Park north of Toronto. Once again, I had Greatest Crawford, Cody Jones, Jimmy Christopher and Lucky Little on board as sparring partners, and by the time we moved the camp to Kutsher's Resort in Monticello, New York, three weeks prior to the fight, I was razor-sharp.

When I wasn't sparring or otherwise conditioning my body, I relaxed and sharpened my mind by reading *The Prophet*, a collection of 26 poetic essays by Lebanese writer Khalil Gibran. I was absolutely blown away by what he had to say about life. It was like reading words from God's mouth. *The Prophet* is still one of my all-time favorite books.

At Kutsher's, the whole atmosphere was electric. My sparring sessions (176 rounds in total) became part of the resort's daily entertainment schedule, and when I wasn't in the ring or noshing on great kosher food, I was running laps on the golf course or chopping down trees in the surrounding woods.

One morning after we'd been at Kutsher's for a couple of weeks, Ungerman got a disturbing message from one of the resort's telephone operators. Part of her job was to screen calls from all the reporters who wanted to do interviews, and in the course of carrying out that duty she periodically eavesdropped on what was being said on the other lines.

The woman told Irving that Greatest Crawford was getting calls from Dan Florio, one of Patterson's handlers. She said Crawford, who had previously worked with Patterson, was passing along advice about not trying to fight me on the inside because, as he put it, "George is way too strong for Floyd." She also said Crawford told Florio that Patterson's best strategy would be "to run like hell"—a strategy that had never been part of Floyd's repertoire.

Although Crawford's treachery surprised and disappointed me, we did nothing about it because I liked Greatest and felt no animosity toward him. Scrawny, with long arms and a wispy goatee, he was a man of very few words, but when he said something in that deep, resonant voice of his, it was usually pretty good. His favorite expression was "I gotta make me some cakes [money], baby!" Crawford was a pretty decent fighter, too—although he would've been a hell of a lot better if he hadn't smoked so much. His breath always smelled heavily of tobacco, and every time I whacked him to the body it was just like somebody blowing smoke in my face.

Why Greatest chose to tip off Patterson's people is anybody's guess, but he never found out that we knew what he'd done. And to Crawford's credit, the telephone operator reported that he only reluctantly gave up information. He was a New York guy, so maybe he felt a kind of loyalty to Florio and Patterson. Either way, he disappeared from camp the day after we found out—and Teddy was convinced he'd been whisked straight to Patterson's headquarters in Marlboro, New York, about 50 miles away. McWhorter even coined a clever name for it for the newspaper guys: "sparnapping"!

Sadly, Greatest was killed in his fight with Marion Connor in Canton, Ohio, the following year.

Another of the little distractions that surfaced during our time at Kutsher's was the endless parade of former fighters and other ring luminaries who dropped by to watch me train before offering their predictions to the hordes of reporters. Joe Louis and Rocky Marciano both predicted I would knock Patterson out, as did ex-lightweight and welterweight champ Barney Ross, who was treated like some sort of Jewish deity when he came around for a visit. Jimmy Braddock, the old "Cinderella Man" who refereed my bout with Julio Medeiros in '58, went the other way, forecasting Patterson would win "a very tough decision."

On January 19, I was in the middle of a sparring session with Cody Jones when we were distracted by a wave of commotion moving across the ballroom in the direction of the ring. Then I heard the voice: "Let me in there! Step aside and let me in that ring!" It was Muhammad Ali.

"There he is! There he is!" Ali shouted, pointing at me. "He insulted me, and now I'm gonna whup him! That's what the champ is gonna do . . . I'm gonna get in there and whup the Washerwoman!"

Like the Pied Piper, Muhammad had about 50 reporters and photographers trailing behind him and he was carrying a mop and pail. He jumped up on the ring apron, handed me the props, then read a "prepared statement," bellowing so that nobody in the big crowd missed a single word: "I have come as heavyweight champion of the world to offer you a chance at becoming the champion, which would bring you great honor and dignity and make you a national hero in your home state of Canada! If you can defeat the Rabbit and look good in defeating him, I may grant you an opportunity to be in a $10 million gate with me!"

It was all in good fun—payback for the stunts we'd pulled on him in Detroit and Miami. After the fuss died down, Ali quietly watched me go four rounds with Jones, then told a TV interviewer, "Up close, George is tougher than I thought. And he hits pretty sharp, too. Maybe I should stop talking and start training. I think from now on, I'll have to call him the Washerman!"

I got the final word, though. After I wrapped up with Jones, Ali doffed his coat and climbed into the ring with gloves on, trying to coax me into going one round with him. "Don't bother me when I'm working, Sonny," I snapped. "I'll give you my autograph later."

While the atmosphere at Kutsher's was somewhat over-whelming, by the time we moved to a hotel in downtown Manhattan the fight had become the talk of the town—literally. Every five minutes, it seemed, Ungerman was fielding another request for an interview or photo session. My mug graced the cover of *Sports Illustrated* for a feature story entitled "The Croatian Candidate," and I was invited to appear on *The Les Crane Show*, which at the time rivaled Johnny Carson as television's No. 1 late-night gabfest.

The Sunday before the bout, snazzily decked out in a crisp new shirt and tie, I was introduced on *The Ed Sullivan Show*. Backstage, Mr. Really Big Shoo told me that he'd be at the fight, and if I won he wanted Teddy and me to do a demonstration of the glove beat on the following week's show. But the best part about that little detour into TV land was that I got introduced to one of Sullivan's other guests: Juliet Prowse, the gorgeous redheaded dancer/actress. What a doll!

Meanwhile, as fight night drew closer, a lot was being said and written about me being the heavyweight division's new "Great White Hope." The stories—almost all of which were penned by U.S. writers—inevitably drew comparisons to the Jack Johnson era, when it seemed like any Caucasian over six feet who could punch was hailed as the next savior of the white race. Well, I'm a white guy and I sure as hell hoped I'd win, but that was the extent of it for me.

Unfortunately, a lot of other folks couldn't leave that angle alone. This was still the era of segregation in many parts of the U.S., and black-vs.-white fights were viewed as "unsavory" in some Southern states (although heavyweight Buddy Turman did a lot to torpedo that in 1955 by becoming the first white fighter to legally take on a black opponent in Texas). Protests by the Ku Klux Klan resulted in some theaters in Alabama, Georgia and Mississippi refusing to carry the closed-circuit telecast of me and Floyd Patterson, and on the day of the fight some idiot phoned a bomb threat into Madison Square Garden.

All the tension and chaos of the buildup culminated with the pre-fight weigh-in, which looked more like a panic sale at the New York Stock Exchange. There were so many bodies packed in the room and it was so noisy I just remember thinking that Floyd and I were like prize cattle or racehorses as we stepped onto the scales and heard our weights announced over the deafening din: "Chuvalo, 208! Patterson, 197 and a quarter!"

The weigh-in provided my first up-close look at Patterson, but we didn't speak. I admired Floyd when I was a kid; I remembered watching him win the middleweight gold medal as a 17-year-old at the 1952 Olympics. I'd always liked the way he could look kind of quizzical by raising his eyebrows and crinkling his forehead. In fact, I even tried to mimic that look when I was a kid. But we weren't kids now.

I felt great climbing into the ring that night, and the sold-out crowd of 19,100 gave me a thunderous reception, even though we were fighting in Patterson's backyard.

My personal cheering section was a few rows back of ringside: Lynne, looking beautiful (if a tad apprehensive), and a handful of my buddies from Toronto. Weeks earlier, I'd told my parents and sister that I didn't want them there because I knew it was very hard on them to watch me fight in person—especially my mother. On the few occasions when they'd attended previous fights I'd found it a distraction, so for this one, my mother and Zora stayed at home, taking care of the boys, while my father had a ticket for the sold-out closed-circuit show at Maple Leaf Gardens.

To this day, I can still see and smell the cloud of stale cigar and cigarette smoke that was suspended high above the ring as announcer Johnny Addie introduced everybody from Joe Louis and Rocky Marciano to Frank Sinatra and Ed Sullivan. Ali was roundly booed when he waved to the crowd from ringside, where he was providing color commentary for the closed-circuit telecast, but I didn't pay any attention to him. However, I did pay distressing attention to the amount of tobacco I was inhaling as I stood in the center of the ring in a billow of smoke, receiving the referee's instructions. I said to myself that I might as well be smoking. The only thing that helped me calm down slightly was the fact that Floyd was in the same boat. I also remember that, as a loyal Canuck, I was a bit surprised when it was time for the anthems and the Garden organist played "God Save the Queen" (badly) instead of "O Canada."

From the opening bell, it was obvious that Patterson's camp had taken Greatest Crawford's surreptitious advice to heart.

Instead of coming straight forward and boxing, as he'd done so successfully against Ingemar Johansson, Tom McNeeley and Eddie Machen, Floyd immediately got on his bicycle and threw flurries of light pit-a-pat punches before sliding backwards or sideways to keep the fight in the middle of the ring.

To compound matters, referee Zach Clayton constantly wedged himself between us to force a break every time I got on the inside. It was almost like he was working to a plan—if not consciously, then at least maybe somebody on the New York State Athletic Commission had put the idea in his head.

When you watch the tape today, the favoritism is pretty obvious. Clayton was a New York guy, working for the New York commission, and Patterson was a New York fighter. They all knew I lived on the inside, that being there played to my strength. Through the first six rounds, every time I managed to get my hands free in close, I ripped Patterson to the body and head—but just as quickly, Clayton moved in to pull us apart.

I'm not taking anything away from Floyd. In terms of quickness, he was one of the best I ever fought, and he threw me off right away by moving around so much. He was extremely agile and a very sharp counterpuncher. He fired a lot of punches, but there wasn't a whole lot of snap on them. That was another shock, to be honest. Floyd had shown murderous power in a lot of his previous fights, particularly against Johansson, but to me his shots felt like a feather duster.

After seven rounds, my corner told me I was leading and I could sense that Patterson was really tiring, but the more I tried to press the action, the more Clayton felt duty-bound to pull us apart.

I was hurting Floyd big time with hooks to the body, but in retrospect, I never zeroed in on his chin the way I should have. Remember, Patterson was knocked down more times than any heavyweight champ in history (and got up more times, too), and most of the shots that dropped him were right on the button. I had my chances to do the same, but I kept missing high. Besides, I figured I was doing enough damage to his ribs that he'd eventually wilt.

Unfortunately for me, that never happened.

Both of us were dog tired after eight rounds, and that's when the fight started to slip away from me—at least according to the judges. Floyd's quick little combinations had raised a pretty good mouse under my right eye, and in the ninth he nicked me beside the left, but I still had enough in the tank to bull him into the ropes and land a half-dozen hooks to the kidneys that buckled his knees.

I knew the body shots were hurting him, because just before the bell rang to end Round 10, I knocked out his mouthpiece before he wobbled over to the wrong corner.

I thought Rounds 11 and 12 were pretty close, though most of the post-fight stories said those six minutes swung the scoring in Patterson's favor. All I know is that he was a desperate fighter, particularly in the last round, and that was the only time during the whole fight that he reverted to his old style, if only for a few moments.

Judge Tony Castellano gave it to Floyd by seven rounds to five, while Joe Armstrong saw it eight to four. What fight was he watching? Ironically, the closest score was turned in by Clayton, the guy who wouldn't let me fight my fight. He had it six to five for Patterson, with one round even.

The details of the scorecards showed how close it actually was. Patterson won only three rounds unanimously, while I got two. With Clayton and the two judges divided over the other seven, it basically came down to the subtle intangibles that color every decision in the ring. And Floyd was no dummy when it came to maximizing his advantages. He had the hometown crowd, two New York judges and a New York referee. That's a pretty loaded deck in anyone's game.

I was disappointed, naturally, but far from disheartened. I felt then (as I do now) that Clayton made the difference by not letting me fight my fight, but what could I do about it?

Floyd never came close to hurting me, but I know I did some major damage to him. An hour after we left the ring, he collapsed in his shower while a bunch of reporters were in his dressing room, but one of the few guys who wrote about it was Dave Anderson of *The New York Times*. All the Toronto writers witnessed it, too, but somehow that little fact never made it into their stories. I could just see the headline: "Winner KO'd in Shower!" It would have made a nice addition to my scrapbook. Oh well.

For his part, though, Patterson was a gracious victor. "Fighting Chuvalo is like trying to chop down an oak tree," he told Anderson. "He hurt me several times, but I was fortunate enough to weather the storm. I thought at one time in the fight I was behind, and my corner told me so. I guess it was around the eighth or ninth round. I wanted to throw a lot of punches, trade with him and then move outside. But every time I tried to fight him inside, he always got the better of it. Had I fought George three fights ago, he probably would have knocked me out. Even two fights ago, he would have stopped me. One fight ago, it would have been a lot closer. This wasn't a title fight, but it's the most satisfying victory of my career—and I'm definitely not looking for a rematch."

Floyd was as good as his word. As much as we tried to get him in the ring again, the answer was always a resounding "NO!" I must have made a lasting impression on him.

In the 1980s, long after both our careers were over, Patterson became a marathoner. In an interview with *The New York Times*, he talked about what it was like to hit the infamous "wall" that long-distance runners often speak about. "The only thing I can compare it to in boxing was the night I fought George Chuvalo at the Garden," he told the reporter. "After five rounds, I was totally exhausted. I couldn't even hold up my arms. I was so tired, I lost the next two or three rounds. But then the crowd started cheering me and chanting my name, and I knew I had to do something special. Somehow I won the last couple of rounds, and that made the difference."

My dance with Patterson ended up being named *The Ring*'s Fight of the Year for 1965, and it was the highest-grossing non-title bout in boxing history to that point, with a live gate of $166,423 and $600,000 from closed-circuit TV. It made for a real nice payday . . . but all I could think about was getting away for a little R&R.

A couple of weeks later, Lynne and I were in Lethbridge, Alberta, where I appeared at a charity event with former Boston Red Sox star Jimmy Piersall. He had a reputation for being a bit of a wingnut (immortalized in the 1957 movie *Fear Strikes Out*, starring Anthony Perkins and Karl Malden), but I found him to be personable and interesting to chat with while we signed a couple of thousand autographs.

But Piersall's demeanor changed once dinner was served. Even though the MC had instructed the audience to hold off on autograph requests until we were finished eating, a couple of guys made the mistake of approaching Jimmy with baseball cards they wanted signed. In the blink of an eye, he transformed from Dr. Jekyll into Mr. Hyde. "Get the fuck away from me! Didn't you hear the MC?" he screamed. "Can't you see that I'm eating?" It was quite a scene.

From Lethbridge, Lynne and I flew to Vancouver and then down to San Francisco to enjoy a mini-vacation. After a couple of days on the beach, we rented a car to drive to Los Angeles. About two in the morning, dead tired from the journey, we decided to get a motel room in the little town of Pismo Beach where, unbeknownst to us, a gas station had been robbed shortly before our arrival.

A few minutes after we checked in, there was a loud pounding at the door. I opened it to find a couple of no-nonsense-type cops demanding to know who we were, where we were coming from and where we were going.

This was too good of an opportunity to pass up. Without skipping a beat, I turned to Lynne, who had just stepped out of the shower. She was wearing a robe, had her hair up in curlers and definitely wasn't in the mood for my warped sense of humor. "Hey doll," I growled. "What did you say your name was?"

ROUND 6

TEN WEEKS AFTER THE PATTERSON FIGHT, I GOT back to business by knocking out Bill Nielsen in eight rounds at Maple Leaf Gardens. It was my first fight at home since being disqualified against Joe Erskine four years earlier, and it felt good.

Nielsen, who hailed from Omaha, was nicknamed "Golden Boy" for his outstanding showings in the U.S. Golden Gloves nationals from 1956–60, and as an amateur he once dropped a split decision to Cassius Clay. By the time we hooked up his record was 22-5-1 and included a KO of former British Empire champion Joe Bygraves in 1963, but he'd since been stopped by Tom McNeeley, Brian London and Billy Walker.

As a pro, Nielsen's biggest claim to fame was being awarded a DQ victory over a guy named Ernie Cab at Madison Square Garden in 1962, after Cab took a bite out of his arm.

Nielsen was rugged, I'll give him that. But he couldn't hit, and his jab was more of a nuisance than a punch. I was rusty and far from being at my best, but referee Jackie Silvers stopped the fight in the eighth after I caught Bill with a good flurry that closed his right eye and opened a nasty cut under the left one.

For me, the most memorable thing about that fight was meeting Bob Hope. Long before he became one of the most versatile entertainers ever, Hope fought a few amateur bouts under the name of Packy East. He was in Toronto for an Easter Seals fundraiser and we ended up having a nice little visit.

Over the next four months, while I stayed busy in Canada with KO wins over Sonny Andrews, Dave Bailey (refereed by the great Barney Ross) and Orvin Veazey, the heavyweight division was undergoing yet another upheaval in the wake of Ali's May 25 rematch with Liston in front of 2,500 fans at a hockey rink in Lewiston, Maine.

Everybody knows the story.

Officially, Ali scored a first-round KO after landing his so-called "anchor punch." It was so sudden and so unexpected that referee Jersey Joe Walcott forgot to order Muhammad to a neutral corner, then lost the count and actually motioned for the fight to continue before Nat Fleischer, publisher of *The Ring*, screamed from his front-row seat that Liston had been on the deck for about 20 seconds.

Five years later, in a story published in *Sports Illustrated*, Liston explained it to writer Jack Olsen: "Clay caught me cold and the count was messed up, and that's all there was to it. Clay knocked me down with a good punch. Anybody can get caught cold in the first round, before you even work up a sweat. And when I was down, Clay stood right over me. No, I never blacked out, not for a second. But I wasn't gonna get up, either, not with him standin' over me. See, you can't get up without puttin' one hand on the floor, and so I couldn't protect myself, and he can hit me on the way up."

That was Sonny's version.

From where I was sitting, about 40 feet away, it was pretty obvious he took a dive. I don't think Ali or his people had anything to do with it, and I'm not saying the fix was in, but I think that whole "anchor punch" story is a crock of crap.

When Ali threw his punch—and there definitely was one—I had a clear view. Liston had his back to me, but the "punch" was more like a swat, just a little tap. It wasn't a murderous right hand or anything even close, but Sonny went down like he'd been shot.

Now, remember, this is a guy who barely blinked when he took the best shots from guys like Mike DeJohn and Cleveland Williams, both of whom were big bombers. To see him collapse from a little tap like that, a pussy punch, was ridiculous. But it all started to make sense when more details about Ali's deep connection to the Nation of Islam surfaced. In a way I couldn't blame Sonny, who was probably thinking, "If I get up, I might get shot."

For me, the real tip-off was seeing Ali's reaction. He looked surprised—and disgusted. Immortalized in a famous photo by *Sports Illustrated*'s Neil Leifer, he stood glaring over Liston, bellowing, "Get up and fight, you bum!"

I think Muhammad did that because he knew it was a pussy punch. Nothing else makes sense. If you hit a guy with a clean shot, you don't scream at him to get up. Ali knew it. So did Angelo Dundee. Anchor punch? No way!

My theory is that, without Muhammad and Angelo knowing anything about it, the Muslims got to Sonny and told him he'd better not win. Liston knew better than to mess with those guys. The word was he probably bet some big money on Ali, even though Muhammad wasn't an overwhelming favorite. If Sonny couldn't win, that was at least a chance for him to make some serious dough, so I think he went for it.

I'd forgotten about jumping into the ring afterward, until I saw the clip in *The Last Round*, the 2003 documentary the National Film Board of Canada made about my first fight with Ali. You can see me climb through the ropes and go directly to Muhammad's corner. I wasn't mad at him, I was just really pissed off that the title shot I'd been promised if Liston won was now in the toilet, thanks to the worst acting job I've ever seen.

In the heat of the moment, with the crowd going nuts and chanting, "Fix! Fix!" my shouting and posturing was a knee-jerk reaction to letting my emotions get the better of me. I could maybe understand if Sonny had taken a big shot, or even a few little ones. But it was a terrible dive off a pussy punch, plain and simple. Ali didn't twist his body into it at all, and his face told the whole story. Muhammad's eyes got wide, like he was saying to himself, "You dropped from *that?*"

Later, both *Sports Illustrated* and *The Ring* supposedly "proved" the accuracy and force of the punch by breaking down the film, but I know what I saw. No matter what Ali or Angelo said later about the anchor punch, I'll go to my grave knowing that shot wouldn't have knocked out Liston's grandmother.

It wasn't just me; everybody was in shock. Angelo did a great job of selling it, but what else was he going to say? It wasn't his fault, or Muhammad's. I just wish I had the Nation of Islam in my corner. They made the rules, and the thought of crossing those guys scared the shit out of Liston. That's my take on it.

It's sad that that's the fight people remember Sonny for, but when you think you might get killed, what else do you do? Liston was a hell of a fighter. In my opinion, at his best, he was absolutely one of the top five or six heavyweight champions ever.

For some people, that fight still kind of sullies Ali's reputation, too . . . but that's not right. I don't for a second believe Muhammad or Angelo had anything to do with Liston lying down—especially after the fantastic performance by Ali in their first meeting, which is what I always recall when I think of Muhammad at his absolute best.

Of course, I never did get to face Liston—and that's the one fight I've always regretted not having. Sadly, it was never meant to be—just like my imaginary dream date with Raquel Welch. But we came very close, six years later.

Fast forward to January 5, 1971, the day Liston was found dead by his wife, Geraldine, in the bedroom of their Las Vegas home. Mrs. Liston, who was returning from an out-of-town trip, told police she noticed a foul odor when she entered the house. On Sonny's death certificate, the coroner wrote "December 30," after estimating the date from the number of milk bottles and newspapers piled up at the front door.

Following their investigation, the police concluded there was no sign of forced entry or foul play. To this day, the official cause of Liston's death remains a mystery, although the cops eventually declared it was the result of a heroin overdose.

A couple of weeks earlier, just before Christmas, I'd gotten a call from Regis Levesque, a promoter in Montreal, offering me $25,000 to fight Sonny at the Montreal Forum on February 19, 1971. That was the same money I'd been offered to fight him years earlier, so I thought I could do a little better. After a solid week of negotiating, Levesque finally said, "Chuvalo, you drive a hard bargain." I had jacked up the measly offer to 30 grand. I had to! If I had fought for a lousy $25,000 I would have been ruined psychologically. Even 30 grand in 1971 wasn't great. But at least I felt I could handle it mentally. "Send me a telegram to seal the deal," said Levesque. So I did.

Sure enough, on January 5, Regis called a big press conference in Montreal, where he pulled out my telegram and told the reporters, "I've got confirmation that George Chuvalo has agreed to fight Sonny Liston." Then one of the reporters asked about Liston's contract, and Levesque said, "I just got off the phone with Sonny this morning, and he's agreed to all terms. The fight is on!"

You can guess the rest.

A few hours later, the lead story on the six o'clock news was: "Body of Sonny Liston, former heavyweight champion of the world, found in his Las Vegas home—believed to be dead seven to 10 days."

Levesque was inundated with phone calls from reporters, asking him if he'd been talking to a ghost.

And promoters wonder why nobody believes them?

Two weeks after Ali beat Liston, Ernie Terrell won the vacant World Boxing Association title in a boring 15-round decision over Eddie Machen in Chicago.

Ali had been stripped of the WBA crown on June 19, 1964, because he had opted for an immediate rematch with Liston instead of making his first title defense against Machen, who at the time was the WBA's No 1 contender. Most people thought it was really because Muhammad had embraced the Nation of Islam.

Unlike today, when it seems like there's a new "title" fight every other month, this marked the first time the world heavy-weight championship was split, and on paper the fight looked to be a good matchup. Machen was 47–5–2 and Terrell was 36–4, but as usual, Ernie's style turned it into a suffocating clutchfest.

At 6 foot 6 and 215 pounds, Terrell *looked* like a guy who could punch, but looks can be deceiving. He only had 18 KOs going in against Machen, and the biggest name on his record was future light heavyweight champ Bob Foster, who was 14–2 when Terrell stopped him in seven rounds in 1964.

Instead of power, Ernie preferred to use his 82-inch reach and defensive posturing to smother opponents and win on points.

Terrell's ace in the hole was that Bernie Glickman was his manager of record, even though Tony Accardo was really the guy pulling the strings. Accardo—also known as "Big Tuna"—had been a fixture in the Chicago rackets since the Prohibition days. He'd risen through the ranks, going from a small-time associate of Al Capone to the all-powerful boss of what became known as the "Chicago Outfit," with partners like Frankie Carbo, who was widely thought to be responsible for engineering the murder of Benjamin "Bugsy" Siegel, the guy who built Las Vegas.

Glickman was a rich businessman who'd been involved in

boxing for several years, most notably as co-manager of Virgil "Honey Bear" Akins, who was world welterweight champ for six months in 1958. Glickman served as Accardo's front man, and that connection scared away a lot of would-be challengers once Terrell became champ.

With limited options for Terrell in the U.S., Glickman and Accardo looked north. I was ranked No. 3 by the WBA, so when Ungerman got an offer of $45,000 for me to challenge for Ernie's title at Maple Leaf Gardens on November 1—the day before my son Stevie's fifth birthday—we jumped at it.

When I think about it now, it's almost comical how the fight unfolded. Even if it was for only a piece of the title, I was ecstatic about finally getting the opportunity, but almost from the second we signed it was obvious to me that Irving had no clue about how to deal with the big boys.

Without even talking to me about it, Ungerman decided to bring in Rocky Marciano and Joe Louis as "special advisers." What a joke! Marciano grabbed $3,000 as his fee, did absolutely nothing for a couple of weeks and then blew town before the fight. My pal Marvin Elkind hooked us up with Warren K. Cook, one of Toronto's top tailors, to get free suits for me, Joe and Rocky. For some reason Ungerman told him I didn't need a suit and Joe—always a gentleman—declined the offer, so Marvin ended up taking just Marciano down to the store. "Gimme a blue one and a brown one," Rocky told the guy. After being informed they only had one suit for him, Marciano didn't miss a beat: "I'm takin' Joe's, too."

That was Rocky. He was so goddamned cheap, he wouldn't spend a nickel for a phone call. Still, he was very charming, very pleasant to chat with. But having him and Louis in camp was just another grandstand move by Ungerman to get some ink for the fight. It was good for publicity, of course. The newspaper guys loved rubbing shoulders with Rocky and Joe, but to me having them around was more trouble than it was worth.

While Irving was playing babysitter to Rocky and Joe, Teddy and I were concentrating on getting ready for the fight. Terrell was slow and couldn't punch a lick, so I had no doubt whatsoever I could outmuscle him. Unfortunately, the same couldn't be said for Ungerman vs. Glickman.

For the first time, Irving found himself dealing with guys who had the backing of major muscle, guys who knew how to turn the screws—and he was way out of his league. As the fight drew closer, Ungerman almost came unglued. He was scared shitless. Why? Because to Glickman and his guys, "doing business" in Toronto wasn't any different from what they were used to in Chicago. If the usual backdoor intimidation didn't work, they had no second thoughts about resorting to more brazen tactics—and they did.

For me, there was a much more worrisome consideration. A week before the fight, Lynne and 18-month-old Jesse were visiting the home of some friends who also had a little guy. The two kids were playing in another room when Jesse bit a live electrical cord and badly burned his mouth. It was a horrible injury that eventually required plastic surgery, and for years afterward my son endured a lot of teasing and name-calling because of his scarred mouth.

On the night of the fight, as we drove along Lake Shore Boulevard to Maple Leaf Gardens, Ungerman barely said a word. He was nervous and fidgety, and I had to tell him to get rid of his cigar because it was making me sick. He was white as a ghost, and every 15 or 20 seconds, staring out at the breakwater, he'd slap the dashboard like he was killing a fly.

Ungerman didn't tell me until after it was all over that his life had been threatened. Basically, Irving had been told that if I won, he would wind up on the bottom of Lake Ontario. No wonder the poor bastard was so nervous as we drove past the water! A few days later, referee Sammy Luftspring said right to my face that he was told he'd be killed if the decision went my way. It didn't matter what happened in the ring; it came down to management muscle. Ernie had it, and I didn't.

The fight itself wasn't what you'd call a classic. Far from it. For 15 rounds, I plowed forward and Terrell retreated. From the opening bell, he fell into his usual routine of sticking out that beanpole jab and then trying to tie me up every time I made a move inside. There was a trickle of blood coming from my nose in the second round, but so what? In the eighth, Ernie thumbed me in the eye and landed a decent right to my chin, but that was pretty much his entire offense.

From Round 11 on, Terrell was strictly in survival mode. In the 13th, I pounded him into the ropes and opened two nice cuts over his left eye. In the 14th and 15th, I trapped him on the ropes and rocked him with big shots to the head, but it wasn't enough for the judges. Fred Norbert scored it 73–65, while Billy Burke had it 69–65 and Luftspring saw it 72–65.

The scoring stank. All Terrell did was beat the hell out of my right glove for 15 rounds. Every time I moved in, he backed away—and you don't keep a title by running backwards. He just wanted to survive the 15 because he knew, with his manager's influence, that he'd get the decision. What I'll never forget is that before the scores were announced, everyone in the joint was cheering and all the photographers, newspaper guys and fans were crowding around in my corner. The only guys in Ernie's corner were his trainer, Sam Solomon, and Bernie Glickman . . . and Ernie looked pretty glum. To me, that was a good sign. After the announcement there was kind of a pause, as if people were letting it sink in, and then a mass exodus from my corner over to Terrell's. But those people knew I won the fight. Why would they want to take my picture and ask me questions if they thought I lost? Nobody talks to the loser first.

That was almost 50 years ago, but it still bothers me. In my heart, in my soul, I know I beat Ernie Terrell that night. Yeah, it was only for a piece of the title, but I know I won a world championship that night. Even if it's only for two minutes, once you win the heavyweight championship of the world, you're *always* a champ.

To get robbed like that in my own hometown still hurts.

I wasn't the only one who thought I beat Terrell. A few days later, Ungerman got a call from Mike Barrett, the preeminent promoter in Britain, who said he thought I was robbed. We accepted his offer to fight former British Commonwealth champ Joe Bygraves on December 7 at Royal Albert Hall in London.

When it came to selling a fight, nothing was too outrageous for Barrett. Bygraves was Jamaican, and as soon as the deal was done, at Barrett's urging the British press dredged up the same old "White Hope" angle that was used when I fought

Patterson. Barrett also said the winner would be "guaranteed" a shot at Henry Cooper's Commonwealth title. That sounded good to me, since I'd been ahead of Cooper in the world ratings for years.

Barrett, whom the British press nicknamed "Barnum" after circus promoter P.T. Barnum, also arranged for me to take a stroll down London's Shaftesbury Avenue with a bear! He thought it was a great idea: a bear from the wild hinterland of . . . Toronto. I can still hear him explaining it in his clipped English accent: "Don't worry, George; perfectly safe, old boy. The beast is tame as a kitten. Got 'im from the circus, I did."

Tame? Maybe. Perfectly safe? Not if the bandaged fingers of one of the bear's handlers was anything to go by.

It was a female cub, borrowed from the Bertram Mills Circus. Barrett got a big kick out of telling the reporters the animal's name was "Max Bear," even though she was really called Susie. By the time the handlers got her harnessed up and handed me the leash to walk the few blocks to the gym, a pretty big crowd was gathered.

I was escorted by Barrett's cute little secretary, who was dressed up as a Mountie, and it quickly turned into quite a spectacle. Barrett had tipped off the press, naturally, but he didn't bother to let the police in on the gimmick. The next day's story in the *Daily Mirror* said that a paddy wagon sent to check on the "Shaftesbury disturbance" nearly caused a multi-car crash when the cops spotted the bear sitting in the middle of the street—with me anxiously tugging on the leash, trying to coax it along.

It took some fancy talking from Barrett to avoid being written up for disturbing the peace, but the stunt got us a lot of ink, including several photos that were picked up by the international wire services.

Bygraves, who beat Tonga's Kitione Lave in a 15-round decision for the Commonwealth title in 1956 and then lost it to Joe Erskine the following year, had a record of 42–26–2 going into our fight. He was a big, strong guy but not a dangerous puncher. In his first title defense in '56 he'd knocked out Henry Cooper, but he had only five stoppages since, including a first-round KO of German champ Albert Westphal the previous February. Joe had a reputation for starting quickly and then running out of gas, and that's exactly how he fought me.

In the opening round he showed a decent jab and surprisingly quick feet for a big guy, but I was still able to walk him down and rake him to the body. He took a good shot, and for four or five rounds he didn't back up much. In the eighth, he went reeling across the ring after a big flurry and late in the 10th I finally dropped him with a left hook. He was still on the canvas when the bell rang to end it. I easily won the decision but would have preferred a clean KO.

A few days before the fight, I made a point of introducing myself to Cooper's manager, Jim Wicks, when he dropped by the gym to watch me spar. Wicks looked like a dapper version of Alfred Hitchcock, the famous British movie producer. "Hello," I said, extending my hand. "I'm George Chuvalo. When are you going to let Henry meet me for the Commonwealth title?"

Wicks gave me the once-over, smiled and replied in that clipped English accent, "He doesn't even want to meet you socially."

He meant it, too. In the 12 years that Cooper held the Commonwealth crown (1959–71), he defended it 10 times, including three fights against Erskine and two against fellow Englishman Jack Bodell. But for 10 of those 12 years, Cooper was ranked below me in both the Commonwealth and world ratings. Despite repeated challenges, Sir 'Enery chose never to fight me. When we offered him $40,000 to defend the title, he said he wanted $120,000. That was just another way of saying there was no way he would ever face me. After watching me demolish Bygraves, Cooper told the British newspaper *The Sun*, "Chuvalo is ugly . . . a dirty rough-houser, like [Sonny] Liston." That was his usual excuse for avoiding anyone he thought was too tough. Years later, he wrote the same thing in his autobiography: "As Jim always said, George was 'too ugly.' We only liked good-looking fighters! Anyway, that was as good an excuse as any. Chuvalo was a rough handful."

Before heading back to Toronto, Teddy and I and our pal Mort Greenberg made a quick trip across the Channel to visit Paris. Mort wanted to check out the Eiffel Tower and the Champs Élysées, while Teddy was on a different mission. He'd long dreamed of getting lucky in the city's famous Quartier Pigalle red-light district, so I went along—strictly for moral support.

We were guided to a place where the girls charged $3, plus $2 for the room—a financial arrangement my trainer found acceptable. While I waited in a nearby café, Teddy went off to do his business. Fifteen minutes passed. Then half an hour. Then 45 minutes. I used to tease Teddy about being the original "minute man" when it came to his romantic interludes, so I was getting a little concerned. Finally, he came walking through the door of the café, bearing a scowl on his face that made him look like a 126-pound version of Sonny Liston.

"What happened?" I asked.

"Well, man, she told me she was gonna wash my privates . . . but then she did this to it," he replied, grabbing my hand and demonstrating by digging his thumbnail into my finger. "It hurt like hell."

"So did you get lucky?" I asked.

A resounding "No!" he replied.

"Okay, but what took you so long?" said I.

Teddy's face winced as he moaned, "Man, I was tryin' to get my money back!"

I flew home to spend Christmas with Lynne and the kids, then returned to London to fight Eduardo Corletti on January 25, 1966, in what was supposed to be a tune-up for a possible showdown with Cooper.

Corletti was a handsome kid who had represented Argentina at the 1959 Pan-American Games and the 1960 Rome Olympics, where he lost in the second round of the tournament to Obrad Sretenovic of Yugoslavia. He turned pro in 1961 and had five KOs in six fights in Argentina before relocating to Italy, where he was trained and managed by Aldo Spoldi, a former European lightweight champ.

Using Rome as his base, Corletti fought all over the continent for the next few years, with mixed success. In 11 fights he was 5–2–4, but the two losses were back-to-back KOs to Ray Patterson (Floyd's younger brother) and Italian journeyman Giorgio Masteghin. By the time we hooked up at the Olympia Circus Arena, Corletti was coming off a knockout win over Billy Walker, who was ranked No. 2 in Britain.

That shows you how deceiving records can be. Maybe I took him lightly, but Corletti beat me fair and square in a 10-round decision. It wasn't a great fight. I always had problems when I couldn't work on the inside, and other than Ali, Corletti proved to be the fastest guy I ever fought in terms of foot speed—even faster than Patterson. I had a lot of trouble trying to trap him because he was so quick. Plus, every time I managed to muscle inside and get a hand free, referee Harry Gibbs pulled us apart. That's how they do it in England; I guess they don't think infighting is very "gentlemanly."

Anyway, at some point I fractured Corletti's cheekbone, but it didn't slow him down much. I'm embarrassed that both Jerry Quarry and Al "Blue" Lewis knocked him out in one round a few years later, but that's how it goes. I'm not denigrating Corletti's style—he was very, very quick—but for some reason he chose to stand and trade with Quarry and Lewis instead of running, like he did with me. As they say, styles make fights.

Corletti went on to be ranked in the top 10 in 1967–68, peaking at No. 3 in the WBA ratings. After getting starched by Quarry in 1972, he was knocked out in three straight fights and retired with a career record of 32–14–5, with 17 KOs.

I was extremely depressed on the long flight home from London, wondering if the loss to Corletti would knock me out of title contention. But then, thanks to the Nation of Islam, out of nowhere I got an offer to fight Ali for the world championship.

Or so I thought.

ROUND 7

I WAS SITTING IN UNGERMAN'S OFFICE ON THE afternoon of March 12, 1966, when the telephone rang. Irving picked it up and told the caller I was there with him, so he put it on the speaker. "Hi, George . . . this is Mike Malitz in New York. I'll get right to the point: How'd you like to fight Ali for the title on March 29?"

Malitz was executive vice-president of Main Bout Inc., a group of investors that also included Ali's manager, Herbert Muhammad; lawyer Bob Arum (this fight marked his first foray into boxing); Nation of Islam national secretary John Ali; and Jim Brown, the great NFL running back who retired after the 1965 season. Their plan for a title showdown with Ernie Terrell had fallen apart, so they were looking for somebody to take Terrell's place.

It was only 17 days' notice, but Malitz knew I'd take it if we were fighting in 17 minutes. Still, I decided to have a little fun. "Sounds pretty good, Mike . . . but I gotta talk to my wife first and see if we're doing anything on the 29th. I'll call you right back."

Then I called Lynne.

"Lynne, what are we doing on the 29th of this month?" I asked.

"Nothing, why?"

"'Cause you're going to the fights."

"Who's fighting?"

"Me"

"Who are you fighting?"

"Muhammad Ali."

My wife started laughing.

"No, doll. For real."

I went back on the other line. "Hey, Mike, it's okay. I'm free."

Actually, I wasn't. A couple of weeks earlier, we'd signed a contract with promoter Chris Dundee to fight Levi Forte on March 29 in Miami. Once the bout with Ali was announced, Dundee threatened to get a court injunction to stop it. It was all for show, because Chris wasn't about to screw his brother Angie out of a payday with Ali, but Ungerman ended up piecing him off anyway. On top of that, there had been a press conference just a couple of days earlier, confirming that it would be Ali and Terrell at Maple Leaf Gardens on the 29th, so this really was an 11th-hour deal.

Malitz's offer wasn't much—20 per cent of the gate, plus a piece of the theater TV sales—but to my way of thinking it was a now-or-never proposition and I didn't want to blow the opportunity. It was a rush job, like having five minutes to get ready for a date with a beautiful woman (like Raquel Welch!). You've got to get shaved and showered, brush your teeth, comb your hair. There's no time to prepare the way you really should.

That's what it felt like when I got the offer, but I knew I had to go for it. Plus, I fully expected to win. I figured once I had the title, the money would follow.

Main Bout's plan for an Ali–Terrell showdown had started to fall apart almost from the moment they announced it.

The fight was originally scheduled to take place in Rutherford, New Jersey, but there was so much heat from war veterans over Ali's anti-Vietnam stance that the plug was pulled almost immediately. The New York State Athletic Commission also refused to license it because of Terrell's connections to Glickman and his cronies, so Main Bout then tried Philadelphia, which slammed the door. Even Muhammad's hometown of Louisville said no after the Kentucky state senate passed a resolution that read, "His attitude brings discredit to all loyal Kentuckians and to the names of the thousands who gave their lives for this country during his lifetime." The next attempt was Chicago, but the Illinois Athletic Commission didn't want the fight, either.

Main Bout then looked north and contacted promoter Loren Cassina, who tried to put together a deal for the fight to take place in Montreal. Cassina got Mayor Jean Drapeau on board, but then the American Legion contacted Drapeau and told him that if the fight took place, they would organize a boycott of Expo 67. Drapeau quickly backed down.

The reception was the same in Verdun, Quebec. Offers came in from Vancouver, Edmonton and two Ontario cities—Kingston and tiny Cobourg—before Main Bout finally settled on Toronto.

For a time everything seemed set for the fight to take place at Maple Leaf Gardens, but then Terrell's manager of record, Bernie Glickman, made a near-fatal miscalculation.

No doubt recalling how easy it was to scare the shit out of Ungerman prior to my fight with Ernie four months earlier,

Glickman went to see Herbert Muhammad, who besides being Ali's manager and promoter was the No. 2 man in the Nation of Islam. Glickman must have posed the same threat that he used on Ungerman ... just a different lake: if Ali won the fight, Herbert would end up in a cement box at the bottom of Lake Michigan.

But Glickman wasn't dealing with the likes of Ungerman this time. All Herbert had to do was snap his fingers and a couple of his Black Muslim henchmen, better known as the Fruit of Islam, would pound Glickman to a pulp. He was interrogated by the police but he wouldn't talk. He went directly from the hospital to a mental institution and never saw the light of day again. The next day, Terrell announced he was pulling out.

That's how I ended up getting my first fight with Ali.

Terrell claimed he pulled out because Main Bout backed down on his guarantee—supposedly $50,000 from the live gate and $100,000 from theater TV, plus training expenses—but I think that's total B.S. Glickman's beating sent a very clear signal that nobody, not even the mob, was going to mess with the Nation of Islam.

Even before we made the deal with Malitz, Conn Smythe, the war hero who built Maple Leaf Gardens in 1931, read about plans for the fight while he was vacationing in Florida. Although he'd recently relinquished control of the arena, Smythe retained 5,100 shares in Maple Leaf Gardens Ltd. and a seat on its board of directors.

Ali was the antithesis of everything Smythe stood for, and when he got the news that Toronto was opening its arms to welcome a draft resister who was being so vocal in condemning the Vietnam War, it was more than Smythe could stomach. He called Harold Ballard to confirm the report, then followed up with a letter to the effect that he would resign his director-ship and demand that his shares be bought out unless Ballard could guarantee that "Clay" would not be fighting in Maple Leaf Gardens.

The cantankerous Ballard, who wanted the fight all along, had no qualms about accepting Smythe's resignation. Harold promptly cut a deal with Main Bout for a share of the closed-circuit TV rights and told the press he wasn't at all worried about negative publicity.

The same day the TV deal was announced, former light heavyweight champ Billy Conn was interviewed by *The New York Times* and said, "I'll never go to another one of Clay's fights. He is a disgrace to the boxing profession, and I think any American who pays to watch him after what he has said about Vietnam should be ashamed. They should stay away from those closed-circuit television shows."

The Ontario Athletic Commission and some mealy-mouthed Canadian politicians felt the same way. The OAC was under the jurisdiction of the Ontario Department of Labour. The commission's chairman, Merv McKenzie, spine-lessly announced he had to consult with Labor Minister Les Rowntree before giving final approval to the fight. McKenzie said he wanted it to be either 14 or 16 rounds so that it couldn't be considered a title bout. With typical Canadian reticence, he told the *Toronto Star*, "I want to clear up what-ever political overtones the government might be sensitive to concerning Clay."

Those "overtones" came from the likes of George Ben, a Liberal member of the Ontario Legislature, who grabbed some ink by arguing the fight "would lower the international prestige of Toronto." The Royal Canadian Legion then got in on the act. In a show of solidarity with its American counterpart, the Legion launched a campaign to pressure theater TV outlets against showing the fight. The political pressure and Legion protests on both sides of the border resulted in nearly 100 of 280 signed outlets canceling the telecast.

In the end, McKenzie and his cohorts decreed that as far as Ontario was concerned, Ali vs. Chuvalo would not be a world championship fight. Instead, they called it a "heavyweight showdown" and ordered that the tickets and souvenir programs bill it as such. There was no concern about posters, because the fight was made on such short notice that none were printed.

The OAC's gutless move really cheapened it for me, making it sound like it was an exhibition. It was so bloody Canadian . . . and it hurt that it was my own province and city that were screwing me. I felt like Gary Cooper in *High Noon,* being left to face the bad guys all alone. It still angers me today when I see that program, with the caption under Ali's picture that says, "The People's Champion." Virtually everywhere else on the planet he was recognized as the one and only true world champion—but not in good old Ontario.

What was really galling was that these guys were basically just writing me off, like there was no way in the world I could win the fight. And if I *did* win, my own hometown wouldn't recognize me as the world champion. Thanks for the support!

With few exceptions, the Canadian media lapped up everything that was spoon-fed to them by McKenzie, and none of the Toronto writers had the balls to write how absurd it was to deny that we were having a legitimate world title fight. A columnist in Winnipeg wrote, "If Clay is permitted to have a 'world championship' bout in Toronto, there isn't enough disinfectant in the Dominion to clean the stench out of Maple Leaf Gardens." The headline over Jim Kernaghan's story in the *Toronto Star* was "Clay hated by millions!" In the *Los Angeles Times,* Jim Murray wrote that Ali was "a Black Benedict Arnold" and advised him to never go anywhere near the Lincoln Memorial in Washington "because those will be real tears running down Abe's cheeks."

One of the few writers who showed any guts was *The Ring*'s Nat Fleischer. He really ripped into McKenzie for letting the WBA dictate Ontario's affairs, telling the Canadian Press, "I'm probably setting myself up to be blasted by Mr. McKenzie and his commission, but I've been blasted by far better men."

Personally, I didn't support the Vietnam War either, but I didn't think Ali's stance on it would stir up such a hornet's nest. I didn't talk about his situation, and nobody asked me about it. Maybe it would've been different if I was an American, but all the politics seemed beside the point.

I'd gotten to know Muhammad a little bit ever since our first meeting before I fought Mike DeJohn in 1963, and I liked him—even though he backed out of the deal to fight me after I whipped DeJohn. We'd kibitzed each other with the "Washerwoman" stuff, had fun with it. The poetry, the boasting . . . he got all that from watching Gorgeous George, the wrestler. But Ali took it to another level, and it was refreshing. Boxing had never had a showman like him, and I thought it was great.

But Muhammad was a different guy in the lead-up to our fight; much more somber and restrained than I'd ever seen him. I remember how quiet and humble he was at the press conference. He told the *Toronto Telegram,* "The people here in Canada are very nice. Honestly, I am not saying that just because I am here. I have never been treated so nice in my whole life. There are no people making wisecracks, everybody is friendly—the children, waiters, hotel people, policemen. Everybody is as nice as they could be. It's a lot different than from where I come from."

You could tell that he felt the sting of being a social pariah in so many ways. Today the man is an icon, the most recognized face on the planet. Everybody loves him now, but it was a much different story in 1966. Back then, a lot of people—white and black—hated him. There were always interviews in the papers and on TV, with people saying, "My kid's in the war, my kid went to Vietnam. What the hell is this guy doing? Who does he think he is?" That kind of thing.

I didn't feel sorry for the guy, but I remember thinking that it must be a hell of a thing when you're despised in your own country and people make it so clear that they don't want you to ever come back home. I thought Muhammad must be a pretty strong guy inside. Here he was, facing the wrath of the U.S. government, the wrath of the army, facing possible imprisonment, facing exile from the fight game and not being able to earn a living in his chosen profession. He was bucking a lot of very powerful people, and for what?

Of course, to the Black Muslims, to millions of black people, Ali was a hero. His courage lifted them up and made them proud. He made them feel good about themselves. I could see how it would be very easy to root for somebody like him, who stood up for what he believed and was willing to accept the consequences. To my way of thinking, Ali was a guy who had some big problems, but I wasn't going to lose any sleep over it. I had enough on my own plate to worry about—and only 17 days to get ready.

In the meantime, Ungerman was in a dither trying to help Teddy and me prepare for the biggest fight of my life. He made sure to let the newspapers know he was "sparing no expense" by bringing Joe Louis and Rocky Marciano into my camp—again—but it was just window dressing, like it had been for the Terrell fight. Marciano was only interested in getting paid and getting laid, and Joe didn't do much more than pose for pictures.

To be honest, it was a pain in the ass having those guys around. I just wanted to concentrate on training, but Irving was always setting up silly photo ops, with Joe and me sipping tea or Rocky and me looking at film. If that wasn't bad enough, Ungerman also brought in Drew "Bundini" Brown, Ali's longtime cheerleader, confidant and cornerman. They'd had a big falling out a few months earlier over Bundini's refusal to accept the Nation of Islam's ban on drinking, and he was finally kicked out of Ali's entourage after he hocked Muhammad's championship belt to a Harlem barber for $500.

Ungerman wanted Bundini in my corner because he thought it would do a psych job on Ali, but I didn't want to have anything to do with the guy. If Bundini was capable of selling out Ali after everything Muhammad had done for him, what the hell would he try with me? A few days before the fight I told Irving, "Get him the hell out of here. It's like having a spy in my camp!" Bundini didn't stick around after that.

My plan for the fight was simple: as the shorter guy, I wanted to stay close to Ali, nullify his speed and prevent him from using the whole ring. I knew I could hurt him to the body, so I wanted to wear him down and immobilize him to the point where I could knock him out.

I wanted to take him past the 12th round, which would be virgin territory for him. I'd gone 15 rounds with Terrell, but Muhammad had never been there before. I also wanted to make it rough. The rougher, the better. There's more body contact at close quarters, and fights have a different feel at that range. When I'm in close, I feel like I'm the boss and I can impose my will on anybody.

It was a good plan, but the mistake we made, which I never realized at the time, was doing all my sparring in the small ring at the Lansdowne gym, which was like a snake pit.

The two quickest guys I worked with—Billy Joiner and Alvin "Blue" Lewis—were both fast, slick guys, but I had no trouble at all trapping them on the ropes and banging them to the body. It's okay for a stick-and-move guy to work in a small ring, but for me it was too easy. Lewis, who was still an amateur, went home to Detroit after I busted him up pretty badly in the rib cage. Joiner, the 1962 U.S. Golden Gloves champion at light heavyweight, was 86–6 as an amateur—and two of those losses were to Ali. His style was pretty similar to Muhammad's, and I was handling him with no problem.

Because time was so short, I did more running for this fight than was normal for me. To help with conditioning, we also brought in the renowned fitness guru Lloyd Percival—the guy who wrote the tips on those Kellogg's trading cards I'd studied as a kid. I didn't want Lynne and the boys being bothered by all the distractions, so I moved out of the house and into the Seaway Towers hotel, where I got up at seven in the morning and did four miles of jogging and wind sprints. In the afternoons, Teddy and I went to Lansdowne to spar with Lewis, Joiner or the other guys we had in camp: Hubert Hilton, Greatest Crawford and Richie Pittman, an old-timer who'd been a sparring partner for Ali, Liston and Patterson.

The day before the fight, the Canadian Press ran an interview with Ali and Dundee in which they called me a dirty fighter. "I know he fights dirty, I've seen it, but if Georgie tries it with me he's going to be in real trouble," Ali told the reporter. "Still, I can't figure on putting him away early. He's never been down, let alone out. I had a dream about it. I kept hitting him and hitting him and he wouldn't go down, and pretty soon I was so tired, I could hardly keep punching. He kept punching and getting stronger. Man, I woke up in a sweat."

Dundee was more succinct. "Chuvalo is dirty—and he's good at it," Angelo said. "He's a tough guy who would fight a lion, and he can punch. We gotta watch out for his left. A guy like Chuvalo, you could hit him over the head with a pipe in a dark alley and he would turn around and hurt you with a left hook. We gotta watch out for that."

That Ali was a 7-1 betting favorite struck me as absurd. I remember thinking, "Why should this guy be such an overwhelming favorite to knock me out?" That had never happened before, so why would it happen now? For people to think this was going to be an easy night for Ali seemed to be pretty unsound judgment.

At the official weigh-in, I was 216 pounds and Ali was 214½. On the afternoon of the fight, I had a nice meal of broiled filet of sole and then took a nap. When the bell rang a few hours later, he came directly to me—and it took all of about 30 seconds for me to realize he was the fastest fighter I'd ever seen.

It's one thing to expect it; it's another thing to feel it, live it. When you experience that kind of speed up close, there's nothing to compare it against.

In the opening round, Ali tried to psych me out by holding me close behind the head while exposing his gut, like he was inviting me to rip out his kidneys. I knew what he was doing, holding me close enough so that my punching a short distance wouldn't have that much velocity, but I gladly obliged him by pounding 15 short rights to his ribs. Today, people say to me, "Wow, the cat opened up and let you nail him to the body!" That's true. But if you notice, he only did it once.

For most of the next hour, that was the story. A crowd of 13,540 (which paid what was then a Canadian record gate of about $165,000) watched as I kept trying to bull my way inside while Ali jabbed and moved, relying on his quick feet to get him out of trouble whenever I tried to trap him on the ropes.

Against the ropes is where I wanted him, so I naturally kept going to his body to try to slow him down. Probably 80 per cent of my punches were body shots. Over the years a lot has been said and written about me supposedly deliberately throwing low blows, but that's not true. A few of my punches did land south of the border (one of which was immortalized in a great full-page photo in *Life* magazine the week after the fight), but in most cases it only looked like they were low because Ali was wearing his cup about six inches higher than normal.

Dundee knew I was a body puncher, so he had a special cup made for Muhammad. It was made to fight George Chuvalo. In order to disguise it, they had to get custom-made trunks. I knew it as soon as I saw Ali in the ring. When I saw the top of his bright red jock a couple of inches above his belt line, I felt like Elmer Fudd when he fought Bugs Bunny. In the cartoon, Bugs wore his trunks up around his ears in order to avoid getting hit.

The referee was a clothing salesman named Jackie Silvers. Like everybody else, he could see that Ali's trunks were way too high, but what could he do about it? Still, I've got to give Silvers credit for letting us fight. He was the complete opposite of what Sammy Luftspring had been when I fought Terrell.

Afterward, in response to Dundee complaining long and loud about my "dirty" tactics, Silvers told the reporters that he "didn't want to ruin a good fight by being too intrusive." I thought that was pretty good. When *The Ring's* Nat Fleischer asked him about it, Silvers replied, "The low punches were of no consequence. They weren't hurting Clay. Chuvalo is not a low-blow hitter, he's a body banger. If you're going to be watching that close for low blows, there would be no fight."

Ali's left hand was like greased lightning, but there wasn't a lot behind it. His jab had more zing than sting, but it was a lot tougher for me to cuff aside, like I did with Terrell. Once in a while he tried to turn the jab into a power punch by putting all his weight behind it, but it wasn't a whole lot harder.

To this day, people say to me, "He really hit you, he really pounded on you." Maybe it looks that way, but I wasn't taking any real hard shots. They weren't nearly as hard as some of the punches I'd taken before, like from Mike DeJohn. And I got hit a lot harder by Mel Turnbow and George Foreman in later fights. But because of Muhammad's speed, because of his movement, a lot of people think I took a real beating. When they ask if I was worried about getting hurt I have to laugh, because in my mind I always said to myself that I couldn't be hurt. In a crazy kind of way, I felt indestructible. If another fighter said that about himself, I'd start laughing, but to my own ego, to my own sense of identity, that's how it was. It made me feel special.

When I say Ali's speed was amazing, I'm not just referring to his hands. When he moved his legs and hands at the same time, when he synchronized them, he was really something. In those days, heavyweights didn't move around very much, so he really looked different. Before him, the only guys I ever saw move around the ring remotely like that were Jersey Joe Walcott and a blown-up light heavyweight, Billy Conn.

What surprised me the most about Muhammad was that he threw so accurately when he was in full motion. He'd be out of punching range, but as he moved back in he would already be starting to throw his punch, right on target. If I waited until he was back in range, it was already too late. I got hit, no question, but I was never hurt and he never landed anything hard in the most dangerous area, which is right along the jawline and up behind the ears. Most of the time he caught me high on the head—and I can take punches high on the head all night long.

As fast as Muhammad was, I still managed to shake him up three or four times. In Rounds 5 and 6 I nailed him with some left hooks that got his attention, and in the 15th I backed him up and had him hurt. He definitely proved he could take a punch—something nobody talked about before our fight, but which everybody wrote about afterward. He had a real talent for riding punches and being able to weather the storm when he was hurt. I know I hurt him to the body at times, and I should have followed up by punching to his head, but he was just too damn quick on his feet.

I'm sometimes still asked why I didn't bob and weave more against Ali instead of going straight forward. The answer is pretty obvious when you watch the film. When you fight a quick guy and try to weave your way inside, you're bent down and not positioned properly to strike, because he's backing up. Bobbing and weaving is only effective when the other guy is right on top of you, but that wasn't where Ali wanted to be with me. At close range I could hurt him—and he knew it.

Under Toronto's five-point must system, Silvers scored the fight 73–63. The two judges, Tony Canzano and Jackie Johnson, had it 74–63. By rounds, Silvers had Ali winning nine and me winning two, with four even. Canzano scored it 12–1–2 and Johnson 13–1–1. *The Ring* scored it 72–62 and gave me Rounds 1, 2 and 12, with Round 8 even.

As the scores were being read, my oldest son, Mitchell, who was six at the time, climbed up into the ring. He gave me a big hug, but he had tears in his eyes. I felt bad for the little guy.

There was a lot of talk about me being the first to go 15 rounds with Ali, and people still bring it up because the fight has been replayed hundreds of times on TV in Canada and the U.S. At first I thought all the talk about my durability was a negative thing, but then I realized it was kind of special. The average person can't conceive what it's like to fight 15 rounds; that was the exclusive property of world champions and top-10 contenders. And now that the championship distance is 12 rounds, it will never happen again, so I guess it was special. And I can't imagine anything that comes close to matching what that feels like.

When people meet me and say, "George, you went the distance with Muhammad Ali!" I say, "No, you've got it wrong. He went the distance with me." When it was all over, he was the guy who went to the hospital because he was pissing blood. Me? I got to go dancing with my wife. No question I got the best of that deal.

In a crazy way, that fight is what defines me for a lot of my fellow Canadians, but it took a long time before I came to appreciate how good it made them feel. It happened almost 50 years ago, but I still hear it all the time, that it made Canadians proud. I feel happy about that, because it means the fight will kind of live forever. A day doesn't go by that I don't get asked about it, and it's always the same: "Hey George, you rumbled with Muhammad Ali! What a great fight!"

Although I was disappointed about losing to Ali, it was nice to finally get some positive press. Not surprisingly, it was mostly from U.S. writers rather than Canadians. Gilbert Rogin's cover story in *Sports Illustrated* was headlined "A Battle of the Lionhearted" and described me as being "far tougher and more persevering than any lion, and it was these attributes which made the fight." The *New York Herald Tribune* story said, "George Chuvalo deserves an apology from all who derided him. One-sided as a fight could be in points, he made this a memorable battle. It was a far, far better show than anyone could have expected. There wasn't anything questionable or distasteful about it." The *New York Times* report took a similar turn: "Some of us said that this Canadian should have been selling peanuts in the aisles rather than throwing punches in the ring. We were wrong. Cassius Clay has never been given a harder, more bruising fight. Chuvalo was the honest worker. He comes to fight. He wasn't scared, or cocky or overconfident. He was willing to take a lot of punishment for the opportunity to give some. And he did."

Even Joe Louis weighed in. He was signed up by the Canadian Press to write a ringside report, which was published under his byline in papers all across the country. "They can run and most of the time they can hide," wrote Joe. "Cassius Clay hid long enough for George Chuvalo to get tired, so he's still heavyweight champion of the world. But don't let anyone say that George didn't make this the best heavyweight championship fight since Rocky Marciano knocked out Archie Moore in 1956."

Ali told the *Toronto Star* I was the toughest guy he'd fought to that point, adding, "I kept saying he was tough—tougher than Liston, tougher than Patterson—but people thought I was just trying to build up the gate. Now you know I was right." That was nice—as was the last word from Dundee, who told the *Star,* "Chuvalo fought the greatest fight of his life. Canadians ought to be real proud of this man. I was proud of him . . . and I was in the other guy's corner."

As for my minuscule payday, it wasn't until decades later that I learned more, after *Globe and Mail* sportswriter William Houston got hold of the old accounting books from Maple Leaf Gardens. According to the MLG records, Ali received $125,000 and I was paid $49,000. Off the top, Irving pocketed $24,000 from my cut as a promoter's fee, even though the Ontario Athletic Commission's regulation that prohibited managers from promoting cards on which their fighters appeared. According to the terms of our contract, that left me with 50 per cent of the remaining $25,000—meaning that I fought 15 grueling rounds with one of the greatest champions in boxing history for $12,500 . . . in Canadian money, no less!

Contrary to his self-proclaimed and carefully cultivated philanthropic image, Ungerman entitled himself to $36,500 from my total purse of $49,000—and for that piece of the action he never had to take a single punch. I can only imagine the kind of creative accounting he came up with for several other of my fights that he promoted.

Oh yeah, one other thing. The night after the fight, Lynne and I, my cousin Eddie and his wife, Millie, were among several hundred Torontonians who reported seeing three UFOs alternately hovering and then moving at high speed across the sky above the city. With colors ranging from a glowing white to red, green and blue, the objects were unlike any commercial aircraft I'd ever seen before—or since.

The authorities never issued an official explanation for the mass sighting, but I like to think that maybe Muhammad and I had some extraterrestrial fight fans tapping into that closed-circuit telecast . . .

ROUND 8

SIX WEEKS AFTER FIGHTING ALI, I KNOCKED out Levi Forte in Glace Bay, Nova Scotia, in the makeup for the bout we were supposed to have down in Miami in March. Right afterward, I signed to meet South American champion Oscar Bonavena at Madison Square Garden on June 23. It was a huge fight for New York because Oscar, who was from Argentina, was popular with the Hispanic community and promised to fill some seats in the Garden.

Bonavena was born on September 25, 1942, in Buenos Aires, and by age 17 he was Argentina's national amateur champ. His amateur career came to an abrupt end when he reportedly bit the nipple of an opponent who was getting the best of him, so he traveled to New York and turned pro under the legendary Charlie Goldman, the guy who molded Rocky Marciano into a world champion.

After winning his first eight fights—seven by KO— Bonavena was knocked down and took a bad beating in a 10-round loss to Zora Folley in 1965, but he rebounded to win

12 of his next 13, including a decision over tough Gregorio Peralta, who was 48–4 at the time.

Oscar was a pretty crude guy—and not just in the ring. He was loud and volatile and had been sued a couple of times for smashing photographers' cameras. Later in his career, before his fights with Frazier and Ali, he tried to psych them out by doing this exaggerated sniffing thing. He'd lift up his chin contemptuously and start sniffing like there was a foul scent in the air, like he was disgusted to be in their presence. He never did that with me—I must've been wearing my best cologne at the weigh-in—but I wish he had, because it might have made for a better fight.

It should've been a helluva match, and on paper it was: two strong wade-in guys who liked to go to the body. Bonavena was built like a tank, and the 17 KOs on his 20–2 record proved he could punch, but against me he did nothing but hopscotch like a rabbit all over the ring. It made for a real lousy fight, one of the worst I was ever in. I never saw him do that before, and he never did it against anyone else.

Bonavena's former manager, Dr. Marvin Goldberg, told me later that Oscar was scared out of his wits going into the fight, so maybe that's why he didn't want to mix. In the second and fourth rounds he tried pushing me to the canvas when I was off balance. The first time, when I kind of skidded backwards, I heard the crowd drawing in their breath in anticipation. Then it raced through my mind that if I stumbled and went down, my record would be gone. I thought, "I'm not going down! I won't let it happen!" And it didn't. It's kind of funny . . . one of those pride things. But from there my reputation for remaining vertical just kind of snowballed without my realizing it.

For the rest of the night Bonavena did more mauling than brawling and never landed anything even remotely powerful. On the few occasions when he stopped running, I nailed him with jabs and one-twos, but then he'd grab me and try to wrestle. It still rankles me that they gave him the decision. Referee Arthur Mercante scored it a draw at 4–4–2, while Tony Castellano had it 4–5–1 and Tony Rossi saw it 3–7.

Under a headline reading "Chuvalo won fight, Bonavena got decision," Lew Eskin wrote in *Boxing Illustrated*, "We scored it 6–4 for George, who outdid Oscar in every department but holding. Chuvalo outfought, outpunched, outbutted and outfouled Bonavena, but the judges saw it differently."

I never saw or spoke to Bonavena again after that night, but he went on to have a pretty decent career. He got stopped by Ali in Muhammad's second comeback bout in 1970, and two years later he broke his hand in a loss to Floyd Patterson before winning 11 of his next 12.

Oscar was in the midst of a seven-fight win streak when he was shot and killed outside the Mustang Ranch brothel in Reno, Nevada, on May 22, 1976. The rumor was that he was having an affair with the wife of his manager, Joe Conforte, who also owned the Mustang. Whatever the real story, one of Conforte's bodyguards, Willard Brymer, pleaded guilty to manslaughter and served 15 months in prison. True to Oscar's larger-than-life persona, his memorial service at the Buenos Aires soccer stadium drew 150,000 mourners.

The rest of 1966 was a whirlwind. In August, I knocked out Mel Turnbow at the Paul Sauve Arena in Montreal, but not before he shook me early with one of the hardest punches I was ever hit with. A few months earlier, Turnbow, who was one of

Floyd Patterson's favorite sparring partners, decked Cleveland Williams before losing a 10-round decision. I'd also seen Mel hold his own in sparring with Liston when Sonny was training for his second fight with Ali, so I knew he could punch. Late in the seventh, I dropped him with a left hook. When he got up, I whacked him with a combination that sent him backwards into the ropes. He sprang off right into another left hook that knocked him cold with five seconds left in the round, and it was about 15 minutes before the doctor got Mel back on his feet. Covered with flecks of resin from lying on the canvas, he walked straight over to where I was talking to the reporters and, out of the blue, said, "George, I still think you won the Terrell fight." Then he exited between the ropes.

Twenty-eight days later in Edmonton, I dropped Bob Avery five times before stopping him in two, then I wrapped up the year with KOs over Dick Wipperman (Montreal), Boston Jacobs (Detroit, with Willie Pep as referee), Dave Russell (Saint John) and Willie McCormick (Labrador City).

I felt bad about knocking out Wipperman, who at 6 foot 4 was one of the taller guys I ever fought. He was a good banger and a nice guy, and I later used him as a sparring partner.

Dick hailed from Buffalo, and he was 32–7 when we fought the first time. He had a reputation for being a crowd pleaser, dating back to October 2, 1964, when he faced 6-foot-9, 250-pound James J. Beattie on the undercard of my fight with Doug Jones at Madison Square Garden.

The previous year, Beattie, who lost to Buster Mathis in the 1962 Golden Gloves, answered a newspaper ad looking for "a future heavyweight champion." Now he was being promoted as the rising star that would pull the fight game up by its boot-

Strolling the streets of London with Susie the bear, prior to beating Joe Bygraves in a 10-round decision to close out 1965.

Relaxing in the Montana wilderness a few days before I KO'd Archie Ray in Missoula on June 22, 1967.

Lynne and I at the Caravan Club, circa 1967. Our involvement in the night-club business was short-lived.

Back in the old country, 1969. I look like a slimmed-down version of King Farouk! The fez was to commemorate my father, who donned the headwear as part of the national dress code when he was back home.

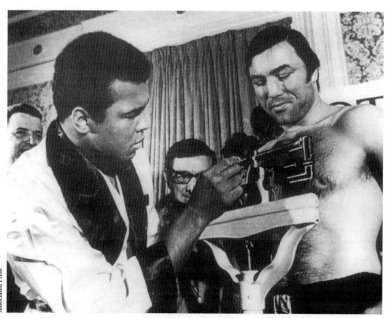

Muhammad Ali checks my weight prior our "Second Reckoning" bout at Vancouver's Pacific Coliseum, on May 1, 1972.

Just 11 days after my loss to Foreman, I knocked out Mike Bruce at Kosevo Stadium in Sarajevo. I'm posing by a waterfall near my dad's old house in the hamlet of Proboj, Bosnia-Herzegovina, the day after the fight.

My inimitable trainer Teddy McWhorter rides a donkey in Proboj. The guy laughing on the left promoted the fight in Sarajevo.

George Foreman and I ham it up at a New York press conference before our fight on August 4, 1970.

Showing Dolly Parton a few of my moves before her 1977 performance in Toronto. She's a very nice lady.

Cue the world-class scream! Jeff Goldblum rips my arm off in *The Fly* (1986).

With Jerry Quarry and my granddaughter Rachel at Jerry's induction into the
World Boxing Hall of Fame in Los Angeles, October 14, 1995.

With Johnny Tapia on August 17, 1996, the day of his fight in Albuquerque. Little
did I know that while I was working Tapia's corner, Stevie was probably dead.

Chatting with Queen Elizabeth about going for a cup of tea after her Golden Jubilee reception in Ottawa, 2002. That's my story, and I'm sticking to it.

My grandson Jesse poses with Earnie Shavers near the Muhammad Ali Center in Louisville, Kentucky, in 2007.

With writer Bert Sugar at the International Boxing Hall of Fame in Canastota, New York, in 2009.

Tryin' to be a wise guy? The one and only Tony Soprano (a.k.a. the late actor James Gandolfini) moves in for a close-up at a charity event in New York City, 2010.

straps. Beattie was 12–1 against handpicked opponents and was fast becoming a favorite with the media—so much so that ABC had featured him in a prime-time documentary.

None of that mattered to Wipperman, who was 36 pounds lighter and five inches shorter than the Minnesota giant. He easily outpointed Beattie over the first six rounds and had him bleeding so badly that the ringside doctors conferred with referee Barney Smith about possibly stopping the bout.

Beattie stormed out of his corner swinging wildly to start the seventh, but after hitting nothing but air he used his massive body to drive Wipperman into the ropes, where Dick simply covered up. That's when Smith stepped in, stopped the fight and raised Beattie's arm in victory.

Well, Wipperman went nuts—and so did the crowd. Dick started yelling and screaming, then broke away from his handlers and took another swing at Beattie. Then he tried to grab the microphone from the ring announcer to plead his case to the fans, who were throwing all kinds of garbage into the ring. The cops finally had to move in to give Smith an escort, and my fight with Jones was late getting started because the mess in the ring had to be cleaned up. The next day's story in the New York *World-Telegram* referred to Wipperman as "the wild buffalo from Buffalo" but noted that he had "a justifiable complaint."

I ended up fighting Wipperman again four months later in Akron, Ohio, and gave him a real bad beating before knocking him out in the third. He had a decent jab but never moved enough. I couldn't have missed him in my sleep. I felt terrible afterward because he had these huge purple lumps on his forehead.

Dick hung up his gloves the following year with a career record of 32–14–1, then became a police officer in the Buffalo suburb of Cheektowaga. If he was as tough on criminals as he was in the ring, I'm sure he made a hell of a cop.

In the 12 weeks after I beat Wipperman in Akron, I KO'd Buddy Moore in Walpole, Massachusetts, and stopped Willie Besmanoff in back-to-back fights in Florida.

Moore—a.k.a. Abdul Haleem—was 6 foot 3 and hailed from Pittsburgh. He had a win and two losses against Wipperman, but the highlights of the rest of his résumé were pretty nondescript: decision losses to Leotis Martin and Al "Blue" Lewis and a split decision over Jimmy Christopher, whom I'd used as a sparring partner.

I dispatched Moore in the second round in front of a nice crowd. Afterward, while we were celebrating the win, I heard a tap-tap-tap in the corridor outside my dressing room. I looked out and saw two guys, the youngest of whom carried a white cane and was obviously blind. "My nephew is a huge fight fan, and he loves you, George," said the older fellow. "We came to ask if you could find it in your heart to give him your gloves from this fight."

I was touched. I turned to Ungerman and said, "Irving, go get my gloves." When he came back a few minutes later and handed over a pair of gloves, both guys thanked us profusely before going on their way.

Shortly after they left, Irving turned to me with a big grin and gleefully exclaimed, "I just fucked the blind kid!"

"What are you talking about?" I said.

"I went to Moore's room and took *his* gloves!"

I was dumbfounded. I'll never forget the look on Ungerman's

face; he was so proud of himself for pulling a fast one. It made me sick.

"How could you do that?" I said. The reply was vintage Ungerman: "Don't worry about it, Georgie; he'll never know the fuckin' difference."

The worst part was that he went on gloating about it for the next half-hour, telling everyone within earshot that he'd ripped off the blind kid. I felt like a piece of crap for letting it happen. I remember thinking to myself that if God was ever going to have a say in the outcome of one of my fights, He would never be in my corner as long as Irving was there.

Between the fights with Moore and Besmanoff, I made a detour to Myrtle Beach, South Carolina, for an exhibition with Giancarlo Barazza as part of what was billed as a "Canada-America Days" celebration. It was a good workout, and I remember being impressed that a couple of thousand people turned out to watch us go six rounds.

Besmanoff, the guy I decked six times in four rounds back in '61, had announced his retirement the day after he was knocked out by Amos Johnson in 1963, but he made a comeback three years later and had won six of seven when we hooked up again on April 4, 1967, in Miami. In a TV interview a couple of days before the fight, Willie, in his thick German accent, solemnly asserted that "this time, I am too *schmart* for Chuvalo"—but it turned out to be pretty much a replay of what happened in Toronto. I finished him in three.

Six weeks later, Besmanoff was the promoter of a card I was headlining in Cocoa Beach. When my opponent, Moses Harrell, pulled out the night before the fight, poor Willie reluctantly filled in and took another beating. I can still remember the look of relief in his eyes when his corner threw in the towel after the second round. He had just one more fight, a KO loss to Dave Zyglewicz three months later, then retired with a career mark of 51–34–8.

Between the Wipperman and Moore fights, Ungerman got a call from Teddy Brenner at Madison Square Garden, offering us a July date against unbeaten Joe Frazier. The money was good—$50,000—and the fight would air live on network TV, so it was a great opportunity to move up in the top 10. We signed right away.

I knew Frazier's reputation. Born on January 12, 1944, he grew up dirt poor in Beaufort, South Carolina, as the youngest of 12 kids. At 15, he left home to live with his brother in New York, and then he moved on to Philadelphia, where he found work in a slaughterhouse and joined the Police Athletic League (PAL) boxing program in order to lose weight.

At the 1964 U.S. Olympic tryouts, Frazier won the Eastern regionals in Washington, then traveled to New York for the finals, only to lose for the second time to big Buster Mathis. In their showdown to see who would fight at the Tokyo Games, Mathis outweighed Frazier by exactly 100 pounds, 295 to 195.

Joe still made the squad as an alternate. Ironically, a week before they were to leave for Japan, Mathis broke a knuckle by punching Frazier in the head during an exhibition in Brooklyn and was forced to pull out of the competition. Joe went on to make the most of his opportunity by outpointing Hans Huber of Germany for the gold medal—the only American boxer to bring home the top prize.

In his pro debut on August 25, 1965, Frazier took exactly 100 seconds to knock out Elwood Goss in a makeshift ring set up in Philadelphia's Broadway Hotel. The left hook that did all the damage against Goss would quickly become Joe's trademark, and by the time we squared off at the Garden on July 19, 1967, he was 16–0 with 14 KOs—including stoppages of Mel Turnbow, Dick Wipperman, Eddie Machen and Doug Jones. His toughest fight to date had been a 10-round decision over Oscar Bonavena 10 months earlier, during which Bonavena twice dumped Joe to the canvas.

With a big payday and the chance to ruin what Brenner was billing as "Joe Frazier's coming-out party" on the line, I signed for a tune-up fight against Archie Ray in, of all places, Missoula, Montana.

Elmer Boyce, who managed light heavyweight contender Roger Rouse, promoted the June 22 card at the University of Montana's Adams Fieldhouse. Rouse fought Bobby Rascon in the co-main event, while the featured prelim was No. 1–ranked middleweight contender Don Fullmer against Luis Garduno.

I'd never experienced anything like Missoula; it was like being parachuted into the middle of nowhere. But Boyce had done a nice job of hyping the card, and the place was packed with a raucous crowd by the time I climbed through the ropes to face Ray.

Archie was from Tucson, Arizona, and had turned pro in 1962. At one point he had a record of 20–4–2, but on May 16, 1966, he was stopped in eight rounds by Mexican champion Manuel Ramos in Phoenix. That fight grabbed national attention because the referee, Dick Moll, had a heart attack in the opening round and died on the way to the hospital. Ray went on to lose five in a row after that and was coming off a seventh-round KO loss to Florida Al Jones when we met up in Missoula.

It wasn't much of a fight, because Ray was in survival mode right from the opening bell. With one second left in the second round, I nailed him right in the solar plexus—and never before or since did I see a guy go down like he did.

After I whacked him in the belly, Archie jackknifed forward. I recall being surprised at how quickly he folded right over; in fact, it happened so fast that I never had time to step back. He was paralyzed, but as he pitched forward his head crashed into my right cheekbone before he crashed to the canvas.

Within minutes, blood started pooling on the spot where Ray's head clipped me, and my right eye started to swell up like a balloon. I thought it would be okay, but it wasn't.

When we got back to Toronto, I got a prescription for a medication called Orenzyme to break down the blood clots around my eye. I'd already resumed heavy sparring to get ready for Frazier, but I was worried because the eye felt injured every time I got hit. It go so bad that I mentioned to Teddy and Irving that maybe we should think about postponing Frazier, but Ungerman wouldn't hear of it. I did have medical clearance to fight. They appealed to my macho side, convincing me there was too much at stake. I knew Teddy needed the money, too, so that was that. I can still hear Ungerman: "We need this fight; we won't get this chance again. It's New York City, the Big Apple . . . and if we beat him, we'll get a world title shot."

They made me feel like a sissy for not wanting to fight; still, I knew something was wrong. Even with big headgear on, my eye was blowing up every time I got hit upstairs, but I sucked it up and hoped I'd be able to take Joe out before he could do any more damage.

In retrospect, fighting Frazier with an injured eye was sheer lunacy. But first, a little historical perspective.

With Ali's political problems canceling him out of the title picture, in May 1967 the World Boxing Association announced it would conduct an elimination tournament to determine a new champion. Frazier was on the original list of tournament invitees, but I wasn't. Sonny Liston, Buster Mathis, Zora Folley and Manuel Ramos were likewise bypassed, despite the fact we were all ranked ahead of some of the other guys who got the call from the WBA.

I didn't particularly care one way or the other because I'd already signed to fight Joe, and beating him would obviously be a shortcut to another title shot. Meanwhile, Frazier's manager, Yank Durham, didn't like the tournament format and basically told the WBA where they could stick it. Durham figured that if Joe got past me, he'd go straight into a fight with Mathis for New York State's recognition of the title, which in some quarters was recognized as the world championship. It would also give Frazier an opportunity to avenge his two amateur losses to big Buster—but he'd have to beat me first.

When Joe pulled out, the WBA filled his spot with another Philly fighter, Leotis Martin.

As we headed into an abbreviated training camp, a puffy eye wasn't the only thing on my mind. Lynne was pregnant again, which meant we had to start thinking about another mouth to feed. And for some reason, Ungerman decided we needed another voice in the corner to go along with him and Teddy McWhorter. Freddy Brown was brought in to work as my co-trainer—and he was a disaster.

You have to understand, the fighter-trainer relationship is based on mutual trust and respect, and those things don't take root overnight. Teddy and I had been through thick and thin together, and I trusted him implicitly. He came across as laid-back, but he always knew what buttons to push to get the best out of me. Most of all, Teddy knew when to back off and just let me work. I loved him for that.

Brown was the exact opposite. He came into camp barking commands like a lion tamer. He was a "do this, do that" kind of drillmaster, which more than irritated me because nobody ever had to light a fire under me in training. If anything, Teddy knew how to pull in the reins in order to keep me from peaking too early.

Brown was just a hard guy to like; he thought the best way to get me to train harder was to try goading me into thinking I wasn't doing enough, which is no way to establish trust or respect. He was a real control freak too, telling me when to eat, when to take a crap, when to go to bed. I just couldn't relax around the guy. I remember he blew up on Teddy and Irving when he found out I liked to eat broiled fish for my pre-fight meal; he thought I should eat steak. It got so bad I threatened to leave camp a few days before the fight unless Ungerman got him to back off.

What I needed more than anything in preparing for Frazier was confidence and direction, but Brown's presence pretty much ensured my training camp was in a perpetual state of chaos. Of course, some of that's on me; after the first day I should have insisted that Ungerman get rid of the guy, but I figured things would work out and we'd find our way. It didn't happen.

Considering what I'd experienced over the previous month,

it was pretty amazing that my heart rate was only 36 beats per minute at the pre-fight medical at Madison Square Garden on the morning of July 19. I chalked it up to being able to put all the disorder of my training camp behind me and finally focus on what I was going to do to Frazier in a few hours. I weighed 217, and despite my bad eye and being an 11–5 underdog, I felt a real sense of inner calm. (By the way, my heart rate was exactly the same at the Toronto hospital a few days later; I remember the nurse screamed because she thought I was dying!)

The bout was televised live, and the Garden was packed with 13,985 screaming New Yorkers. As expected, Joe came out throwing his left like a battering ram. It was kind of a half jab, half hook, and accurate as hell. There wasn't a whole lot to pick between us in the first two rounds (some of the ringside reporters had me winning both), but Frazier was fast and difficult to hit cleanly. He nicked me on the forehead about a minute in, and I responded by trying to go with my bread and butter, working him to the body.

I went back to the jab to start the second, but Frazier wasn't nearly as stationary as he'd been in other fights. He bobbed and weaved, slipped punches and countered very well while plowing forward the whole time. Joe isn't usually remembered as being particularly good defensively, so a lot of you might be surprised when I say he had the best defense of any guy I ever fought. He moved his head extremely well coming at you side to side, left to right, fighting out of that crouch. It's awfully hard to nail a guy who can move like that.

Frazier landed a couple of nice hooks and an errant elbow late in the second round that opened a gash on my right cheekbone, but it was nothing serious. Early in the third, I pinned him against the ropes and shook him with a left-right-left-right flurry to the head and body, but he was able to spin out of trouble before I could really unload.

By now there was a steady flow of blood from my eye and I was having a lot of difficulty picking up Joe's lefts. My peripheral vision was gone; I could still see the start of his punches, but then they just kind of dropped off the radar. Still, I managed to land a couple of decent uppercuts that backed Joe up, but before I could reload, he charged back to the attack and landed another big left that really blew up my eye. In the last 30 seconds it was sticking out about three-quarters of an inch. I looked like a one-eyed cat peeping into a seafood store.

Before Round 4, the doctor came into my corner to check on the damage and I told him I was good to go—even though I couldn't see a thing out of my right lamp. When the bell rang, Frazier stormed across the ring and landed two sharp left hooks square on the eyeball. The pain was excruciating, so I turned my head sideways and took a couple of steps toward my corner. That's when referee Johnny Colan jumped in and waved it off. My initial reaction was to tell Johnny he was nuts, but in retrospect it's a good thing he stopped the fight. If Joe had nailed me again, I probably would've been permanently blinded.

As it was, Frazier's final punch shattered the orbital floor of the eye socket and pretty much drove my eyeball south of the border, where it got lodged in the crack. They practically had to pick it up off the canvas. I got a temporary patch job right after the fight, but I waited until we got back home for the surgery, which was performed at Toronto Western Hospital. There, they cut through the socket bone, lifted out my eyeball, and then inserted a piece of silicone underneath to hold it in place.

The night after the fight, Lynne and I watched a replay in our hotel room across the street from the Garden. After the second round it looked like Frazier was hitting me with four hands, but it was also painful to see all the chances I missed. Joe kept punching and pressuring, but I could see—even with one eye—that I hurt him with my uppercut, especially in Round 3. I don't know why I stopped throwing it.

As mad as I was at myself, I was more upset with Ungerman, who really showed his true colors in the dressing room afterward. He kept telling the reporters that I didn't take much punishment and wasn't hurt too much—like he was the one getting hit by Frazier's punches.

When Dave Anderson of *The New York Times* asked if I was going to retire, Irving said something I'll never forget, a statement that was immortalized in Mark Kram's story for *Sports Illustrated:* "No, Georgie's gonna be around for a long time. Every kid on the way up is gonna want a piece of Georgie boy. He'll be a great opponent for 'em . . . a great and rich trial horse."

I was dumbfounded. There I was, lying on the dressing room table, wondering if I'd ever see properly again, listening to my manager expound on how I'd be a "trial horse" for years to come. I wanted to get up and tear his miserable head off. Why not just offer to sell off my organs, too? I was so upset that I couldn't go back to the hotel after they patched me up. Instead, I just roamed the streets until dawn.

A lot of memories of that night came flooding back on November 7, 2011, when a reporter called to tell me Frazier had died of liver cancer. Joe and I had grown pretty close over the years, and we saw each other as often as our busy schedules would allow. He was always a gentleman and a real sweet guy. On the 40th anniversary of our fight, he came up to Toronto for a $600-a-plate charity banquet and auction to raise money for my Fight Against Drugs foundation and the youth programs he sponsored in Philadelphia.

The last time we were together was at a gala in New York in June of 2010, and he looked great. In fact, I remember saying, "Hey Joe, let's get the gloves back on!" Like always, we talked about the old days and had a lot of laughs. But in all the years since we rumbled, we never once talked about fighting each other—even though I can't help thinking about it almost every day, because I still have vision problems. In fact, thanks to Joe, I have to close my right eye every time I parallel park a car.

By the way, that little piece of silicone that the doctors used to repair my eye socket is destined to survive me. As I once told an interviewer from *The Globe and Mail*, one day, if I'm not cremated and I'm lying in a grave, when all the tendons and ligaments have worn away, that little chunk of plastic will eventually pop loose and ricochet into the back of my skull. And it will make a little noise, just a little tinkle. Maybe the termites that are around, or the insects, will hear the clink.

Perhaps that sounds macabre, but I think it's kind of cool, too, knowing that a tiny piece of me will be around for centuries.

The Frazier fight also marked the last time I crossed myself in the ring before the opening bell. As a good Catholic I'd done it almost unconsciously since I first started boxing, but then I realized how absurd it was to ask God to help me beat up the guy in the opposite corner. I'm sure the man upstairs has more important things to do.

ROUND 9

RECOVERING FROM THE EYE INJURY KEPT ME out of the ring for the next 11 months, and in the interim the WBA conducted its heavyweight elimination tournament with eight participants: Floyd Patterson, Jerry Quarry, Oscar Bonavena, Karl Mildenberger, Jimmy Ellis, Thad Spencer, Ernie Terrell and the guy who was brought in to replace Frazier, Leotis Martin.

The main sponsor of the tournament was a promotional group called Sports Action Inc., which agreed to pay $50,000 per man for the four quarter-final bouts, $75,000 for the semi-finals and a guarantee of at least $100,000 each for the final.

Televised live on ABC, the tournament opened on August 5 with a doubleheader at the Houston Astrodome that saw Spencer beat Terrell in a boring 12-round decision, followed by Ellis stopping Martin in nine. Martin, who would make headlines two years later by knocking Sonny Liston colder than an Alberta winter, was 24–1 when he fought Ellis—the best record of the eight invitees.

Six weeks later in Frankfurt, Germany, Bonavena manhandled Mildenberger in a 12-round decision, and on October 28 in Los Angeles, Quarry floored Patterson twice en route to winning the rematch of their June fight, which had ended in a draw.

The quarter-final bouts temporarily shifted boxing's spotlight away from Ali's political problems and focused it on what the WBA was dubbing "the showdown for succession," but during the break between the two semifinal matches (Ellis dropped Bonavena twice in winning a decision in Louisville on December 2; Quarry stopped Spencer in Oakland on February 3, 1968), the tournament's media profile was bushwhacked by Ed Dooley, the cagey chairman of the New York State Athletic Commission.

Since the WBA had already announced that the much-hyped finale between Ellis and Quarry would take place April 27 in Oakland, Dooley called a press conference in early January to announce that Frazier and Mathis would square off March 4, with the winner earning New York's recognition as world heavyweight champion. In short order, five other states— Pennsylvania, Texas, Illinois, Maine and Massachusetts— agreed to follow New York's lead.

Dooley's smooth move pretty much harpooned any hope the WBA had of its tournament winner being recognized as the best heavyweight in the world. A lot of fight fans—probably a majority—already figured that with Ali out of the picture, Frazier was the "uncrowned" world champion, and his spectacular 11th-round knockout of Mathis, who went into their fight with a record of 26–0 and 17 KOs, only solidified that standing. A crowd of more than 18,000 turned out to watch—along with Nino Benvenuti regaining the middleweight championship from Emile Griffith in the co-head-liner—on the first card staged at the "new" Madison Square Garden at West 33rd Street and Seventh Avenue.

Six weeks later, when Ellis defeated Quarry in 15 rounds in the anticlimactic WBA tournament finale, hardly anybody noticed—even though it gave Ellis "world champion" status in 44 states and most of Canada, too.

A couple of weeks after my fight with Frazier, the American Medical Association published the results of yet another study that concluded professional boxing should be banned once and for all. The story cited my eye injury as "proof" of the potential for permanent impairment and included a recommendation that George Chuvalo never again be licensed to fight in the Land of the Free and the Home of the Brave. Shortly after that, not knowing if I would ever fight again, Teddy McWhorter boarded a flight for England to become head trainer for former British Commonwealth champ Brian London.

Recuperating from the eye surgery gave me a very welcome opportunity to spend more time with Lynne and the boys while I contemplated my next move. It was great to live a "normal" life for a change and not really worry too much about what I was eating or if I was getting enough sleep. My training regimen wasn't nearly as active as when I had a bout lined up, but I maintained a routine of light workouts until I could start sparring again.

On January 19, 1968, Lynne gave birth to our beautiful daughter, Vanessa, at Mount Sinai Hospital in Toronto. It was kind of a shock after four sons, but in a way it was easier because we were running out of names for boys. We both thought Vanessa was a pretty name (for a very pretty little girl), and the middle name Lynne was for her mother. Of course, Vanessa and Lynn were the names of the famous Redgrave sisters, two of the top movie stars of the 1960s. The new arrival was an instant hit with her four brothers, all of whom grew to be fiercely protective of their sister.

Four days later, I was in Regina, Saskatchewan, to referee a Canadian light heavyweight title bout between Al Sparks and Leslie Borden. Sparks decked Borden in the opening round for a mandatory eight count and never looked back. What I remember most about that fight is that when Borden got knocked down again in the 11th, he looked up at me and yelled, "Foul!" I almost started laughing; I'd never seen a fighter do that before.

With our family growing and no guarantees that my eye would heal well enough for me to ever fight again, Lynne and I started to think about alternative sources of income. Shortly after the Frazier fight I signed a deal with a Canadian company to market George Chuvalo Autograph Model boxing gloves and speed bags, and later that year Ungerman talked me into putting a chunk of dough into the Caravan Club, a restaurant/ nightclub in downtown Toronto that he had a stake in and assured us was destined to become the most popular in the city. My official title was "host" and my duties consisted of a lot of glad-handing, smiling, posing for pictures and eating dinner with the well-heeled clientele.

Irving flew Rocky Marciano up from Miami for the official opening, but, as usual, Rocky was more interested in getting laid and getting paid than in helping us publicize the new venture. He did a couple of newspaper interviews and put away a lot of free meals, but that was about it. His sage advice to me consisted of three words: "Quit boxing, George."

The nightclub venture was fun while it lasted—which turned out to be not very long at all. Within a few months it became a money pit, so instead of helping smooth the path to my life after boxing, the investment ended up costing us a bundle before we got out. As they always say, live and learn.

By the spring of '68 I was getting a little restless, so when Labatt's brewery invited me to join a goodwill mission to visit Canadian troops stationed in Soest and Lahr, Germany, I jumped at the opportunity. There were a half-dozen or so athletes making the 10-day trip, and my traveling companions included the legendary Maurice "Rocket" Richard, who had retired from the NHL's Montreal Canadiens in 1960, and Toronto Argonauts offensive lineman Bill Frank.

While all of us were honored by the opportunity to help brighten the lives of our guys in uniform, the trip was especially meaningful for Richard, who at the age of 18 had been turned down for military service at the beginning of World War II. Rocket told me he was heartbroken when X-rays taken during his medical exam showed that the pounding he took for being the best junior hockey player on the planet had damaged his ankles and wrists so much that he was deemed unfit for active duty.

Big Bill Frank, on the other hand, was no stranger to trench warfare. At 6 foot 5, he was 260 pounds of mean muscle who'd been a junior college All-American in San Diego before starring for the University of Colorado. He broke into the CFL with the B.C. Lions in 1962, had a cup of coffee with the NFL's Dallas Cowboys in '64, and then came back up north to star for the Argos from 1965–68 before moving on to the Winnipeg Blue Bombers. Bill was named a CFL all-star seven times, and in 2006 he was voted one of the league's top 50 players of all time by Canadian sports network TSN.

It was a fun trip. For the most part, we just spoke to the troops, did Q-and-A sessions, that sort of thing. The base gyms had heavy bags set up, so I trained a little bit, too. The soldiers seemed to get a kick out of our being there—especially Richard, who was mobbed like a rock star. The Rocket was a real gentleman, very polite and humble. Listening to him, you'd never guess he was one of hockey's all-time greatest players.

Frank and I hit it off right away, and we ended up bunking together. We teased each other mercilessly. Bill was a party animal, and as soon as he got up in the morning, he'd crack his first beer—then drink almost nonstop until the wee hours . . . with no visible effect. I don't know how the hell he did it. But on the bus ride to Frankfurt to fly home to Trenton, Ontario, big Bill's iron constitution finally went *kaput*.

We boarded the bus at seven in the morning, and about 15 minutes into the ride Frank jumped up and yelled at the German driver, "*Stoppen sie bus! Stoppen sie bus!*" I asked him what was wrong. "Gotta take a dump!" he boomed. Meanwhile, the driver had no idea what the hell was going on . . . and Bill was in a serious state of, uh, discomfort. "Stop this fuckin' bus!" he roared.

Too late.

Bill was wearing tan trousers, so you can imagine the scene as he lost control, surrounded by a bus full of horrified onlookers. The poor driver finally pulled over, and Bill jumped out. There was a road crew digging a trench nearby, so he ran over, plopped himself down in the trench and tried to clean himself up—with those tan trousers down around his ankles. Figuring this would make a nice photo for his opponents to put up on their locker-room walls, I grabbed my camera and started clicking away. "Hey Billy, nice ass!"

You get the picture.

The funniest thing was that after he cinched up his drawers and made his way back on the bus, Frank asked me if I thought Labatt's would pay to get his pants cleaned. He finally ended up reluctantly throwing them away. What a guy!

Even though it was peacetime, that trip to Germany really made me appreciate the sacrifice made by members of the armed forces who are posted overseas. As tough as it is for their families back home, I imagine it's worse for the men and women who have to endure months and months of separation from their loved ones. I had the same feeling 40 years later when I was asked to send a video greeting to Canadian troops fighting in Afghanistan.

I made my comeback on June 5, 1968, with a defense of my Canadian title against Jean-Claude Roy in Regina, Saskatchewan. If that date sounds familiar, it's because about 20 hours before we stepped into the ring, New York Senator Robert F. Kennedy had been critically wounded by an assassin in Los Angeles, right after winning the California primary in his bid to become the Democratic Party's nominee for president of the United States.

As you can imagine, the crowd at Regina's Exhibition Stadium was pretty small and pretty subdued. The promoter, my buddy Nick Zubray, was beside himself. "If I didn't have bad luck, I'd have no luck at all," he sniffed. Kennedy was very popular in Canada, and people stayed home to watch TV updates on his condition as surgeons fought to save his life. The senator ended up dying three days later.

It was a crappy fight, and I looked bad. Roy was a southpaw from Montmagny, Quebec, who'd made a name for himself by launching his pro career in 1964 with an eight-round decision over tough Yvon Durelle, who was 87–23–2 at the time. That was Durelle's last fight. The only other "name" on Roy's record was former world title challenger Tom McNeeley, who beat him in a split decision in 1966.

Even though I hadn't fought in almost a year, I didn't expect to have much trouble. Boy, was I wrong! From the opening bell, Roy was in survival mode; all he did was run and grab. It's very tough to fight a guy who just wants to do that. Joe Louis was the referee, but not once did he warn Roy about holding, nor did he threaten to deduct a point. Still, that's no excuse for how bad I looked. I won the fight by decision, but I remember Zubray telling me afterward that I should think about quitting. "I think your career is over, George," he said. It was that bad of a performance on my part.

Three weeks later, I knocked out Johnny Featherman in 95 seconds in Penticton, British Columbia. Featherman, who was from Bisbee, Arizona, had a record of 27–11 . . . and a reputation as a head-butter. He tried butting me about 10 seconds after the opening bell, and I got mad. I bent him over with a series of body shots before ending it with a beautiful left hook that almost took his head off. Ironically, Featherman's next fight was a TKO over Richard Steele, a pretty good southpaw from L.A. who compiled a 12–4 record before going on to become a highly respected referee, judge and member of the World Boxing Hall of Fame.

September of 1968 turned out to be the busiest month of my entire career. On the 3rd, I knocked out Levi Forte in two rounds in Miami Beach, followed on the 17th by a three-round KO of Vic Brown in Toronto in the co-main event to world middleweight champion Nino Benvenuti's non-title bout with USBA champ Art Hernandez (Nino won a boring 10-round decision). One week later, on the 26th, I was back in New York, headlining at Madison Square Garden against the biggest Mexican I'd ever laid eyes on: 6-foot-5 Manuel Ramos, who was ranked No. 4 in the world.

Born in Hermosillo, Sonora, Ramos had been a soccer phenom as a youth before he started amateur boxing in his late teens. He turned pro in 1963 and won five in a row before going 0–6–2 over his next eight fights. But starting in the spring of 1966, he reeled off an impressive string of 15 straight wins (12 by KO), including a split decision over Eddie Machen and a unanimous 10-round verdict over Ernie Terrell, in which he decked the former WBA champ. He also knocked out James J. Woody, who was a pretty tough customer.

The win over Terrell earned Ramos a shot at Joe Frazier for the New York State version of the world championship on June 24, 1968. Ramos went toe to toe with Smokin' Joe and staggered him with a big right uppercut in the opening minute, but Frazier came back to deck Ramos for the first time in his career before stopping him in Round 2.

My fight with Ramos was the main event on what was billed as "The All-Star Night of Heavyweights." The Garden was packed to the rafters and there was a palpable sense of excitement in the air. I was pumped up, too; it was great to be back in the Big Apple!

On the undercard, Buster Mathis knocked out James J. Woody, Chuck Wepner stopped Forest Ward, Billy Marquart beat Don Waldheim on a decision, and Johnny Gause got off the deck to KO big-punching Jeff Merritt in the third.

For a lot of reasons, I think the Ramos fight was the best of my career. It was just one of those nights when all my moves were clicking like a clock. Staring across the ring at him during Johnny Addie's introductions, I felt very calm. Only 15 months had passed since Frazier busted up my eye in the very same ring, but that seemed like an eternity ago. This was a chance to get back in the top 10, and I intended to make the most of it.

At the bell, Ramos met me flat-footed in the middle of the ring and threw a jab that missed the mark. I responded with a left hook to the body that got his attention and then, like he did against Frazier, Manuel tried to use his long arms to keep me on the outside. It didn't work. His jab was slow and easy to time, and by the end of the first round I was pounding him almost at will on the inside.

That trend continued through the next couple of rounds: me jabbing my way inside, getting him to back up, then raking him with hooks to the body and head. By the fourth I was really teeing off on Ramos, and I sensed he wouldn't last much longer. Early in Round 5 I shoe-shined six shots to the belly, followed by a hook and as good a right to the head as I'd ever thrown. A minute later I got him bent over the ropes and landed 17 consecutive punches before referee Zach Clayton moved in to wave it off. Ramos slid down the ropes and hit the canvas in a sitting position.

Unfortunately, the only known film of the fight is the last 30 seconds of Round 4 and all of Round 5—but at least my wild victory celebration survives on celluloid. When Clayton signaled that the bout was over, I cut into an impromptu version of the Watusi, which on the film looks like my upper body and lower body are kind of disjointed. I don't know where all those weird voodoo-like moves came from, but hey, I was a very happy guy. And they said I couldn't dance!

Ramos was never the same after our rumble. He was out of action for 12 months, then he won a decision over Tony Doyle before losing to Jack O'Halloran and Wepner. In 1970, he traveled to Argentina and was destroyed in one round by Oscar Bonavena. After that he became a stepping-stone for guys on the way up, including Ron Stander and Ron Lyle.

After his boxing career ended, Ramos returned to Mexico, where he worked as an office manager for the navy and acted in a handful of movies. He was only 56 when he died of chronic health problems in 1999.

In keeping with the year's international theme of my opposition (a French-Canadian, three Americans and a Mexican), I capped 1968 by knocking out 6-foot-4 Italian champion Dante Cane in seven rounds at Maple Leaf Gardens on November 12. The card was billed as an "international doubleheader" because a couple of hours earlier Sonny Liston dispatched Roger Rischer in Pittsburgh in a bout that was televised by closed-circuit on a big screen at the Gardens before Cane and I squared off.

There were 10,000 people in the stands, and I swear to God it was like fighting in Cane's hometown of Bologna. As it does today, Toronto had a huge Italian community in 1968, so Cane was the "hometown" hero! Big surprise, eh? When we were introduced, the crowd cheered a lot louder for him than they did for me. I remember thinking to myself, "Where the hell am I?"

No matter. Cane might have been big and strong, but he was slow and predictable, too. For such a big man his jab was almost nonexistent, and after the first couple of rounds it was obvious to everyone in the joint that he moved about as well as one of Michelangelo's statues. He was willing to mix it—as evidenced by the cut he opened under my right eye in the sixth—but I was landing virtually every body punch I threw, including a big right hook that knocked him through the ropes in Round 7. To his credit, Dante pulled himself off the ring apron and tried to fight on, but I instantly dropped him again. He'd just made it back to his feet when his corner threw in the towel.

Well, you can imagine the reaction. Within seconds, my hometown "fans" were screaming bloody murder and throwing stuff into the ring. The next day, Toronto's Italian newspaper had a front-page photo of me hitting Cane low, and there was a long interview in which his manager, Bruno Amaduzzi, accused me of deliberately fighting dirty. "Next time we meet Chuvalo, we bring a pistol!" he fumed.

A couple of days later, when I walked into Ungerman's office to get paid, Irving was being berated by one of a long string of irate callers on his speakerphone: "Hey Ungerman, you ass-a-hole, that Chuvalo . . . he's a dirty sonofabitch! He hit-a poor Dante right-a in da balls! Fuck-a you, Irving—I'm-a gonna go buy my chickens somewhere else!"

It took about a week for the Italian community to calm down. In the meantime, I got a big kick out of the way a writer for the *Toronto Telegram* described Cane as "one of the most colorful boxers to ever appear in our city. After being tenderized by Chuvalo, his nose was red, his eyes were deep purple and his body seemed to be made from some strange, quivering thing that was sort of lavender."

Eight years later, the *Telegram* photo of my punch lifting Cane's feet off the canvas just before I knocked him out of the ring got me a part in the first *Rocky* movie. Well, sort of.

The photo was picked up by the United Press International wire service, and in the movie, Rocky (Sylvester Stallone) shows a clipping of it to Adrian (Talia Shire) when he takes her skating on their first date. To illustrate why he has a dislocated finger, Rocky pulls the clipping from his wallet and says, "I originally done it in the Baby Crenshaw fight. Look, I carry pictures from all my fights. Big Baby was about the size of an airplane, and I broke both my hands on his face. I lost the fight ... but that's a nice picture, don't you think?"

Decades later Stallone avoided a lawsuit by paying Chuck Wepner some big dough for being the "inspiration" for Rocky Balboa, but I've always thought the Italian Stallion bore a closer resemblance to me ... at least in the first movie. For example, Rocky trains in a slaughterhouse—I trained in the slaughterhouse at Canada Packers. Rocky gets a shot at the world champion on short notice—I got my first fight with Muhammad Ali on 17 days' notice. Maybe what tilts it in Wepner's favor is that Rocky was more journeyman than top-10 contender.

At any rate, by using my photo (for free, by the way) Stallone inadvertently turned my name into a great piece of movie trivia. And when we finally met in person at his 2011 induction into the International Boxing Hall of Fame in Canastota, New York, Sly shook my hand and said, "George, you're my idol."

As pleased as I was about knocking out Cane to put an exclamation mark on my 6–0 comeback year, the coming Christmas season didn't promise much cheer around the Chuvalo household. Quite the contrary, in fact.

Back in October, I was showering after a workout at the Lansdowne gym when Lynne telephoned with some devastating news. She'd just come back from taking my mother to a medical appointment, and the doctor had confirmed that my mother had colon cancer. Instantly, I started crying like a baby. How could I not? I was a mama's boy if ever there was one, and the thought of her not being around was just too much to process. Today, more than four decades later, I still tear up when I think about her.

From the day I first put on those boxing gloves she bought for me at Eaton's, my mother was my biggest booster—but she never saw me punch or get punched. She always said she couldn't bear to look up, even in the early days when she sat at ringside. Just couldn't do it. For a while, she attended all my fights at Maple Leaf Gardens, and I also flew her down to New York for my MSG debut against Pat McMurtry, but she always sat staring at the floor, never at what was happening in the ring. She told me she could tell what was going on by the reaction of the crowd.

The cancer finally took my mother on February 6, 1970. At the end, she was just skin and bones, having dropped from 215 pounds to just 67. That hit me harder than anything I'd experienced to that point in my life.

❖   ❖   ❖

THANKS to those six wins—five by KO—in the five months since I beat Jean-Claude Roy, by the end of 1968 my record was 52–14–2 and I was rated No. 4 in the world by both the WBA and *The Ring*. Just before Christmas, Irving got an offer that potentially would put me right at the head of the line for another title shot: Teddy Brenner called and said he would pay us $20,000 to fight No. 6–ranked Buster Mathis on February 3 at Madison Square Garden.

Mathis was quite a story. The youngest of eight children, he was born in 1943 in Sledge, Mississippi, but his family moved to Grand Rapids, Michigan, when he was still a baby. His father abandoned them a short time later, leaving Buster's mom to raise the family. She died when Buster was 15, and soon afterward he quit school and for a time supported himself by playing defensive tackle for the Grand Rapids Blazers of the semi-pro United Football League. At age 16, carrying 275 pounds on a six-foot frame, he took up boxing at a police youth center in order to slim down.

For such a big kid, Mathis was real quick. His success in regional amateur tournaments caught the notice of Al Bachman, the New York–based manager of Montreal heavy-weight Bob Cleroux. Bachman was impressed enough to send Mathis north for a couple weeks to help Cleroux prepare for his fight with Zora Folley in 1962.

By 1964, Mathis had shot up to 6-foot-3 and won the U.S. amateur championship. He beat Joe Frazier in a showdown to see who would fight at the Tokyo Olympics, outweighing Frazier by exactly 100 pounds—295 to 195—but Joe still made the team as an alternate. A week before they took off for Japan, Mathis broke a knuckle during an exhibition bout with Frazier and was forced to pull out of the Games. Joe went on to win the gold medal.

Buster turned pro in June of 1965 after signing a four-year agreement with Peers Management, a syndicate that included Bachman. His first three fights were in Quebec: a KO and a four-round decision over Bob Maynard, and a KO of Johnny Shore. In his sixth fight, on January 7, 1966, Mathis stopped Chuck Wepner in a four-rounder at Madison Square Garden.

Mathis was 16–0 with 12 KOs when trainer Cus D'Amato joined his management team in 1967, and that's when Buster really started to gain notice in the heavyweight division. For starters, D'Amato trimmed him down to 235 in order to take full advantage of Buster's natural speed. He also encouraged Mathis to embrace his sense of showmanship, which included dancing a little jig in his corner before fights and blowing kisses to the crowd. D'Amato also taught him to growl when he threw punches—a trick Cus supposedly picked up by watching Sonny Liston train.

Ungerman set up my training camp at Grossinger's Catskill Resort Hotel near the village of Liberty, smack dab in the middle of the borscht belt in upstate New York. Because Buster was a tall guy, I brought in a couple of sparring partners who were about the same size as him: Dick Wipperman and Everett Copeland. Wipperman had dropped a 10-round decision to Mathis a few months earlier and Copeland had been knocked out by Buster in '66, but I figured both guys would give me good work.

A couple of days into camp, a short, stocky Italian-looking guy showed up and asked to see me. He was wearing one of those heavy flannel shirts and looked like a truck driver. Before I could even ask his name, the guy started talking excitedly in a real thick New York accent: "Hey George, I hitchhiked all the way up from the city because I wanna spar witchya!" I had to stop myself from laughing out loud. The guy was maybe 5 foot 7, but I didn't want to be a rude jerk.

"See those big guys over there?" I said, pointing at Wipperman and Copeland. "Those are the type of guys I need in order to get ready to fight Mathis. Nothing personal, but you're the exact opposite of what I need. You can't help me." But he was persistent. "Oh George, please," he pleaded. "I know I can help. I'm broke, but I thumbed up from the city because I know I can help you. All I want is for you to give me a chance."

What could I do? I felt kind of sorry for the guy, and he seemed sincere enough. "Okay," I said. "Let me work with those other guys first, and if I've got a little steam left afterward, you can go a couple of rounds."

I needn't have bothered. He was a tough enough kid, but green and fairly easy to hit. Still, he was an engaging guy, polite and friendly. Everybody in camp liked him. He told me his name was Jose and that he was Puerto Rican. We kept him around for a couple of days before sending him on his way with a couple of hundred bucks in his pocket.

Just before he left, however, Jose and I went for coffee. The tab came to a grand total of 60 cents—pretty steep for java in 1969—and he handed over a pair of one-dollar bills and told the waitress to keep the change! As we said our goodbyes, I asked Jose what he did for a living. When he replied that he was an actor, I thought to myself, "If you act as well as you box, you'll starve to death." (Boy, was I wrong about that!) But I never forgot that generous tip.

The next time I saw the guy was eight years later, in the fall of 1977. I was invited to be on the Canadian Broadcasting Corporation's *Bob McLean Show* to talk about my upcoming fight with Earl McLeay, and as I sat in the green room in the CBC's Toronto studio, waiting to go on, the talent coordinator came over and said, "George, guess who Bob's interviewing right now? Burt Young!" The name didn't register. "You know—the guy from the *Rocky* movie. Rocky Balboa's brother-in-law! Would you like to meet him?"

You guessed it. Burt Young was "Jose" . . . but I didn't recognize him at first.

"Hey Georgie, you remember me from Grossinger's?" he asked—still with that thick New York accent. "Sure," I lied. He tapped his chest and said, "I always held you in my heart here. You were nice to me, and I don't forget." We chatted a bit, but he had a cab waiting to take him to the airport for a flight back to Los Angeles. It wasn't until he walked away that it dawned on me who he was. I ran down the hall, calling "Jose! Jose!" but he didn't make the connection. Oh well. At the very least, I figured his cab driver was going to get one hell of a tip.

Years later we ran into each other again, and when I mentioned that day in the studio, Burt asked why I kept calling him Jose. "When you were at Grossinger's you told me that was your name, and that you were Puerto Rican," I said. Burt let out a big laugh. "Nah . . . My real name is Dino and I'm Italian!"

✧   ✧   ✧

GOING into our fight, Mathis had a record of 28–1—his only loss being the stoppage by Frazier 11 months earlier. Since then,

Buster had knocked out Mel Turnbow, Jim Beattie and James J. Woody, beaten Dick Wipperman in a 10-round decision and won a split verdict against tough Amos Lincoln.

A crowd of 14,155 packed the Garden to watch former middleweight champ Emile Griffith beat Andy Heilman in the semi-main event before our fight, and in the dressing room I remember thinking how terrific it was to be back at MSG just a few months after my big win over Ramos. If I could bust up Buster the same way I whipped Ramos, I'd probably get another title shot before the end of the year.

But it wasn't to be. And I have only myself to blame.

My performance against Mathis ranks right up there with the loss to Pete Rademacher (1960) as the worst of my career. When I see the film today, I can't believe I fought such a dumb fight.

For starters, I was far too erect. I'd been so successful standing straight up against Ramos that my new trainer, Maxie Kadin, figured the same strategy should work against Mathis, who was two inches shorter than Ramos. But Buster was a lot quicker. I should've crowded him the way Frazier did, but Kadin thought the best way to keep Mathis at long range and neutralize his jab was for me to attack from a much straighter stance than what I was used to.

At 232, Mathis had a 25-pound advantage, but that didn't bother me in the least because I could see he was soft in the middle. In the opening round, I hammered him to the body and backed him into the ropes, then shot a left hook downstairs that landed a little south of the border—unintentionally, of course. As referee Harold Valan started to warn me about the low blow, Mathis pushed him aside and tried to land one of his own. Game on!

For the rest of the first round and into the second, I forced the action, but big Buster was much faster than he looked. He was a pretty decent sharpshooter from long range, but I shook him every time I got inside. By Round 6 his left jab and quick combinations opened cuts over both my eyes, but I still felt that I was holding my own.

Everything changed after he caught me with a head butt that raised a big lump on my right cheekbone. As it swelled up, I started having difficulty picking up his punches—just like I did with Frazier. Another head butt split the cut over my right eye wide open in the 11th, but I came back to rock Mathis with a big left hook to the head. We were going toe to toe when the fight ended.

The fans were on their feet and roaring with bloodlust when the final bell sounded, but the cuts looked a lot worse than they were (it only took 10 stitches to sew me up). I knew I'd lost, but I thought it was much closer. Valan scored it 10 rounds to two, while judges Al Berl and Jack Gordon had it 9–3 and 8–3–1, respectively.

At the post-fight press conference, Mathis apologized for shoving Valan out of the way in the first round. "I was in pain and Chuvalo kept hitting me low and saying he was sorry," he was quoted by the *New York Post*. "I told the referee, 'Let me hit him low and tell him that.'"

I don't actually recall telling Buster I was sorry, but it sounds like something a polite Canadian boy would do, right? As for those head butts, Mathis, along with his manager, Joe Fariello, Valan and Ungerman were summoned to a hearing convened by the New York State Athletic Commission the next day, but there were no repercussions.

According to the follow-up story in *Boxing Illustrated*, Valan told the hearing he never considered stopping the fight "because there would have been a riot." The story also said the referee was called on the carpet, not for letting the bout get out of hand, but for removing his tie at the end of the second round!

I was still having some vision problems several weeks later, so I ended up taking a five-month hiatus to make sure there was no permanent damage. Then, in August, I got a call from McWhorter, inviting me out to Napa Valley, California, to spar with Brian London, who was preparing to fight Jerry Quarry on September 3 in Oakland.

On the flight to San Francisco I was really looking forward to seeing Teddy again . . . and also to finally getting in the ring with London, who had pulled out of our fight in Toronto in 1961. It would be fun kicking his ass as payback for ducking me. Unfortunately, I never got that chance. Ten minutes after I arrived at the hotel, Teddy told me that London didn't want to spar. Just like that. No explanation other than the obvious, unspoken one: I would've beaten the crap out of him.

London's refusal to spar annoyed me, but I stuck around for a few more days and ended up boxing with a guy who had once fought Jerry Quarry in a six-rounder and was now making a living running a soul food restaurant. It was good work for a few days, and I needed it because Ungerman had lined up a fight with Jamaican champ Stamford Harris on September 8 in Lethbridge, Alberta.

Before I left San Francisco, I visited Quarry at his motel to wish him luck against London—not that he needed it. Jerry had a sense of self-assurance that bordered on cockiness, but he seemed like a nice kid. It was basically just a "Hi, how you doing?" thing, and we talked about boxing in general. He'd become very popular by beating Patterson and making it all the way to the final of the WBA tournament the previous year, and since then he'd won a decision over Mathis and been KO'd by Frazier in what was voted *The Ring*'s Fight of the Year for 1969. Little did either of us realize we'd be squaring off just over three months later.

On the morning of September 1 I arrived in Lethbridge, where my buddy, promoter Nick Zubray, had booked Irving and me into the luxurious (for Lethbridge) El Rancho Motel. Shortly after checking in, I got a call from Teddy in California, telling me that Rocky Marciano had died the night before when the private plane flying him from Chicago to Des Moines crashed in a cornfield near the town of Newton, Iowa. Marciano, the pilot and another passenger were killed on impact. There were no survivors. An official investigation blamed the crash on pilot error.

I was stunned . . . and saddened. We had our differences over the years, and I knew Rocky felt dissed when I turned down his overtures to manage me, but I liked the guy. He was cheap as hell but very entertaining and fun to be around. Ironically, September 1 would have been his 46th birthday.

McWhorter arrived in Lethbridge on September 4, the day after Quarry KO'd London in two rounds in Oakland. Between Teddy being down in the dumps over the beating that London took and Irving being shook up about Marciano's death, things were pretty somber for a day or two, but Teddy was soon back to his old self and I was happy to have him with us again.

We didn't expect any surprises from Stamford Harris. I'd sparred with him ahead of my fight with Ramos a year earlier, so we weren't too worried. Harris was a durable guy with a blocky build that made him look like a taller version of Frazier (George Foreman sparred with him a lot before his fight with Smokin' Joe), and he had a decent punch. He turned pro in 1953 as a 15-year-old middleweight, but two years later he was fighting as a full-fledged heavyweight and making a name for himself in Jamaica, Barbados and Haiti. He didn't fight outside the Caribbean until 1968, when he beat Everett Copeland on the undercard of my bout with Dante Cane in Toronto.

On fight night we were sitting in my dressing room at the Lethbridge Exhibition Pavilion when Zubray burst through the door, white as a sheet. "George, they're gonna fuckin' kill me!" he wheezed.

"What are you talking about?" I said.

"The fans! They want my blood!" snorted Zube. "All the Mexicans we brought up from Arizona are dropping like flies," he said of the prelim fighters. "If you knock this guy out quick, they'll lynch me. You've gotta carry him, George. You've gotta go at least three or four rounds."

I thought it was pretty funny. Nick had nickel-and-dimed on the undercard, as usual, and now his chickens were coming home to roost. The featured prelims had likewise ended quickly: Nafiz Ahmed, who was my sparring partner, knocked out Hugh Mercier in the first round, and Billy McGrandle, a world-class featherweight from Edmonton, stopped Gabe Espinoza in the second.

"Okay, Nick," I said. "I'll take it easy for a couple of rounds, then I'll go to work." No big deal, right? Wrong!

When the bell sounded, my plan was to just pussyfoot around and feel Harris out a little in order to time his jab. It's what every fighter does when he wants to catch his breath or buy some time, but Harris had other ideas. Two minutes in, he whacked me on the temple with a good left hook that made my eyeballs spin like a slot machine. It happened in the flash of just a second or two, but when I blinked, I saw seven Stamfords. And when I walked back to my corner at the end of the round, I saw seven Teddys and seven Irvings. What an awful sight!

At first, McWhorter and Ungerman didn't understand what was happening. "I can't focus my eyes," I said to Teddy. "I see seven of him." McWhorter could sense the concern in my voice. "Hit the one in the middle," he said.

It's a horrible feeling to have your vision go from perfectly normal to totally screwed up in the flash of a second, but that wasn't my main concern at that point. I was more worried about losing the fight. I wasn't supposed to lose to Stamford Harris, not in a million years. But if I didn't take care of business, that was a distinct possibility.

When I walked out of the corner to start Round 2, I looked like Boris Karloff playing Frankenstein: both arms fully extended, pawing hesitantly at the closest of the seven Stamfords lined up in front of me. He didn't try to back away, so after I grazed his forehead with a short jab to measure the distance, I pitched a hook to the chin that landed with full force.

As soon as I felt Harris wobble, I went nuts. He was hanging on the ropes right in front of me, so I cut loose with everything I had, nailing him with 15 consecutive punches, machine-gun style. He was draped over the middle rope and sliding halfway out of the ring when the referee waved it off at 2:09.

Zubray was crestfallen. He understood perfectly well why I didn't want to risk losing the fight by letting it go longer, but that didn't make him feel any better. Every bout on the card had ended in three rounds or less, and poor Nick was scared to death that the good folks of Lethbridge would tar and feather him before he could get out of town. Much to his relief, those fears proved unfounded.

With my vision back to normal, on November 16 I headlined another Zubray promotion in another out-of-the-way place: the tiny ski resort town of Kimberley, British Columbia. We almost didn't make it because of a mechanical glitch on the three-seat propeller plane Nick had chartered to bring me and my buddy Chuck Scriver across the Rockies from Calgary, but Chuck was able to fix the problem in 10 minutes—or about one minute longer than I needed to KO Leslie Borden at the Kimberley hockey rink. Good thing, too. I was anxious to make short work of Borden because I had a much bigger date circled on my calendar: a showdown with No. 4 world-ranked Jerry Quarry on December 12 at Madison Square Garden.

ROUND 10

I T'S NO STRETCH TO SAY THAT QUARRY WAS PROBABLY the most popular fighter on the planet in 1969. In fact, two separate polls conducted by *Boxing Illustrated* conferred that title upon the good-looking 24-year-old Californian, and he did his best to live up to it. Everywhere you looked, it seemed, there was Quarry—and not just in boxing-related settings. His picture made the cover of entertainment papers and teen idol magazines, and when he wasn't doing the rounds of TV talk shows and variety programs, he was guest starring on hit series like *Batman, I Dream of Jeannie, Adam-12* and *Land of the Giants*.

Quarry's father, James, got Jerry started in boxing when he was three years old, and by the time he was eight he'd won a junior Golden Gloves 45-pound championship. At age 13 Jerry was diagnosed with nephritis, a serious kidney ailment that required massive injections of penicillin and hospitalized him for three months. The doctors told him to forget about boxing and said he'd never be able to do a hard day's work for the rest of his life, but Jerry wouldn't accept that. He not only regained his health, he resumed his stellar amateur career and wound up winning the 1964 U.S. national Golden Gloves title.

Co-managed by his father and Johnny Flores, a longtime L.A. fight guy, Quarry turned pro in 1965 and reeled off 12 straight wins before being held to a draw by Tony Doyle. Jerry made his Madison Square Garden debut with a draw against Tony Alongi in March of 1966, fought another draw with Alongi a month later back in California, then lost for the first time in 20 fights when Eddie Machen beat him in a 10-rounder at the Olympic Auditorium in L.A.

In 1967, Quarry's wins over Al Jones, Brian London and Alex Miteff and a draw with Floyd Patterson earned him an invitation to participate in the WBA tournament, which he opened with a majority decision over Patterson in their rematch. He then KO'd Thad Spencer to reach the final, which he lost to Jimmy Ellis. "I just didn't have it," Quarry told a reporter for the *Los Angeles Times*. "I didn't have my rhythm and I couldn't put any punches together."

Not everyone bought that explanation. In fact, *Times* columnist Jim Murray publicly pilloried Quarry for not being properly prepared. "As far as young Jerry is concerned, roadwork is just something done by the state highway department or a lot of guys sitting on skiploaders under a parasol," wrote Murray. "Jerry thinks jump ropes are for little girls with ribbons in their hair and lollipops in their mouths. The only bag he punches has cookies in it . . . and his idea of getting ready for a fight is to shave and get a haircut."

Pretty harsh words for the guy a lot of other columnists were already dubbing the new Great White Hope.

Quarry rebounded from the loss to Ellis—and the bad press—to beat Buster Mathis in a 12-rounder in March of 1969, but three months later he got stopped on cuts by Frazier in a challenge for the New York State version of the world championship.

With Ali in exile and Frazier and Ellis still largely perceived as gatekeepers of the fragmented title, Quarry's colorful persona and boy-next-door demeanor struck a chord with fans. Being white certainly didn't hurt, either. In fact, the day our fight was announced, one of the New York papers referred to Jerry and me as "the two toughest white men on the planet" and predicted the winner would become "the new hope of the heavyweight division."

I was bound and determined it would be me.

The press conference to officially announce the fight was held at Madison Square Garden, and both of us made the usual speech about it being our big chance to secure another title shot. Quarry was ranked ahead of me, so he was the betting favorite. Jerry was very popular in New York, so there was already a lot of buzz about the fight—much more than for my bouts with Mathis or Ramos.

I usually never put much stock in stuff that was said at press conferences, but when Quarry wrapped up his comments by making a crack that compared me to Canadian bacon, it got my dander up a little bit—not because of the context, but because I never touch swine meat. If Jesus wouldn't eat it, why should I? So it kind of bugged me that he'd make such an inference. But I kept my mouth shut and just filed it away. I was confident I could make him eat those words.

I think the fight more than lived up to its advance billing, starting with the great ring introductions by Johnny Addie. I can still hear his voice reverberating through the big arena: "Recognized as the heavyweight king of Canada . . . George Chu-val-o . . . Chuvalo!" Standing in the corner, I remember thinking how cool that sounded . . . and that I'd have to remind Lynne of my regal status when I got home: "Hey doll, sweep the floor! Do the dishes!"

I came in at 217 pounds; Quarry was 202. The referee was my old pal Zach Clayton, and if you watch the film you'll notice that after his final instructions, just before Quarry and I touch gloves, Zach asks, "Are there any questions, *Chevalier?*" I felt like Rodney Dangerfield (again). Clayton had refereed my fights with Ramos and Patterson, but he still pronounced my name like I was a French movie star.

From the opening bell, it was a fast-paced fight. Quarry met me in the middle of the ring and landed a pretty good one-two to get things started. I guess if I had to compare his punching, he was similar to Frazier: a steady diet of left hooks. In the early going I relied mostly on my jab, which he couldn't get out of the way of. Of course, if you listen to Don Dunphy's blow-by-blow account—"Where did Chuvalo find that jab? Where did that come from?"—you'd think I'd never thrown one before in my life.

Just before the first round ended, I opened a cut on Quarry's nose, giving me a target to shoot for. In the third, we had a nice exchange of left hooks in the last 30 seconds and Jerry's right eye started to swell up a little, but he came back in the fourth and nicked me under my right eye—just before he landed a low left hook that got him a warning from Clayton. By the middle of the fifth, my eye was pretty much completely closed, but it looked a lot worse than it really was. Despite Jerry bouncing around a lot, I was still able to cut off the ring and nail him to the body, but I knew the aesthetics weren't good.

At the end of Round 6, I figured I was ahead—as I still do today—even though the scorecards showed that Clayton and judge Bill Recht had it 4–1–1 for Quarry, while the other judge, Tony Castellano, had it an even 3–3. Because my eye was such a mess, Dr. Harry Kleiman of the New York State Athletic Commission took a look at it between rounds and told Clayton he'd stop the fight if I took one more direct hit.

That's all I needed to hear.

Quarry must have figured out what was going on in my corner, because he came out for Round 7 with a look of confidence, perhaps underestimating the recuperative power of "Canadian bacon."

We both landed some good shots, but in the last 30 seconds I opened up with one of the best sequences of my career.

Here's what to look for on the film: just before I knock him out, I trap him on the ropes and throw a flurry of punches to the body and two upstairs to the head. I shoeshine him with seven or eight shots to the belly, then come up with a right hook to the head. That stuns him. The punch is hard to see because Clayton blocks most of the view on the camera angle. Quarry bounces off the ropes and circles toward the center of the ring. As I move in, he hits me with a good uppercut, then another one. My balance is bad because I'm only peeping out of one eye, but as Jerry pulls his right hand back to telegraph a third uppercut, I step over on my left foot. He's bent over a little bit, so I throw a short left—no more than six or seven inches. The punch doesn't look that hard, but when it landed flush on his temple, I felt the shock go all the way up my arm.

Immediately after he got hit with that left, Quarry stumbled backwards, then dropped to the canvas. He got back on his feet as Clayton tolled three, but even with one eye I could see he looked woozy and very unsteady. When he dropped to one knee and took out his mouthpiece, I remember thinking that he was probably okay and just waiting for Clayton to reach eight before he popped back up.

Meanwhile, Zach continued counting—with some blatant favoritism thrown in for good measure: "... four ... five ... six ... seven—are you okay, Jerry? Are you okay?—eight ... nine ... ten!"

Unbelievable! Why not just ask Quarry if he needed something for his headache, or maybe a pillow to kneel on?

Officially, the knockout came with one second left in Round 7—and the crowd went berserk. As Teddy and Irving mobbed me in the middle of the ring, Quarry's handlers stormed out of his corner and tried to get at Clayton. Cops and security guards materialized out of nowhere as people tried to climb through the ropes.

Quarry's post-fight comments to the reporters were predictable. "Nobody knocks me out," he said. "I wasn't hurt. I was looking at the clock and I couldn't hear the count because the crowd was yelling so much. I got gypped. I got ruined. This has destroyed me. I could have gotten up, but I couldn't tell if he was at eight or nine or 10 just by his fingers."

Like I said, predictable.

In an interview with *The Ring*, Clayton said, "I was signaling and calling the count right in Quarry's ear. If I had allowed him to continue, I would have been crucified. They would have blown the place up."

Lew Eskin broke down the KO this way in his report for *Boxing Illustrated:* "Jerry was seemingly on his way to victory when George dropped him with a smash to the head. Jerry went sailing backwards, hit the ropes, slumped to the canvas, then bounced up at the count of three before dropping to one knee. He removed his mouthpiece, holding it in his right hand as he rested the arm on the ropes and listened to Zach Clayton count him out. A fraction of a second after Zach shouted '10!' into his ear and waved his hands in the out signal, Quarry jumped up and started screaming that he had been 'short-counted.' He wasn't."

All I can say is if Quarry couldn't tell nine from 10, it must have been a pretty good punch. Jerry's brother Mike, who was a world-ranked light heavyweight contender, came to my dressing room afterward and said, "My family is complaining, but you won the fight fair and square, George." That made me feel pretty good.

Quarry had 25 more fights after I knocked him out. In his very next outing (March 3, 1970), he was decked by Rufus Brassell (my old sparring partner) at the end of the first round in Miami before coming back to stop Brassell in the second. Seven months later, after knocking out Mac Foster and Stamford Harris, Jerry was handpicked to be Ali's opponent in Atlanta after the U.S. Supreme Court ruled that Muhammad's banishment from boxing was unconstitutional. Ali's jab carved up Quarry's face, and his corner stopped the fight after Round 3. Ironically, one of the judges for that bout was Lew Eskin of *Boxing Illustrated*—the same guy who had so astutely analyzed my KO of Jerry in the magazine story.

Quarry then strung together six straight wins before being stopped by Ali again in their 1972 rematch. He rebounded to win a tough 12-rounder over Ron Lyle and starched big-punching Earnie Shavers in one round in '73, but after being knocked out for the second time by Frazier (1974) and stopped by Ken Norton (1975), Jerry called it quits—at least for a while. Two years after the loss to Norton, he returned at age 32 to KO fringe contender Lorenzo Zanon—after which he officially announced his retirement—only to come back again, this time as a cruiserweight, to knock out Lupe Guerra and beat James Williams in 1983.

While he was preparing for that comeback, Quarry was featured in a *Sports Illustrated* story about health problems among retired fighters. When he scored poorly on a series of cognitive tests, the experts concluded he was in the early stages of *dementia pugilistica*, an atrophy of the brain from repeated blows to the head. He retired for the third time after winning a majority decision over Williams, but on October 30, 1992, Jerry was back in the ring for one last fight, a six-rounder against somebody named Ron Cranmer in Aurora, Colorado.

Cranmer's record was only 3–4–1, but by that time Quarry was 47 years old and his physical and mental decline was painfully obvious. He lost all six rounds and reportedly pocketed only $1,050 to serve as a human punching bag.

The last time I saw Jerry was on October 14, 1995, at his induction into the World Boxing Hall of Fame in Los Angeles. When I went over to say hello and shake his hand, he had no clue who I was; he just stared at me blankly and mumbled, "You look like you could be a fighter."

Between Christmas and New Year's 1998, after being hospitalized with pneumonia, Jerry went into cardiac arrest and never regained consciousness. He died on January 3, 1999, at age 53.

ROUND 11

FIVE MONTHS WENT BY BEFORE I FOUGHT AGAIN. Those uppercuts that Quarry landed just before I put him away had ripped open the scar tissue on my chin from the cut Don Prout originally gave me in 1964, so I took some time off to let it heal. Then my mother passed away from her terminal cancer in early February (I was glad she'd been able to watch me beat Quarry on TV), so Teddy and I didn't return to a regular training schedule until the spring. I got back in the saddle with a 10-round stoppage of Billy Tiger in Detroit on May 1, 1970.

Tiger was from Miami, where he worked as a regular sparring partner for Ali and Jimmy Ellis at Angelo Dundee's 5th Street Gym. After showing good knockout power as an amateur, he turned pro in 1964 and won his first eight, but then for some strange reason he ended up fighting the same guys over and over again, which kind of stunted his progress. By the time we fought he was 15–14–2, including five bouts with Willie Thomas, three with Duke Johnson and two with each of Sammy Stone, Florentino Fernandez and Art Miller. But after I knocked him out in the 10th, Billy never fought again.

A week later I was back in Kimberley, British Columbia, to fight a guy named Gino Ricci, who hailed from Noranda, Quebec. Zubray was promoting the show, so I knew it would be . . . different.

With visions of a sold-out arena dancing in his head, Nick had scheduled the card for the afternoon of May 10, a Sunday, expecting that the entire population would turn out. What Zube didn't figure on when he made the fight was that the date corresponded with game four of the National Hockey League's Stanley Cup final series between the Boston Bruins and St. Louis Blues. I can still hear him moaning in my dressing room: "That fuckin' Bobby Orr! He just scored in overtime to give the Bruins their first championship since Christ was a cowboy! George, everybody's watching the celebration on TV! You're gonna be fighting in an empty barn!"

That wasn't Nick's only surprise of the afternoon. Ten minutes before the main event, he burst into my room to ask if I had any spare trunks. "Why would I have spare trunks?" I replied. Zube looked like he was about to have a stroke. "Because that asshole Ricci doesn't have any. He thinks somebody stole them," he said.

Picture the scene moments later: as the lights are dimmed and the sparse—and I mean *sparse*—crowd settle into their seats, I'm loosening up in the ring when I look across and see Ricci stripping off his robe. Underneath, he's wearing hockey pants, held up by oversized suspenders, complete with an overstuffed waistband and thick foam kidney pads. I couldn't believe my eyes; it was the most absurd thing I'd ever seen in the ring. I started laughing so hard it was all I could do to make it back to my corner.

When the bell rang, I was still chuckling. I cuffed Gino around a little bit, then nailed him with a payoff punch to the solar plexus, right between the kidney pads and those oversized suspenders. That was about the only vulnerable spot south of his shoulders. It was all over at 2:17 of the first round.

I've always enjoyed visiting the beautiful Pacific Northwest, so after the quick win over Ricci, I spent some time in Vancouver before heading down to Seattle to fight "Sweet" Charlie Reno a couple of weeks later.

Reno worked as a teaching assistant at a high school in nearby Renton, Washington. He turned pro in 1968 and had mixed success, getting stopped by Quarry in five rounds in '69, then battling tough Thad Spencer to a 10-round draw in March of 1970. A short, stocky guy, Charlie was a pretty good boxer, but he had problems with his weight, at one time ballooning to over 250 pounds. The day before our fight, a reporter for the *Seattle Times* described him as "sort of a combination of Archie Moore and Tony Galento."

The card at the Seattle Coliseum attracted a nice crowd (including George Foreman, who was at ringside), and the referee for the main event was Tacoma native Pat McMurtry—the guy who had beaten me on a decision when I ran out of gas in my New York debut 12 years earlier. Maybe Pat was thinking that Reno might get the same result if our fight went long enough, because he waited until I nearly killed poor Charlie before stopping the bout. I dumped him with the first decent punch I landed and had him on the deck four times in the third round before McMurtry moved in.

In the dressing room afterward, I had a visit from Quarry, who came up from California to take in the show. Two weeks earlier, Jerry had scored a big KO over Mac Foster in New York. We didn't talk about our fight, just exchanged pleasantries and wished each other luck.

Shortly after we returned to Toronto, Teddy Brenner came calling again, pitching a rematch with Quarry. Ungerman was all for it, of course; he couldn't wait to get back to New York and act like a big shot. I was somewhat less enthused, and told Brenner that if he couldn't guarantee us $100,000, he could forget about it. What would be the point? I'd have been happy to fight Jerry for peanut money when nobody thought I could beat him, but the KO had dramatically changed my bargaining position. I had nothing to prove and nothing to gain by beating him a second time. On the other hand, if I took a rematch for chump change and lost, where would that leave me? Why take that risk?

When Brenner finally figured out that I wouldn't budge on my terms for a rematch with Quarry, he asked if I was interested in taking on George Foreman at the Garden.

Foreman had turned pro the previous summer after winning a gold medal for the U.S. at the 1968 Olympics in Mexico City. Fighting every two weeks or so, he was already 21–0 with 18 KOs. Brenner's offer of $51,000 sounded all right, but to be honest, I just wanted to rest on my laurels for a while. We'd heard rumblings for weeks that Ali was on the verge of getting his license back and that his management team wanted to maximize the publicity by having his first comeback fight against a white guy in the Deep South. Being the highest-ranked white heavyweight on the planet, I figured they just might pick me.

But Ungerman, as usual, was anxious to pose as a big wheel in New York again. Brenner convinced him that Ali was several months away from launching his comeback, so Irving cajoled me into taking the offer for Foreman. And what happens? A week after we signed the contract to fight at MSG on August 4, Ali's people held a massive press conference to announce Muhammad's comeback on October 26 in Atlanta. The opponent? Jerry Quarry—who was guaranteed a cool $400,000!

Foreman was a big, strong 21-year-old with an Olympic gold medal, but other than that, I knew very little about him or his style. In those days there wasn't the easy access to film that there is today, so fight strategy was often based on stuff your trainer knew about an opponent, or information picked up from sparring partners who had previously worked with him.

When McWhorter found out that George was a converted southpaw, he figured Foreman might go back to "thinking left-handed" if I could keep the pressure on him. With that in mind, we planned to fight him the same way I'd gone after Quarry, by pressuring him with the jab until I could get inside and bang him to the body. The big difference, of course, was that George was a lot taller than Quarry and had a much longer reach, so it figured to be more difficult to get inside. And the fact he sparred a lot with Sonny Liston told us he was probably no stranger to getting pounded to the body.

We set up training camp in the Catskills, and one of the sparring partners Irving brought in was Charley "Devil" Green, a tough light heavyweight from the streets of Harlem who'd supposedly worked with Foreman.

Though he didn't have a great record, Charley packed a big punch. Earlier that year he'd won a decision over Henry Hank, and before that, as a last-second substitute for Jimmy Ralston, he'd come out of the crowd at Madison Square Garden (after munching on a couple of hot dogs and swilling a couple of beers) to put former world champion Jose Torres on the deck twice before Torres came back to knock him out.

Green was always a wild dresser, very hip for the time. On his first day in camp, he showed up in a frilly white shirt with a long collar, and a lime-green jumpsuit, like a pair of overalls but made with nice material. To this day, when I think of Charley I think of that song "The Age of Aquarius," by the Fifth Dimension.

Here's a little aside: in the spring of 2009 I had a presentation scheduled in Hudson Falls, New York. My buddies Mike and Bernie Slattery, huge boxing fans who were accompanying me on the trip, mentioned that Green was incarcerated at the Shawangunk Correctional Facility in Wallkill, a couple of hours' drive from Hudson Falls. Charley had been handed a sentence of 45 years to life after being convicted of killing three people in a Harlem cocaine den in 1983. He always maintained he got a raw deal, but apparently there were eyewitnesses. A few hours after the murders, the cops nabbed Charley, who had taken refuge at his lawyer's office in Manhattan. When they found him, he was hiding in an airshaft, bare-chested, snorting coke out of a plastic bag and threatening to jump 15 floors to his death.

Anyway, we drove out to the prison and spent an hour with Charley. A practicing black Ethiopian Jew from Mississippi, he shuffled into the visitor's center wearing a prison-issue shirt and pants and a yarmulke. He looked like a wizened old man on his way to the synagogue—not at all like I remembered him. He didn't really know who I was, but it was a nice reunion nevertheless. We kibitzed and told old stories for an hour, and he seemed happy that we were there. And I was allowed to give him $50, which is the most a prisoner can accept.

The Foreman fight marked the last time I headlined at Madison Square Garden, and to this day it bugs me that my final appearance there was so unsatisfying—both for me and, if crowd reaction is anything to go by, for a lot of the 12,526 fans who paid to watch it. I truly believe it might have ended differently if referee Arthur Mercante hadn't been so quick to wave it off.

That's certainly no knock against Foreman, who proved to be a terrific, heavy-handed puncher. He didn't always maximize his leverage, but his massive arms were so powerful, it didn't matter. When I'm asked to compare Foreman and Joe Frazier as punchers, my answer is this: Frazier's punch was like getting hit at 100 miles per hour by a Pontiac; Foreman's punch was like getting hit at 50 miles per hour by a Mack truck. Either way, it's not pretty.

In the opening round I nailed George with a couple of good left hooks to the body, but by the middle of the second, when he started pressing forward behind those big telephone-pole arms, it broke my rhythm. I caught him with a solid right to the head just before the round ended, but it didn't slow him down much.

Foreman's jab was straight and very heavy . . . and believe me, it was no fun being on the receiving end of it. I don't know if I was more surprised by that jab or by his quick movement, but about a minute into the third he cut off the ring and cracked me with as good a left hook to the jaw as I was ever hit with. *Boom!* It put me on the ropes in his corner, and as I tried to slide sideways he came back with a right-hand body shot. If you look at the film, I've got my right hand up as he lands a good one-two to the head, but I take those punches and then start shooting back to the body because I can see his breathing is getting heavy.

I fought my way off the ropes, but he kept coming forward, pursuing me into my own corner. By now George was missing more punches than he was landing, and while I'll concede he connected on more than a few of them, at no time did I think I was going to be knocked out—or even really staggered. Quite the opposite, in fact. I knew exactly where I was and what was happening, and I could see that he was getting wild. It's called "throwing punches out the window." He was pitching from all angles, but not many were getting through. I don't think I was hit by one good shot after that big left hook, but for some reason that's when Mercante decided to stop the fight. I turned to him and barked, "Are you fucking nuts?"—hardly the reaction of a fighter who supposedly was out on his feet, wouldn't you say?

I was furious. Sure, a few of George's big bombs landed with pinpoint accuracy, but it's not like I was on the verge of being decimated. On the other hand, Foreman breathing through his mouth in just the third round was a sure sign that he lacked stamina, and I figured he'd punch himself out sooner rather than later. Some of the newspaper stories played up the fact that Lynne was screaming for the fight to be stopped because she thought I was badly hurt, so maybe that had something to do with Mercante's decision. Either way, I wasn't happy.

Now fast-forward to the spring of 1974. My buddy, sportscaster Mike Anscombe, put together a fundraising banquet in Sarnia, Ontario, with me and future NFL Hall of Famer Larry Csonka as guest speakers. When Csonka canceled at the last minute, Mike lucked out and was able to get Ali to come up from Detroit, where he was on a press tour to publicize his upcoming title challenge against Foreman in Zaire.

As soon as he saw me, Muhammad asked, "George, what do you think about me and George?"

"He throws punches out the window," I replied.

"That's what I been hearing," Ali said. "I've got something special in store for him."

I didn't know it at the time, but Muhammad was referring to the extraordinarily brilliant rope-a-dope tactic he employed in Kinshasa a few months later en route to knocking Foreman out in the eighth round to win the world championship for the second time.

As he was starting to do with me just before Mercante stopped our fight, Foreman completely exhausted himself against Ali by giving way to emotion. Whether it was frustration or simply bad judgment, he didn't try to establish a punching rhythm or any real targeting strategy, he just let 'em fly. Probably for the first time in his career, he discovered that punches that miss the mark tire you out a lot quicker than the ones that land.

I never for a moment thought that Ali would beat Foreman, even after Muhammad hinted that he knew how to do it. When he first started leaning on the ropes and inviting George to pound on him, even Angelo Dundee was surprised . . . and angry. On the film, you can hear Angie screaming at him to get off the ropes. But Muhammad definitely knew what he was doing; by the end of Round 3 Foreman was already gassed.

So is it any wonder I'm still piqued at Mercante?

By the way, as much as I doubted that Ali had a snowball's chance in hell against Foreman, years later I was even more skeptical about George's comeback, which he launched in the spring of 1987 with a fourth-round KO of Steve Zouski—10 years after his first retirement.

As he kept chalking up the wins, however, I was really impressed by the way George transformed himself—both as a fighter and as a person. When he was a young guy, he wasn't that likable; he was surly, almost arrogant. But when he came back, he was like a different person; always affable and smiling. People identified with him. He went from being a menacing, brooding Sonny Liston wannabe to a self-effacing, roly-poly jokester who seemed more interested in scoffing down cheeseburgers than knocking out opponents. But knock them out he did: 23 in a row, until he dropped a title challenge against Evander Holyfield in 1991. But three years later, after Holyfield had been dethroned by Michael Moorer, Big George became the oldest lineal heavyweight champion when he KO'd Moorer just two months shy of his 46th birthday. That capped what for my money is the greatest comeback in all of sports history.

I was one of several of Foreman's opponents from the 1960s and '70s who were interviewed for a story in *Sports Illustrated* a week before his fight with Holyfield. We were asked to rate George's punching prowess, and while most of the guys said he was the hardest hitter they ever faced, one notable exception was Levi Forte, whom I KO'd twice, in 1966 and '68. He'd dropped a 10-round decision to Foreman six months before my fight with George in 1970.

"It was close," Forte said. "He had me down in the first round and he broke three of my ribs, but I still went the distance. Foreman's a heavy hitter, but not the heaviest. George Chuvalo hit the hardest."

✧ ✧ ✧

ELEVEN days after my date with Foreman, I was back in the ring—halfway around the world.

The previous year, on my first visit to my parents' homeland of Bosnia-Herzegovina I'd basically just toured around and soaked up the warmth and hospitality of relatives and family friends who'd been following my career from long distance for more than a decade. It was overwhelming . . . and humbling, to say the least. In Zagreb and Sarajevo, I'd been embraced like a prodigal son. In Ljubuski, the closest town to my father's village of Proboj, they closed the schools and public buildings and declared a civic holiday so that everyone could attend the mayor's reception for me.

It was during that initial visit that a promoter named Ivan Lakoseljac hatched the idea of having me headline a card at the soccer stadium in Sarajevo. We'd actually tossed it around for a couple of months and worked out a deal before I signed to fight Foreman, so Ivan was none too happy about me taking the fight in New York so close to his August 15 date. Losing to George put a bit of a damper on the idea for a splashy homecoming bout, but there was no way I was going to cancel the trip.

My opponent was Mike Bruce, a former U.S. national Golden Gloves finalist from Springfield, Massachusetts, who'd turned pro with great fanfare in 1964 but never came close to fulfilling his potential. In just his fourth fight, Bruce was showcased on the undercard of the Ali–Liston rematch (he won a six-round decision over Abe Brown), and two outings later he made a name for himself by dropping Joe Frazier for an eight count in the opening round of what was Smokin' Joe's second pro fight. Frazier came back to KO him in the third.

As it turned out, the weigh-in was more memorable than our fight.

The day before, in front of the press and hundreds of curious onlookers, the head of the Sarajevo boxing commission, an older gent named Hajrudin Mehmedbasic, seemed genuinely concerned about my safety. Sizing up Bruce's chiseled 6-foot-3 physique as Mike stepped on the scale and the photographers clicked away, Mehmedbasic leaned over and whispered slowly and emphatically in Croatian, "George [long pause] . . . he's taller than you!" A minute later, after another official called out Bruce's weight—245 pounds to my 215—he leaned over again and whispered, with the same dramatic concern, "George . . . he's heavier than you!" After Mike and I posed for a photo together, he sidled up to me one last time. Shaking his head, he quietly muttered, "George . . . he's *younger* than you." In his mind, he couldn't see how I could possibly beat this guy, who was indeed nine years younger, taller and heavier. Just the same, I thought his fatherly concern was kind of cute.

The commissioner needn't have worried. Five minutes after the national anthems finished reverberating through the packed Kosevo Stadium—which was adorned with a massive portrait of Marshal Josip Broz Tito at one end—I knocked Bruce out with a left hook to the head. The referee didn't even bother to count.

As soon as Bruce hit the deck, the place exploded. I'd never fought in front of such a partisan crowd in my life—and I never would again. They were yelling and chanting my name like I'd just won the championship of the world. It went on and on, until a bunch of my relatives who had come up from Herzegovina came pouring into the ring and carried Teddy and me back to the dressing room on their shoulders. That's something I'll never forget.

The next day, I took Teddy back to Proboj, the village my parents were from. Everybody turned out for the party, and as I was introducing McWhorter around, one of the older residents asked me what "bloodline" Teddy was. Since there were a lot of North Africans in Yugoslavia in those days, I simply replied, "He's a black person." The man gave Teddy the once-over and said, "What kind of black person? He's a gypsy!"

The sight of McWhorter donning a fez and riding around on a donkey only endeared him to the villagers. Teddy loved it there . . . and they loved him. One of my cousins even lined up a woman for him in a neighboring village so that Teddy could get lucky, but when he showed up at her place there were a bunch of dogs running around the yard, yapping like crazy. He got scared and high-tailed it back to Proboj.

I think every resident of the village turned out for the celebratory feast to mark our visit. My aunt Janja's contribution to the menu was a young lamb, but when she killed the poor thing by slashing its throat, Teddy was mortified. "Man, I can't eat that," he said. After it was dead, Janja cut out its knee joints and hung the carcass on a tree branch. By blowing into the hollowed-out joint in each leg she was able to peel the skin right off, exposing the bare flesh. In minutes, there was a mouthwatering aroma wafting from the barbecue—and Teddy had an instant change of heart. He said it was the best lamb he'd ever eaten.

I thought about Teddy and how much fun we had on that

trip when I was invited back to Ljubuski in 2011 for the unveiling of a granite-and-bronze statue of me in front of the town's sports center. Just like in 1970, it was a very humbling experience to be so warmly greeted by relatives and friends, most of whom I hadn't seen in decades.

The statue—a life-size rendering of me throwing a left hook—is mounted on a block of granite adorned with a carved maple leaf. In his dedication speech, Ante Simovic, president of the Boxing Federation of Bosnia and Herzegovina, said my career had stirred national pride in my parents' homeland all those years ago: "Back then, everyone in my generation imagined George somewhere on the other side of the planet, with unbelievable strength in body and soul, contending against the biggest and strongest in the world," said Simovic.

Former European heavyweight champ Zeljko Mavrovic unveiled the statue, which was sculpted by renowned artist Fabijan Tomic. It was very moving. When it came my time to speak, addressing the big crowd in Croatian, I said, "I was born in Canada, I live in Canada, but a piece of my heart and soul will forever remain here in this monument. You have made me very proud."

I know my mother and father would've been proud, too. That statue is as much a tribute to them as it is to me.

Teddy and I enjoyed a short detour through Italy on our way back to Toronto, then took a few weeks off before getting back to work. In the interim, I was asked by *The Canadian Magazine* to pick the 10 best fighters in the National Hockey League for a cover story. My choice as the NHL's "heavyweight champion" was Montreal Canadiens left winger John Ferguson, of whom I wrote:

"What makes Ferguson the champion is his tremendously aggressive instincts. For instance, he destroyed Chicago's Eric Nesterenko twice, once knocking him cold with one punch and then hitting him with a second punch before Nesterenko even reached the ice. Ferguson has terrifically fast hands. Judging by the effect they have, they must be very hard as well. Gordie Howe is probably the closest threat to Ferguson, but since Ferguson repeatedly defends his reputation, I'd have to say he's the champion. His one weakness is that nose of his. Few boxers ever made it with a nose like that: hit it with one good punch and the blood runs out like a faucet. I'm surprised more hockey fighters haven't found the mark."

Maybe I shouldn't have been so effusive about Fergie's fighting ability, because a few weeks after the story was published, a *Toronto Telegram* columnist named Paul Rimstead floated the idea of promoting a three-round exhibition between me and Fergie at the Canadian National Exhibition. It got a lot of media attention for a couple of days, until Canadiens general manager Sam Pollock issued a statement saying that under no circumstances would the hockey club agree to allow Ferguson to get in the ring with me.

Not that it would've been even remotely competitive. Fighting on skates in hockey is completely different from boxing, and more than once I've watched so-called "tough guy" hockey players get taken apart by boxers half their size when they've squared off between the ropes. The best example was in 1978, when my pal Benny "Red" Randall, a 43-year-old lightweight who'd retired 10 years earlier with a record of 4–14–1 (one of those losses was a 10-round decision to the great Willie Pep), laid a one-round boxing lesson on 25-year-old Toronto

Maple Leafs enforcer Dave "Tiger" Williams during a private sparring session at Sully's Toronto Athletic Club.

A week before Halloween, I was back in action, defending my Canadian title with a first-round KO of Tommy Burns (no, not *that* Tommy Burns—not even a reasonable facsimile!) in Hamilton, Ontario. The most memorable thing about it was that I didn't throw a single punch in the first minute after the bell rang, which was probably a record for my career. Burns ran like a thief until I dropped him face-first with a body shot. As the correspondent for *The Ring* put it, "It took Chuvalo longer to lace his boots than it did for him to end the fight." Three weeks later, I stopped tough Tony Ventura in four rounds in Montreal. Ventura had wins over Dick Wipperman and Levi Forte and was coming off a decision loss to Joe Bugner.

My last fight of 1970 was supposed to be on December 11 against Mike Boswell, from Youngstown, Ohio, who turned pro earlier that year after a stellar amateur career that saw him lose just nine of 170 fights. I heard he'd decked Ken Norton and beaten Earnie Shavers in the amateurs, so it was no surprise he won his first 12 pro outings, scoring 11 knockouts— including two stoppages of J.D. McCauley, the uncle of future heavyweight champ Buster Douglas.

Dean Chance, a veteran major league pitcher who was just winding down his career with the Detroit Tigers after stops in Los Angeles, Minnesota, Cleveland and New York, was Boswell's manager. Chance was known for never looking at home plate once he received the sign from his catcher. Halfway through his windup, he'd turn his back fully toward the hitter before whirling around and unleashing a blazing fastball with pinpoint accuracy. Apparently, Chance didn't have the same control over his fighter.

Two days before Boswell was supposed to fight me, he was shot twice in the back during a bar brawl over a woman. According to a report in *The Ring*, Mike calmly took the gun from his attacker and then beat him with it until the cops showed up. With Boswell out of the picture, Chance, who was also promoting the show, scrambled to find a replacement. He came up with a guy named Charles Couture, who would never fight again after I got through with him at the Austintown Fitch High School gym in Youngstown. It took me all of four minutes to end Couture's boxing aspirations with a second-round KO.

Much more memorable than the fight was the warm reception I got in Youngstown, both from the fans and the commission, which was headed by a great guy named Blackie Gennaro. He presented me with a long leather overcoat, which was just the thing to take home to face another Toronto winter.

Oh, by the way, Dean Chance remained in boxing long after Boswell's career had run its course. He managed Earnie Shavers through much of the '70s, and later founded the International Boxing Association, which he still heads.

ROUND 12

BY THE SPRING OF 1971 I WAS TAKING CARE OF all my own expenses and was no longer contractually obligated to give Ungerman a piece of my purses. He was still working my corner because he loved to be seen, but from then on he was strictly a front man.

It was around this time that Ungerman formed All Canada Sports Promotions to get his paws on the lucrative closed-circuit TV pie. For a while, he partnered with Alan Eagleson, the head of the National Hockey League Players' Association, who also served as the agent for Boston Bruins superstar Bobby Orr. That's why Canadian closed-circuit posters for many of Muhammad Ali's bouts in the mid-'70s carry a dual promotional banner reading "All Canada Sports Promotions and Bobby Orr Enterprises present . . ."

I wonder if Bobby ever realized he was briefly in the boxing business?

In March, Ungerman offered me a May fight in Toronto against top-10 contender Jose Luis Garcia, a hulking 6-foot-4 southpaw from Caracas, Venezuela. Eight months earlier,

Garcia had shocked the boxing world by knocking out previously undefeated Ken Norton, and he also had a KO win over Thad Spencer. A week or so after I told Irving to go ahead and make the match, he decided Garcia wasn't a big enough name to draw a full house at Maple Leaf Gardens, so he came back with another offer: $40,000 to fight Jimmy Ellis. I immediately agreed, but Lynne had other ideas, figuring I should be paid more to take on the former WBA champ. But when she started to argue the point, Irving cut his offer by $5,000. "Take it or leave it," he said. So I reluctantly took it.

To be honest, I don't remember much about fighting Ellis, who won the 10-round decision by scores of 48–46, 48–44 and 49–43. I'm not making excuses, but the post-fight medical revealed I had a lack of potassium in my system, which made me feel totally drained, like a bad case of the flu.

What I do recall is that Ellis moved very well. He was slick and hard to trap, but I hurt him with a head shot in the fourth or fifth round. Angelo Dundee, who was Jimmy's trainer/manager, told me afterward that Ellis was ready to go, but I didn't realize it. Angie kept yelling at him to stay out of the corner, but I didn't have the energy to keep him there anyway. I wasn't surprised by the result; I didn't win decisions.

Excuse me; I should say I *rarely* won decisions.

One of the few exceptions came six months after the Ellis fight, when I beat the Big Cat, Cleveland Williams, in a 10-rounder on the undercard of Ali's win over Buster Mathis at the Houston Astrodome. Mike Boswell was also on the undercard, dropping a 10-rounder to Joe Bugner, the statuesque Hungarian-born No. 2 contender—behind me—for Jack Bodell's British Commonwealth title. I say "statuesque" because

Bugner was a big guy—6 foot 4—and very strong-looking, like a statue. But he threw a punch about every half-hour. He was just another in the long line of Commonwealth contenders who wouldn't fight me.

I was happy to take on Williams. It was a big promotion, with international TV, and I knew he'd come to fight. Williams was a good puncher with a huge wingspan. He was built like a black Li'l Abner: massive upper body, very muscular arms . . . and skinny legs. And, of course, he still had a bullet lodged in his abdomen from his altercation with a Texas Highway Patrol officer seven years earlier. After a long recovery, he'd returned to the ring on February 8, 1966, knocking out Ben Black in the first round. Before that fight, Williams received a 10-minute standing ovation from his hometown fans that began when he walked down the aisle and didn't end until he motioned for them to sit down. The *Houston Post* called it "the greatest single ovation ever paid one man in the history of Houston athletics."

But that was all ancient history by '71. All I knew was that I'd have to stand close to Cleve if I wanted to stay on top of him and not give him any punching room—which was much easier said than done. In the first round he cut me under the right eye with a booming hook, and in the second he nicked me on the nose. I almost had him out when I caught him with a big right hand later in the round, and that kind of took the steam out of him. For the rest of the night, I loaded up with combinations while he threw just one punch at a time.

I was aiming for the bullet when I ripped a left hook to Williams's liver in the eighth, dropping him to one knee, and even though the punch wasn't even close to landing below the belt, the referee, a guy named Earl Keel, gave me a warning before awarding Williams a one-minute rest. "Earl, what the hell y'all doing?" I said, working on my newly found Texas accent. His reply sounded like an apology: "George, y'all kickin' the shit out of this ol' boy anyway, so I'm gonna give him a minute's rest." Keel scored it 98–93, as did one of the judges. The other had it 97–94.

There was at least one spectator who didn't agree with the verdict—and who went to great lengths to make me aware of her opinion. Now remember, this was in the Astrodome, where the walk from the ring back to the dressing room was about a quarter of a mile. As Teddy and I were making our way back, with Williams about 20 feet ahead of us, walking with his wife and kid, a hysterical older white woman came running up and got right in my face. "Cleveland won that fight!" she hollered, half out of breath. "Cleveland won that fight!" She must have been a close friend of theirs.

Having just been screwed out of a knockout because of the referee's sympathy for Williams, I was in no mood for niceties. "You think so?" I snarled. "Ask him who just kicked his ass!" Williams had his head bowed down and didn't say a word. I don't know if it even registered. He just kept walking.

The Big Cat had just three more fights after I beat him, and he retired in 1972 with a record of 78–13–1, with 58 KOs. On September 3, 1999, while crossing a street in Houston, he was hit by a car. He died from his injuries seven days later.

I OPENED 1972 by defending my Canadian championship with a sixth-round KO of Charley Chase on January 28 in Vancouver. It was the headliner on a card at the Pacific Coliseum that also featured Clyde Gray defending his Canadian welterweight title with a four-round KO of Lonnie States, and as an added attraction Ali toyed with Tracey Summerfield and Jeff Merritt in a pair of five-round exhibitions. Three weeks later, on February 21, I knocked out Jimmy Christopher in two rounds at the Winnipeg Arena. I think that was the only time in my career that I didn't get top billing on a Canadian card, but that date brings back a much darker memory: it was the night I saw Stu Gray, the older brother of Clyde Gray, get killed in the ring.

Stu's record was only 14–14–2, but that was good enough for him to get a title shot against Canadian light heavyweight champ Al Sparks. Sparks was a southpaw and not a big puncher himself, with only seven KOs on his 21–10 record. But Al was a dedicated, workmanlike fighter who always showed up in terrific shape. He turned pro the same year as me (1956) and won nine of his first 12 fights before getting knocked out by former world middleweight champ Bobo Olson in 1960. In 1969, Sparks dropped a 15-round decision to Bob Dunlop in Australia for the Commonwealth title, after decking Dunlop twice.

After making short work of Christopher in the semi-main event, I had a ringside seat that terrible night in Winnipeg. Both guys came out punching, but Sparks was doing most of the landing. Gray was taking some good licks, and he looked foggy at the end of six rounds. When he sat down on the stool, his right leg was draped over the bottom rope. Teddy was working the corner, and he pulled Stu's leg back inside.

When the bell rang for round seven, Gray came out of the corner staring straight ahead. His gloves were up, but he didn't look right. He just kept staring. Being a southpaw, Al circled to his right, out of Gray's field of vision, but Stu didn't even move his head. After a few seconds, Al moved back to his left and threw a long overhand left. Gray took the punch and turned, almost in slow motion, to his right. When he collapsed slowly to his knees, his backside was on the back of his heels. He grabbed the middle rope and his head was tilted at a 45-degree angle. I remember thinking that his pose looked like Jesus Christ on the cross. Then he went twisting around backwards. I'd never seen a guy knocked out that way. It was eerie.

As soon as referee Steve Trojack counted Stu out, at 24 seconds, a doctor jumped into the ring. He wasn't even the ring doctor, just a fan who was sitting behind where Gray went down. He immediately depressed Stu's tongue, but it was obvious something was very wrong. I turned to my sparring partner Nafiz Ahmed and said in Croatian, "He's going to die."

We all went to the hospital afterward. Stu underwent a two-hour operation to relieve intracranial pressure from a severe concussion, but he died of massive brain trauma a few hours later.

Sparks was devastated. He had just three more fights before retiring in 1977 with a career mark of 23–12–1. I know Gray's death must have haunted him, but I never heard him talk about it. It was a hell of a thing for him to live with all those years, but Al was one of the kindest, gentlest guys I ever met in the fight game. He was aces. When he died of a stroke in 2008, boxing lost one of its true gentlemen.

ROUND 13

GRAY'S DEATH WASN'T THE ONLY THING THAT put a dark cloud over the Winnipeg show. The following day, Christopher informed the Manitoba Boxing and Wrestling Commission that, prior to our fight, "a mysterious stranger in a long white overcoat" had threatened his life and ordered him to take a dive.

It was all a product of Jimmy's fertile imagination, of course, but the commission immediately issued Canada-wide suspensions for all the fighters and trainers, along with promoter Jack Keller, until an inquiry could be completed. Besides being ridiculous, I thought the investigation was callously inconsequential in the wake of Stewart's death, but they went ahead with it anyway.

A few days later, after extensive interviews with Christopher, referee William Cozman and other "persons of interest" (curiously, Teddy, Ungerman and I were not questioned), the commission issued a statement saying, "Christopher's testimony exonerated Chuvalo and his mentors from all guilt, and indicated that they could not have in any way known about the alleged threat against his life."

In response, the Canadian Boxing Federation ordered the three-man Manitoba commission to rescind the suspensions, but chairman Norm Coston refused, telling the *Winnipeg Free Press,* "If we did that, we'd look like a bunch of donkeys." Instead, all three guys resigned.

The fight with Christopher was supposed to be a tune-up for a rematch with Ali on March 13 in Vancouver, but in the aftermath of Gray's death and the commission investigation, on my behalf Ungerman requested a postponement until later in the spring. To be honest, Stewart's death really shook me up, and I just didn't feel like fighting for a while. The promoter, a Vancouver stockbroker named Murray Pezim, had already brought my pal Nick Zubray on board to help front the show, and while the postponement initially threw a monkey wrench into their plan to cash in on the boxing interest Ali helped ignite in the city after fighting those exhibitions in January, it turned out to be a blessing in disguise.

The following week I flew to Yugoslavia with a business associate. Following up on some good connections I'd made during my visit in 1970, we were negotiating a deal to purchase aluminum, which we planned to resell back home. A few days after we arrived, however, Irving called to say the bout with Ali was set for May 1, so I had to cut out early in order to resume training.

Unfortunately, my associate, who didn't speak Croatian and had no clue about how to grease the appropriate wheels in the Communist bureaucracy, ended up getting bogged down in red tape. The end result was that a deal that could have netted us hundreds of thousands of dollars never got off the ground, and he returned to Toronto empty-handed.

I grabbed a flight from Zagreb to London, where arrangements had been made for me to spar with Billy Aird, an up-and-comer from Liverpool whose claim to fame to that point in his career was that he'd won two of three fights with compatriot Richard Dunn. Four years later, in Munich, Dunn would challenge for the world championship and go down in history as the last fighter to be KO'd by Muhammad Ali.

I handled Aird rather easily. He wasn't big or particularly quick, but what he lacked in speed and stature, he made up for in enthusiasm. Still, after pretty much toying with him for a few days, I knew it was time to get back to Toronto to put in some serious rounds with my regular sparring partners. As it turned out, that plan would have to be put on hold.

I started feeling a little queasy just before leaving London, and by the time the transatlantic flight touched down in Toronto, I was sicker than I'd ever been in my life. And it lasted for a full week. I remember dragging myself home and telling Lynne how horrible I felt, then collapsing into bed and feeling so weak that I couldn't even get up to use the bathroom. I actually crapped the bed! Lynne somehow managed to get me up long enough to change the sheets, but when I crawled back into the sack I didn't even care if I died. Looking back, it's hard to believe. I never thought I'd say something like that in a million years, but my will to live was almost nonexistent. I was so tired and weak that I couldn't begin to muster the energy to make myself fight back. I just didn't care.

The illness finally ran its course, but it wasn't until decades later, when I had a blood test prior to getting inoculated for a trip to Africa in 2008, that I found out why I'd gotten so sick: acute hepatitis A. I must have eaten some bad food over in

Europe, and when the virus took hold of my liver, it was like a death grip.

But there was no time to contemplate the whys or what-ifs. The hype was already building for my rematch with Ali—dubbed "The Second Reckoning" by Pezim and Zubray—and I had about seven weeks to prepare for what I realistically knew was my last opportunity to earn another shot at the title Joe Frazier had claimed when he beat Muhammad the previous March.

ROUND 14

MY FIRST CLUE THAT "THE SECOND RECKONING" was going to be a somewhat unorthodox promotion came at a press conference following the formal signing ceremony in New York, where Pezim actually managed to outtalk both Ali and Howard Cosell. Believe me, that took some doing!

I liked Pezim right from the start; he reminded me of a smaller, more hyper version of Zube. An excitable little guy, Murray went on and on about how the fight would transform Vancouver into "the boxing capital of the world" (quite a bold statement, considering we were in a hotel adjacent to Grand Central Station, just blocks from Madison Square Garden), and how he had already received confirmations (or so he boasted) from all the biggest stars in Hollywood and New York to attend what he promised would be a "90-hour A-list all-star party" at the Bayshore Inn, the swanky seaside resort that eccentric billionaire Howard Hughes had moved into a couple of years earlier.

Grandiose plans were part and parcel of Pezim's personality.

Born in Toronto in 1920, he didn't make his first investment until he was in his 30s. After serving in World War II, he was working in his father's butcher shop when he sank his life savings—$13,000—into stock of a company that prospected for gold and copper mines. By the time the company went broke six weeks later, Murray was hooked on the markets. He took an unpaid apprenticeship at a Toronto brokerage firm and eventually learned enough to move to New York and earn a living in the financial district. He later returned to Toronto and struck it rich after buying up stock in northern Ontario's Denison Mines for 40 cents a share. When Denison went on to develop the vast uranium deposits at Elliot Lake, the stock peaked at $85.

After that, there was no stopping "The Pez." In 1963 he relocated to Vancouver where, in addition to making and losing several fortunes, he became one of the city's most beloved and recognizable raconteurs while cultivating a lifelong love of sports—and the spotlight. Years later (1989), he bought the B.C. Lions of the Canadian Football League, then made more headlines by signing former New York Giants defensive end Marc Gastineau. In addition to suiting up for the Lions, Gastineau—along with his girlfriend, actress Brigitte Nielsen—was made a minority owner of the team. After one season, however, Gastineau was gone. "Marc had two problems," Pezim told *Sports Illustrated* writer Douglas Looney. "He didn't try, and he's not too bright." When Gastineau later launched a brief pro boxing career, whom do you think he asked to be his manager? Murray Pezim!

Like Ali, Pezim never met a microphone he didn't like, and at the New York press conference I got quite a kick out of watching him interact with the media guys. It didn't matter if the question was about me, Ali or the state of boxing in Vancouver; at some point Murray always wound up telling the reporter that he had discovered more gold than anyone in history—"more than 40 million ounces . . . you can look it up!"

When it was Ali's turn to take the microphone, he opened by saying I hit him low "26 times . . . or 30 . . . or 60 times" in our first fight, six years earlier.

"Wait a minute," I interjected. "How many times?"

"I guess about 30 times," replied Muhammad.

"Hell, that's only twice per round," I shot back. "Don't tell me you can't take that!"

When a bunch of the newspaper guys started snickering, Ali took it as a cue to jump up and start swinging his arms the way your sister might throw a bowling ball.

"The first time you hit me low, I'm gonna hit you low right back," he barked, glaring at me. "There will be no low blows, or there will be a lot of them. It's your choice, George." Warming up to his shtick, he turned to the crowd and added, "Chuvalo is a dirty fighter, and this time I'm gonna knock him down. I want him out on his back, out unconscious—in the first round, if I can get him. I'm not gonna let it be said there was ever a heavyweight that didn't fall. They have pictures showing my heels. Jack Johnson fell. Jack Dempsey fell. Joe Louis and Joe Frazier, they fell. And on May 1, George Chuvalo is gonna fall! I know you've never been knocked down, George, but you've been on one knee, haven't you?"

"Only in church," I said, playing the straight man.

"Well, you better do some more prayin', 'cuz this time you've got to go! I won't name the round, but it rhymes with four. They are selling ads for the closed circuit on this fight, and I'm going to tell them to put the ads on the soles of your shoes so the people will see that Chuvalo at 34, the veteran of 85 fights, knows when he's whipped."

Then Ali's tone turned quietly serious. "You know, last night I had a bad dream," he told the throng. "There was a news flash: 'Muhammad Ali dies of a heart attack at age 30.' I woke up sweating. I'm sure glad it was a dream. So do me a favor, press people: don't get me too excited! I don't want that dream to come true up in Vancouver."

After the conference wrapped up, Howard Cosell asked me if I'd join him for a drink at a bar on the other side of Grand Central Station. We'd worked together a few times when ABC hired me to provide color commentary for boxing coverage on *Wide World of Sports*, and I always enjoyed talking to him. Howard liked to say of himself, "Arrogant, pompous, obnoxious, vain, cruel, verbose, a showoff. I have been called all of these. Of course, I am."

As we walked briskly through the crowd (well, I sort of half-jogged while Cosell, who stood about 6 foot 5, kind of loped along at double time), wide-eyed fans kept shouting greetings at him. One guy breathlessly ran up beside us and gushed, "Oh, Mr. Cosell, you're absolutely brilliant on *Monday Night Football!*" Without breaking stride, Howard gave him a dismissive glance and tersely huffed, "Well, naturally!"

When we finally sat down for our drink (I had orange juice, he had a beer), Cosell said he thought Muhammad's serious tone hadn't been a put-on. "Ali doesn't joke about dreams, and he never talks about death," he said. "Maybe you're already inside his head, George."

Either way, I had my work cut out.

In the five months since I defeated Cleveland Williams on the undercard of Ali's win over Buster Mathis in Houston, I'd only banked eight rounds of real fighting: the quick KOs of Charley Chase and Jimmy Christopher. Muhammad, on the other hand, had gone seven rounds in knocking out Jurgen Blin in Switzerland in December and then followed up with a 15-round decision over Mac Foster on April 1 in Tokyo.

Anxious to get a rematch with Frazier (it wouldn't come until 1974, after Joe lost the title to George Foreman), Ali wanted to keep busy. Our fight would be for the North American Boxing Federation title he claimed in his second comeback fight by knocking out Oscar Bonavena in 1970, and he'd already announced his intention to take on Jerry Quarry, Al "Blue" Lewis and Floyd Patterson in rapid succession, regardless of what happened in Vancouver.

Unlike for our first fight, when I had only 17 days to get ready in an atmosphere that bordered on complete chaos, this time my camp was calm and workmanlike. Ungerman brought in Bill Drover to join my regular roster of sparring partners, and he proved to be a useful addition. Drover hailed from Wabush, Newfoundland, and in the previous year he'd beaten Jean-Claude Roy, fought to a 10-round draw with Joe Bugner and dropped a decision to Jack Bodell. Lanky and quick on his feet, he did a good job of emulating the way Ali carried both hands low before flicking out his jab.

A few days before the fight, Muhammad showed up at the gym just as I was getting dressed after a sparring session. Accompanied by a TV camera crew and a small army of reporters, he started shouting about how he was going to knock me out, and then he threw a half-assed punch across the closed half-door that separated us. I knew he wasn't serious, but for the benefit of the cameras I braced myself by putting my hand on top of the partition, then lunged at him. When I made my move, the thing collapsed—and I immediately felt a sharp pain in my side. I didn't let on that anything was wrong, and we continued jawing at each other for another minute or two (the reporters ate it up) before going our separate ways.

When Teddy checked me out afterward, he discovered I'd separated a couple of ribs and likely torn some cartilage. Despite the injury, we never considered not going through with the fight. If it had been Joe Frazier or George Foreman, I would have asked for a postponement, but we knew Ali had never been a body puncher, so it was really no big deal. A little ice and I was good to go. Besides, I was making $65,000—the biggest payday of my career. That was a far cry from our first bout when, after expenses—and Irving scalping me under the contract—I pocketed something like $700 a round. When I think about that today, I have to laugh—otherwise I'd cry!

Ali's pre-fight antics didn't surprise me; in fact, I started to think maybe Howard Cosell was right when he'd suggested I might be messing with Muhammad's head. At the Hotel Georgia, when Ali got in the elevator to ride down to the weigh-in press conference, the only other occupant was Teddy McWhorter. Dead serious, Muhammad asked my trainer, "Your man ain't gonna hit me in the body again, is he?"

At the weigh-in, Ali was 217 pounds—his best weight and shape since his loss to Frazier 14 months earlier. I scaled 221. There was no jive at the weigh-in, and when the reporters asked Muhammad why he appeared so serious, he replied, "There's $5 million at stake for me in a rematch with Frazier.

You watch Wells Fargo guards when they unload a payroll . . . they look serious, too."

The weigh-in is also where I was introduced to PR coordinator and ring announcer Shelly Saltzman for the first time. A former sportscaster for the U.S. Armed Forces Network who'd also dabbled in promoting, he was kind of a flamboyant guy who struck me as trying a bit too hard to be noticed. A couple of years later, Saltzman was one of the principals in a company called Invest West Sports, which cut a deal with Top Rank's Bob Arum to put up the money for stuntman Evel Knievel's rocket-cycle jump across the Snake River Canyon in Idaho. As part of the deal, Saltzman made himself media coordinator for the event.

During the months of promotion for Evel's jump, Saltzman carried a cassette tape recorder with him in order to get stuff for an upcoming book. Knievel, Arum and others involved in the promotion were interviewed daily on the recordings, and Saltzman later claimed they were fully aware of his intention to write about his experience.

In late 1977, when Dell Publishing released Saltzman's book—*Evel Knievel on Tour*—it included information that Knievel claimed damaged his image and was misleading to the public. Evel was outraged. A few weeks after the book's release, Knievel visited the lot of Twentieth Century Fox Studios in Los Angeles, where Saltzman was an executive, and attacked him with a baseball bat, fracturing his arm. Evel received a sentence of six months on work furlough for the assault, and in a subsequent civil lawsuit Saltzman was awarded $12.75 million in damages. Knievel declared bankruptcy and none of the civil award was paid.

A few months before Evel died in 2007, Saltzman released a second book entitled *Fear No Evel: An Insider's Look at Hollywood,* in which he told his side of the assault, as well as his involvement in American sports and media.

On fight night, Shelly Saltzman's over-the-top preamble—"Introducing the gladiatorrrrs!"—was about what you'd expect from a guy who enjoyed being in the spotlight so much. He introduced Ali first—for some reason stating Muhammad was from Cherry Hill, New Jersey, instead of Louisville, Kentucky—and then, turning to me, he boomed, "And his worthy opponent . . . his worthy opponent . . . the great Toronto hard-rock . . . Canadian heavyweight champion . . . George Chuvalo . . . Chuvalo!"

I've got to admit it: the guy had style.

When the bell rang, my strategy was what it had always been: crowd and punch, crowd and punch, and keep crowding and punching until something gives. Neither of us expected any surprises, but right away I realized the 1972 version of Ali was a mere shadow of what he'd been six years earlier.

In our first fight, I tried to slow Muhammad down by throwing maybe 75 to 80 per cent of my punches to his body, and that's what I planned to do this time, too. But after the first round I could see he wasn't nearly as fast as he'd been back then, so I kind of switched things around and started shooting my jab. Nobody ever talks about it, but when you look at the film, you'll see that I landed a lot of jabs. In fact, my jab was working so well that I kind of forgot to go to his body as often as I should have—at least through the first six rounds.

The biggest difference I noticed (and remember, Floyd Patterson and I were the only guys to fight Ali both before and after his forced exile) was that Muhammad just didn't have the same energy or fluidity. In '66, he threw a lot more punches and had more verve, in a sense. The second time around he tried to get by on guile, because he didn't have the same physical attributes. There were flashes of his old style, for sure, but he couldn't sustain it. He was just a much better conditioned athlete the first time we fought.

I tagged Ali with a hard right cross off two left hooks late in Round 5, and he fell back on the ropes and waved me in to slug it out. That had always been one of Muhammad's reactions when he was hurt, but I figured he was just playing possum, so I waited for him to bounce back on his toes. That was a huge mistake—which Angelo Dundee later confirmed when he told me that Ali was genuinely hurt at that point and was ready to go.

In the sixth, Muhammad opened up with his combinations for really the only time in the fight, including a couple of backhands that referee Dave Brown chose to ignore. At some point a cut opened above my right eyebrow, but it wasn't a factor. The last half of the fight played out like a cat-and-mouse chase, with Ali relying mostly on his jab while I went back to my original plan to try to pin him on the ropes so I could bang to his body.

When the scoring was announced—judges Tom Paonessa and Tom Keyes had it 60-46 and 58-51 respectively, while Brown saw it 59-51—I was disappointed but not surprised. I thought it should have been much closer; in fact, some of the writers had me winning, but writers don't count. And when you're battling a legend, you never get any breaks.

At the post-fight press conference, when somebody asked me if I was going to retire, Muhammad interrupted before I had a chance to answer: "Going on what he did tonight, George doesn't have to think about quitting," he said. "In fact, he ought to be ranked higher than he is . . . maybe even third."

That wasn't all Ali had to say. "George hurt me three times," he told a reporter from the *Vancouver Sun*. "If I hadn't been in such good shape, he might have beat me. He took all my best shots. You know I don't like to brag, but anybody who can take my best shots and still be on his feet at the end has to be great, and Chuvalo was that tonight."

Remember what I said about fighting a legend? An hour later, after I had showered and was getting ready to leave, my buddy Chuck Scriver dropped by my dressing room to report that he'd just seen referee Dave Brown exiting Ali's room with a souvenir of the fight. Author Tom Henry described the scene in *Inside Fighter*, his 2001 biography of Brown: "Dave was thinking he might get a shoelace, but Ali had something else in mind. He scooped his blood-spattered satin boxing shorts from the floor and held them out. 'You're pretty good for an old guy,' said Ali."

Even though he fought for another nine years and twice regained the world championship that had been stripped from him in 1967, Ali never got back to being the fighter he was before he was forced into exile. When he beat Foreman in Zaire in 1974, he won by using his brains. He sucked George in with the rope-a-dope; he didn't beat him on physical ability as much as by employing a brilliant fight strategy. He used his intelligence and general boxing savvy and let Foreman punch himself out, then he just took over. Against Frazier in the "Thrilla in Manila," Muhammad won on pure guts. For the most part, his speed and movement were just memories, but he showed the world he had the heart of a champion. In terms of raw courage, I think it was the best effort of his entire career.

Ali and I have seen each other off and on over the years—the last time was when the Toronto Argonauts hosted a fundraiser for Parkinson's research in 2002—but we never discussed our fights. Even though Parkinson's has pretty much shut him out from interacting with the world, Muhammad retains a certain grace about him no matter what happens. I don't feel sorry for him, mainly because I see him as a happy person. I see him as a spiritual person. I see him with his family. I see him surrounded by love—just like me, in a way. And that's what makes life worth living.

When I see Muhammad today, I see a caring person . . . a person surrounded by people who love him. He's always receiving constant adulation, no matter where he goes—and so he should. He's got to feel good about a lot of things, even though he has difficulty communicating those feelings. Take a look at his face; does he look unhappy? I don't think so. He knows he's loved and appreciated. He knows he's still the center of attention. He looks at peace with himself, despite the physical impairment.

When Ali lit the torch at the 1996 Olympics in Atlanta, I thought it took a tremendous amount of courage. Even with his shaking and tremors, there was something profoundly touching and dignified about it all. And for a few beautiful moments, the whole world celebrated with him.

✧   ✧   ✧

THREE weeks after "The Second Reckoning"—May 25, to be exact—I was ringside at the Civic Auditorium in Omaha,

Nebraska, to provide color commentary for the TVS network's coverage of Joe Frazier's second defense of his undisputed title, against Ron Stander. Les Snider did the blow-by-blow coverage, while Don Chevrier, a fellow Torontonian, was the host.

The first fight I worked as a color man was with Howard Cosell: Ali vs. Ernie Terrell at the Houston Astrodome on February 6, 1967. I'd also been behind the microphone for a few bouts on ABC's *Wide World of Sports*, which I thoroughly enjoyed. That subsequently led to ABC hiring me to provide color commentary alongside Keith Jackson and Chris Schenkel on a weekly fight show from New York for seven weeks in 1973. The network flew me in from Toronto in the morning, picked me up in a limo at the hotel, and then I'd do the show at Madison Square Garden's Felt Forum before flying home the same night. They paid me pretty good money, too.

I was proud of my commentary work—and judging by the fan mail ABC passed along, the viewers appreciated it, too. All I tried to do was comment from a fighter's point of view— tell what was happening and convey what both men might be thinking. Is the other guy hurt? Is he taking advantage of his opportunities? That sort of thing. There wasn't a lot of prep work involved because, unlike today, there was rarely any film to look at ahead of time, so I'd just kind of wing it.

It's amazing what a different perspective you get from ringside. When you're in there throwing punches, trying to take the other guy out, you can't see what you're doing wrong. You perform by instinct and reflexes. On the other hand, when you're describing a fight from right up close, you see a lot more—and sometimes it almost looks like it's happening in slow motion. I found it very interesting.

Concurrent with my appearance on TVS, Don Dunphy penned a lengthy column in *The Ring* entitled "Give Up the Gloves and Grab a Microphone, George!" He wrapped up his treatise with the following:

"If George Chuvalo is to continue fighting, and I'll bet he does, why don't they give him a chance to win the title by bringing back fights to the finish? I can just see the news report: Jan. 8, 1975: MIAMI (AP)—Heavyweight champion George Chuvalo successfully defended his crown tonight when former champ Muhammad Ali dropped from exhaustion after three hours and fifteen minutes of a brutal scrap. Although beaten, Ali was jubilant in his dressing room when he learned that he had gone farther with Chuvalo than anyone in boxing history. 'I told you,' Ali said over and over again. 'You wouldn't believe me when I said that I would last longer with Chuvalo than Joe Frazier did. I beat his time by half an hour! I hope George gives me another chance.'"

Well, Frazier vs. Stander wasn't going to be a fight to the finish, but it did promise to be a little different—and I was pleased to be invited to be part of the show. For starters, Omaha was far off the beaten path for big-time boxing. Joe Louis (exhibition) and Sugar Ray Robinson (vs. Don Lee and Benny Evans) had fought there way back in 1949, but for the next 20 years the city was pretty much in the twilight zone when it came to showcasing the sweet science. But then Stander arrived on the scene.

At a blocky 5 foot 11 and 230 pounds, Stander—a.k.a. "The Bluffs Butcher"—was built like a tank. Hailing from Council Bluffs, Iowa, right across the Missouri River from Omaha, he'd turned pro in 1969 and reeled off 13 consecutive wins, including a six-round decision over my one-time sparring partner Joe Byrd, the father of future IBF/WBO world champion Chris Byrd. By the time he got his title shot with Frazier, Stander had fought in Omaha 17 times en route to compiling a record of 23–1–1, which included a knockout of Earnie Shavers and wins over Thad Spencer, Manuel Ramos and Mike Boswell.

If ever a fighter personified the hopes and dreams of his hometown fans, it was Stander. Unpolished but disarmingly polite, he said all the right things to visiting reporters anxious to find a new angle to write about. "I'll fight any human being alive . . . and most animals," was his trademark expression. When somebody asked if he'd ever been knocked down, Stander's response was, "Yeah, by a cop with a nightstick." And like his hero, Two-Ton Tony Galento, Stander had a well-documented taste for beer: "How much do I drink? I lose count after the first case." It got to the point where the "Who Is Ron Stander?" storylines emanating from Omaha were so numerous that on fight night thousands of his supporters were decked out in souvenir straw hats bearing the inscription "Who The Hell Is Joe Frazier??"

Stander's wife, Darlene, was equally quotable for the gentlemen of the press. Mark Kram of *Sports Illustrated* reported that the night before the fight she barged into her husband's hotel room just as Ron was showing Kram "how he was going to twitch when Frazier knocked him out."

"We're $250 overdrawn at the bank. What do you think of that? And we're two months behind in our mortgage payments. What do you think of that?" shouted Darlene. "God, I'm telling you . . . it's a good thing I know Frazier's going to do it, or I'd whup you myself!"

That's exactly what Smokin' Joe did, of course.

An hour or so before Frazier entered the ring, when I dropped by his dressing room to wish him luck, I found him totally focused on destruction. Then I went to Stander's room. We chatted for a minute or two, and when I turned to leave, Ron asked, "Don't you have any advice for me, George?" I told him to try to get inside and shoot his uppercut.

That turned out to be a pretty good tip—at least for the first round. Stander staggered Joe in the opening minute, but by Round 3—when Les Snider memorably observed, "And the claret begins to flow!"—Frazier's piston-like jab and murderous left hooks were making mincemeat of Stander's face. "It's a sheet of claret!" Snider effused, in case there was a viewer out there who missed his colorful call the first time.

Referee Zach Clayton mercifully put an end to the carnage in the fifth.

Decked out in a snappy checked sports jacket that made me look like a 220-pound speckled trout, I climbed into the ring with Snider to do the post-fight interviews. Frazier said he was considering retiring for a while, "until somebody comes down to my plantation with Cassius Clay's signature on a contract and three and a half million dollars for me," while Stander allowed that "Joe didn't hurt me too bad, just cut me up pretty good. He can crack!" Fittingly, the best post-fight quote came from Darlene Stander, when a reporter asked her what she thought of her husband's effort. "I'm a realist," she deadpanned. "You don't enter a Volkswagen in the Indy 500 unless you know a hell of a shortcut."

Stander went on to fight for another 10 years before retiring with a record of 38–21–3. Ironically, his biggest post-Frazier win came three years later, when he KO'd Terry Daniels in the one round. Daniels had gone four with Smokin' Joe in his first title defense earlier in '72.

I wrapped up the summer by defending my Canadian title against Tommy Burns on August 10 in Nelson, British Columbia. In our first fight, two years earlier, Burns had managed to survive until 2:40 of the opening round. This time I knocked him down four times and busted a couple of his ribs before Dave Brown counted him out at 2:36. Frank Allnutt's report in the November 1972 issue of *The Ring* put it this way: "Burns should never have been allowed in the same building as Chuvalo, let alone the same ring. Only the quick action by referee Brown saved Burns from serious injury."

What made it even more laughable was that poor Tommy had plotted a secret strategy to beat me.

Six months earlier, after knocking out Charley Chase in Vancouver, I'd accompanied Burns to the town of Creston, British Columbia, to speak at a sports banquet. While we were there we worked out at a local gym, and Tommy picked up on the fact that the higher elevation was bothering my breathing more than a little bit. When he heard me wheezing, he got it into his head that if we had a rematch in one of the neighboring mountain communities, he'd have a shot at taking my championship. That's how we wound up fighting in Nelson. And he would have been awarded the title by default if not for some fancy seamanship on the part of, ahem, *Admiral* Chuvalo.

The day before the fight, a gentleman in Nelson offered a friend and me the use of his houseboat to do a little fishing on the stretch of the Kootenay River that runs between Nelson and the nearby town of Castlegar. He couldn't accompany us, but we assured him that a couple of Toronto landlubbers were old hands at boating and that if the fish were biting we might even stay out on the river all night. The weigh-in at the Nelson Civic Centre wasn't scheduled until 10 o'clock the following morning, so we figured to have plenty of time to catch our limit.

With me at the helm, we chugged out into the middle of the river (I thought it was a lake!) and spent a leisurely day enjoying the sunshine and solitude. When darkness fell I dropped anchor . . . and interpreted the resultant *clunk* to mean it had hit bottom.

Not quite, as it turned out.

When I rose shortly after sunrise and turned the key to start the engine . . . nothing. The battery was completely dead because we'd fallen asleep with all the running lights on. No big deal, right? Just row ashore in the dinghy and call the owner.

Well, there was a problem. By the time we made it to shore and found a phone, the houseboat had drifted out of sight downriver. The owner nearly had a stroke when somebody else called to report that it was heading toward the rapids and a high waterfall (apparently, one of the highest in Canada). Fortunately, the owner's sons were on hand to speed out in a motorboat, and they were able to get aboard the runaway craft and steer it out of danger.

Thus ended my first—and last—naval command. And the closest chance Burns would ever get to become heavyweight champion of Canada.

ROUND 15

A COUPLE OF WEEKS AFTER MY NELSON ADVENTURE, I was relaxing at home when I got a phone call from a guy purporting to represent a promotional group based in Montreal. We set up a meeting the following day, where he introduced me to a French-Canadian fellow who said that he and some Tunisian associates had acquired the exclusive rights to sell Labatt's beer in Haiti, of all places. Their idea was to put on a big boxing show to mark the start of a sales blitz, and they wanted me as the headliner.

But that wasn't all. "The fight will be for the heavyweight championship of Haiti and will be held at the national soccer stadium in Port-au-Prince on September 5 . . . and you can pick your opponent, George," the promoter said. "How much do you want?"

I could sense there was something shady about these guys, but I decided to play along, just to see what happened. "Give me $5,000; but I want it in cash and I want to be paid before I leave Toronto," I said. They agreed. The promoter handed me a list of potential opponents and asked me to pick one. None of them were household names, so I told him it didn't matter which one of them I fought, just as long as I got paid beforehand. Then he asked if I could bring down a couple of other fighters to fill out the undercard.

"Haiti is the poorest country in the western hemisphere and all of this is going to cost some serious dough," I said. "How are you paying for it?"

"I am well connected with one of the most powerful generals in the country, and he has guaranteed to provide 15,000 soldiers, each of whom will buy a $5 ticket to the fight," said the promoter. "They will see great boxing, they will drink Labatt's beer . . . everybody will be happy. And we will all make some money!"

A few days later, still not quite sure of what we were getting ourselves involved with, Lynne drove me to the airport, where we met our contact. As promised, he paid me $5,000 in cash, which I handed to Lynne. "Here you go, doll," I chuckled. "Don't spend it all in one place."

An hour later, with my pals Ronnie Edwards, Ron DesRoches and Andy McCrory in tow, along with my sparring partner Nafiz Ahmed, Teddy McWhorter and my father, we boarded a jet bound for Port-au-Prince.

We landed around 10 at night, and I remember being shocked that the airport—in fact, the whole city—was almost completely dark. We piled into waiting cars and were whisked over pothole-riddled roads to the Plaza Hotel in the center of the city. When I went outside for a stroll the next morning, the place looked like West Africa. There were vendors selling fruit and vegetables and scrawny kids with really bad rickets playing in the shadow of huge billboards extolling the virtues of

President for Life François (Papa Doc) Duvalier and his son/ successor Jean-Claude (Baby Doc). It was like something out of a Federico Fellini movie.

And members of the Tonton Macoute were everywhere.

The Tonton Macoute were the voodoo-inspired militia created by Papa Doc in 1959 to counter a perceived threat to him posed by the regular armed forces. After an attempted coup in 1958, Duvalier dissolved the army and all law enforcement agencies and ordered the execution of several high-ranking generals. In 1970 the militia was officially renamed the Milice de Volontaires de la Sécurité Nationale (Militia of National Security Volunteers), but Haitians called it the Tonton Macoute after a mythological Creole bogeyman (Uncle Gunnysack) who was said to snare misbehaving children in a *macoute*, or gunnysack, before carrying them off to be eaten.

Members of the Tonton Macoute wore straw hats, blue denim shirts and dark sunglasses, and they were armed with machetes and pistols. Anyone who spoke out against Duvalier risked disappearing at night—or being attacked in broad daylight. The militiamen routinely stoned and burned people alive, often leaving the corpses hung in trees as an "object lesson." Their victims ranged from supporters of banished politicians to businessmen who balked at "donating" money for public works—a source of funds for corrupt officials.

The Montreal promoter and his Tunisian pals hosted wild parties at the hotel every night, and Tonton Macoute militiamen were the main guests. I stayed away in order to concentrate on getting ready to fight, but Edwards and DesRoches told me that after the militiamen complained about not having any white girls at the party one night, the following evening the promoter—who had promised to provide white girls—brought in a bunch of light-skinned black girls from the neighboring Dominican Republic . . . and had them all wear blonde wigs!

All the incongruities were making me suspicious. A couple of days before the fight, I asked the promoter why there was no advance publicity—not even a poster. "We don't need it," he said in his thick French-Canadian accent. "My friend, the general, he will have his 15,000 soldiers there. It's no problem, George." That was on September 3. Later that day we met a dentist from Quebec who was staying at the hotel, and he informed us that the Russians had defeated the National Hockey League's Team Canada the previous night in the opening game of the Summit Series in Montreal. Combined with the other absurdities that were unfolding around us, that disturbing news seemed oddly appropriate.

The fight venue was Sylvio Cator Stadium, a 30,000-seat facility named for the Haitian who brought home the silver medal in the long jump at the 1928 Olympics and was later elected mayor of Port-au-Prince. When we arrived on the afternoon of the fight, there were thousands of people milling around outside the walls—always a good sign—but I was horrified to see the Tonton Macoute using their clubs to beat on kids who were trying to climb over the two-storey walls.

When we got inside the stadium a few minutes later, the enormity of the sham hit me like one of Joe Frazier's left hooks: there were 68 people in the stands.

Sixty-eight!!!

The general and his 15,000 soldiers were no-shows, and since tickets hadn't been readily available to the public, we were essentially fighting in front of an empty house. To make matters worse, Ronnie Edwards's opponent bailed out, so Ron DesRoches volunteered to step in as a last-second substitute. They were buddies, but we figured the show must go on, even if nobody was watching. DesRoches never fought pro and his last amateur bout had been about 15 years earlier, so you can imagine the scene. After being introduced as "Marcel Villemain from France" (the name was a combination of popular middle-weights Marcel Cerdan and Robert Villemain), he collapsed in a heap when Edwards tapped him with a jab 10 seconds after the opening bell. It was such a terrible acting job that the "crowd"—all 68 of them—started loudly guffawing while the referee pleaded at Ron to get up and fight. DesRoches managed to beat the count, only to flop down again a few seconds later.

My fight with Charlie Boston wasn't much better. I knocked him out in two rounds, and in the shower afterward he moaned about getting ripped off. "Man, I got fucked by a promoter in New York just last week. Now I come all the way down here to get fucked again! I was supposed to get $1,000, but all they gave me is $340."

I did the math in my head: 68 tickets at $5 each—yup, that's $340. Well, at least they weren't fudging the numbers. Thank God I'd asked to be paid up front!

Back at the hotel a little while later, I told Nafiz to pack his bag. "We gotta get out of here . . . and fast!" I said. I knew the chickens were coming home to roost because every-thing the promoter had charged was about to come due: the rooms, the meals, the booze . . . not to mention those parties! My father, along with Teddy, Edwards, DesRoches and one of the Tunisians, joined me and Nafiz for the mad dash to the air-port, where we jumped on the first flight headed north.

I don't recall ever being happier to get back to Toronto; and the look on my father's face showed he was relieved to be home, too. Still, despite all the madness, the old man had a good time on that trip, and I was glad to have him there with us.

As it turned out, our departure came not a moment too soon. Shortly after we took off, the promoter and his cronies were arrested and thrown in jail. They'd racked up a bill for more than $30,000 (plus my $5,000, which they'd borrowed from a Montreal loan shark), and nobody was going anywhere until the debt was cleared. Fortunately, one of the Tunisians owned property in Toronto, which he mortgaged to raise the money. With the help of the Canadian consulate in Port-au-Prince, he was able to pay everything off.

Oh, yeah: I was never challenged to defend the title I won by knocking out Charlie Boston, so as far as I know I'm still the official heavyweight champion of Haiti!

NEXT up on my dance card was supposed to be Earnie Shavers, the 29-year-old knockout artist from Warren, Ohio. Nicknamed "The Black Destroyer" (and later, by Ali, "The Acorn") he won the national AAU heavyweight championship in 1969 and then turned pro under co-managers Dean Chance and Blackie Gennaro. Shavers opened his punch-for-pay career by knocking out Red Howell in Las Vegas on November 6, 1969 and over the next four years he notched 42 KOs in 44 wins, including 17 first-round stoppages. His only losses were a six-round decision to Stanley Johnson and—somewhat surprisingly—a fifth-round KO at the hands of Ron Stander.

Shavers really started to move up the ladder after the ubiquitous Don King paid $8,000 for Chance's share of Earnie's contract shortly after he KO'd Jimmy Young on February 19, 1973, in Philadelphia. A couple of weeks later, promoter Don Elbaum called me at home with an offer of $20,000 to fight Shavers on May 9 at the Cleveland Arena. I accepted immediately. Eight months had already passed since Haiti and I'd accumulated a bit of ring rust, but I figured a couple of months was more than enough lead time to get into decent shape.

Shavers had certainly earned his reputation as a big puncher. We'd sparred together in Youngstown before I fought Charles Couture in 1970, so I was familiar with his style. Since then, he'd reeled off eight KOs in nine fights, with only the tough Venezuelan Vicente Rondon able to last the 10-round limit.

By the time I arrived in Cleveland for a press conference to announce the formal contract signing in early April, the fight was already being hyped as "The Unstoppable Force vs. The Immovable Object." A sharp-looking poster, designed by artist Dick Dugan, featured a sketch of Shavers throwing his left hook with "42 KOs" written on his glove, with me leaning out of the way below a speech balloon that read, "Foreman, Frazier, Ali, Quarry and 100 others couldn't knock me down!"

That poster apparently got some people thinking they could turn a buck on the bout. I didn't take it seriously, but shortly after I checked into the hotel I got a telephone call from someone who said he was "well enough connected" to the Youngstown underworld to offer me a hefty sum to take a dive. He said the gamblers could get great odds on Shavers being the first guy to knock me down, but they needed it to be a sure thing before they placed their bets.

With Lynne and our boys, carving up the Thanksgiving turkey, 1965.

Reading to my sons during a break from training for Floyd Patterson in 1965.

Stevie (*left*) and Mitchell look on as I wrap Georgie Lee's hands, in 1970.

The Chuvalo brood at summer camp.

My granddaughters (*from left*) Rachel, Michaella and Adelayde, posing for Grandpa George.

Vanessa gives me a good-luck kiss, 1972.

Christmas at the Chuvalo household, 1977. Mitch had just come home from college in Florida.

My father holds his grandson Jesse. Check out my dad's right elbow, which never healed properly after a childhood injury.

My youngest son, Jesse, age 18. Ever since he died, I can't go to sleep without having a light on. Darkness concentrates my misery, like I'm suffocating.

Jesse on the dirt bike he crashed just a few weeks after his 20th birthday, in 1984. The knee injury he suffered put him on the road to heroin addiction.

Georgie Lee worked himself into terrific shape by lifting weights at the Collins Bay penitentiary in the mid-1980s.

Joanne and I are surrounded by Joanne's daughter, Ruby, (*far left*) and son, Jesse (*far right*), along with Stevie's kids, Rachel and Jesse, in 1995.

Joanne and I in the heart of Toronto's Junction neighborhood, 1994. Joanne's love brought me back to life.

Rachel and Stevie, just days before he died on August 17, 1996.

Steven, with his son, Jesse, and daughter, Rachel, in 1992.

The last photo ever taken of Stevie shows him with Jesse, outside the hospital where my dad was convalescing.

Joanne at the summit of Tanzania's Mount Kilimanjaro in 2006. She made the climb in support of the Canadian Liver Foundation.

A relaxing time spent with my two grandchildren Rachel and Jesse.

Mitchell's beautiful sons: Aaron (*left*) and Elijah.

Mitch and his nephew Jesse on the verandah outside Elvis Presley's house in Tupelo, Mississippi, in 2001.

My granddaughter Rachel was offered a scholarship to go to university. Sadly, she passed away from cancer as this book was being completed.

I let the guy say his piece and then gave him my wordless answer by slamming down the receiver.

The press conference attracted a nice crowd of reporters and TV crews, and I was impressed by their genuine enthusiasm. I hadn't fought in Cleveland since my loss to Zora Folley in 1964, but some of the media guys who had been at that fight wanted to talk about it. Not surprisingly, my big edge in experience emerged as their main storyline. In his column in the *Plain Dealer*, Dan Coughlin wrote, "The difference between Chuvalo and Shavers was exemplified in this seemingly innocuous question: what was your toughest fight? For Chuvalo, it was going 12 rounds with Floyd Patterson. For Shavers, it was a 10-round knockout of Chuck Leslie. For this one, promoter Don Elbaum has matched a prince with a peasant."

Unfortunately, we never got to find out if that was true.

Shortly after returning to Toronto, I sprained my back during a sparring session. We requested a postponement of the fight, but King and Elbaum were anxious to keep Shavers on a tight schedule. They said thanks, but no thanks. On May 12 he KO'd Harold Carter in one round, and five weeks later, after doing the same thing to Jimmy Ellis at Madison Square Garden, Earnie looked ready to step right into a title challenge against Foreman (at our press conference Shavers had recited a poem about one day beating Big George). That dream came crashing down in December when Jerry Quarry starched him in one round. That was followed by a loss to journeyman Bob Stallings, a draw in a rematch with Jimmy Young, then a brutal KO at the hands of Ron Lyle.

Shavers finally did get his title shot, against Ali on September 29, 1977, at Madison Square Garden. While I provided color commentary alongside Don Dunphy for Telemedia radio in Canada, the bout aired on the NBC television network (Dick Enberg called the blow-by-blow, with Ken Norton doing color). In a first for TV boxing, the network made special arrangements with the New York State Athletic Commission to show the 70 million prime-time viewers a graphic with the official scoring after each round, and that proved to be Earnie's undoing.

In a stroke of genius, Angelo Dundee put a guy in Ali's dressing room to watch the telecast, and he had a couple of other guys stationed at strategic points near the ring. They used hand signals to relay the scoring to the corner. Simple, but brilliant.

Midway through the second round, Shavers hurt Ali when he unleashed a crushing right hand over Muhammad's jab. "Ali took a great punch and he had remarkable recuperative powers, but I held back when I should have jumped on him. I thought maybe he was faking it," Shavers said later. "I regret that." Hmmm. That sounded just like what happened to me five years earlier in Vancouver.

After Muhammad danced like the Ali of old in Round 5, the pace slowed considerably. Instead of running out of steam, however, Shavers got his second wind in the championship rounds to make it close.

After the 14th, Dundee told Muhammad, "You don't look so good; you gotta go out and take this one." When the bell rang for the 15th, Ali looked like he was on his last legs. Still, he had enough left in the tank to launch his most relentless attack of the fight, landing punch after punch on Earnie's head over the final minute and nearly dropping him with 20 seconds left. That sealed the deal on a unanimous decision.

The next day, Garden matchmaker Teddy Brenner told the media he thought Shavers had won it. He also said he thought Ali should quit for good. Of course, Muhammad went on to fight for another four years—and Shavers was there for the finale. Earnie rebounded from a first-round knockdown to KO Jeff Sims on the undercard of Ali's swan song, the "Drama in Bahama" decision loss to Trevor Berbick on December 11, 1981.

Earnie had plenty left after that. On September 28, 1979, he got a title shot against Larry Holmes. That came after Shavers had KO'd Ken Norton in one round in March. He dropped Holmes with a huge right hand in Round 7 before Larry stopped him in the 11th.

In 1981, while casting for *Rocky III*, Sylvester Stallone invited Shavers to spar with him because he thought it would be a nice touch to use a real heavyweight to play the role of Clubber Lang (which eventually went to Mr. T). Shavers initially refused to hit Stallone with anything more than a soft jab, but Sly kept egging him on until Earnie responded by landing a single hard shot to the liver. "That nearly killed me," Stallone told the Associated Press. "I went straight to the men's room and threw up."

Shavers retired in 1983 because of eye problems but then returned in 1987 to notch a first-round KO of Larry Sims in Cincinnati. Another long layoff followed, during which he became an ordained Christian minister; then, in the fall of 1995, he beat Brian Morgan in an eight-round decision and was stopped in two rounds by Brian Yates—after which Earnie retired for good.

✧   ✧   ✧

WHAT I thought would be a short break to allow my back injury to heal turned into a 12-month hiatus between knocking out Charlie Boston in Haiti and my next fight, a three-round stoppage of Tony Ventura on September 25, 1973, in Cheektowaga, New York. I came in at 230 pounds—the heaviest of my career to that point—and definitely felt the effect of the long layoff. Ventura was slower than when I knocked him out in Montreal three years earlier, but because of the ring rust, I had a little trouble catching up with him this time. When I finally managed to trap him in his corner late in the third, a double left hook to the chin dropped him like a stone.

Five weeks later, I was back in Cheektowaga to take on Mike Boswell, the guy who'd been forced to pull out of our scheduled fight in 1970 after being shot in the back during a barroom brawl. At 195 pounds, Boswell was a bit of a speed merchant. He'd just come out of camp with Frazier, so he was in terrific shape. I, on the other hand, was not. My weight was still 230, and I felt slow and sluggish.

My only sparring partner for that fight was the inimitable Chuck "Spider" Jones—my future co-host on *Famous Knockouts*. Actually, referring to him as a sparring partner is a bit of a stretch. Chuck would dutifully walk into Sully's gym in Toronto, but as soon as he saw me he'd turn around and run back down the steps. I don't know how many times I had to chase after him to coax him back into the ring, but our little game went on for about a week.

My lack of preparation was very evident in the fight with Boswell, which ranks alongside my bouts with Pete Rademacher and Buster Mathis as one of the worst of my career. Boswell hopscotched like a rabbit for the first couple of rounds, which, combined with my lack of conditioning, made for very few meaningful exchanges. I had difficulty hitting him with clean shots, which made him more confident as the fight wore on.

That should never have happened. Truth be told, Mike didn't belong in the same ring with me, but he fought a smart fight. Finally, midway through the seventh round, I landed a decent left hook and he wobbled. He was in the corner, pinned against the ropes with his head over the turnbuckle, and I knew I had to suck it up and just keep punching. I wouldn't let him fall, because I wanted to be sure he was out cold. After ripping him with more than a dozen clean shots, I stepped back to survey the damage and he slithered down and out. It was a nice, clean finish, but I was disappointed that it took so long.

Looking back, the only good thing about that fight was that it marked Ungerman's last appearance in my corner. By that time he hadn't had a say in whom, where or when I fought for a few years, but he still liked to be seen between rounds, feeling important. When we'd first hooked up I sincerely appreciated Irving's financial commitment and his enthusiasm in helping advance my career, and I'd stuck with him because of that. But over the years our relationship had soured to the point where we were at odds more often than not.

Afterward, Irving told the *Toronto Star*, "Against Boswell, I saw things that really bothered me. George knocked him out in the seventh, but he didn't look good at all. His reflexes were slow and his timing was bad. Boswell was nothing, but he was scoring points with his jab. If George hadn't knocked him out, he might have won."

As much as I hated to admit it, Ungerman's critique was right on the money—but I had no intention of retiring at age 36. What I didn't know at the time was that I would be in boxing limbo for the next three and a half years and would be pushing 40 before I again climbed through the ropes with bad intentions.

I never announced my retirement, but there wasn't anyone to fight on the Canadian scene, and nobody was calling from the States.

One day in the spring of 1974, Ungerman phoned to see if I was interested in a rematch with Jerry Quarry in Cleveland, but I knew it was never going to happen.

With no contenders to challenge me, in late 1975 the pipsqueaks in charge of the Canadian Boxing Federation voted to strip my title for inactivity. They subsequently declared the championship vacant, but since nobody wanted to fight me, I remained the de facto titleholder.

I still trained—albeit sporadically. Usually just light calisthenics or hitting the bag. Instead of working out, I devoted most of my time to taking care of business. I obtained my real estate broker's license in 1976 and had pretty good success buying and selling properties (which continued until the real estate market went south in the early '90s). I also opened an import stationery firm called Office World Supplies, but it didn't last very long. My most promising business venture was also the wackiest: George Chuvalo Fruit Punch.

In the spring of 1976, I connected with a guy named Arnold Foote, a native Jamaican who'd recently relocated to Toronto. Foote owned a successful marketing and promotions firm in Jamaica and was anxious to put his expertise to work by launching some new ventures in his adopted homeland. Within minutes after we were introduced, he asked me what I thought about using my name to sell a fruit beverage.

It sounded intriguing. We quickly worked out a deal, and in short order Foote, who was putting up the money, enlisted the participation of SunPac, a well-known independent Canadian food processor. With the company's help we set about developing a line of vitamin C–enriched fruit drinks in lightweight, middleweight and heavyweight sizes.

By the end of the year Foote signed distribution deals with a couple of national supermarket chains and we were ready to launch, but then the whole venture kind of fizzled out when his marriage broke up. Just as the first cases of George Chuvalo Fruit Punch were hitting the Ontario market, he had to hightail it back to Jamaica. A month or so later, we were out of business.

In November of '76 I signed a contract with a Toronto group called Gemini Promotions Inc., headed by Norm Diflorio, a local guy who made his money in trucking and heavy construction. The deal called for me to be paid $10,000 to fight Bobby "Pretty Boy" Felstein for the "vacant" Canadian title on March 7 at the suburban North York Centennial Centre. Diflorio had no experience in boxing or promoting but he struck me as honest and sincere . . . and the 10 grand didn't sound bad, either.

The fight was formally announced at a press conference at Toronto's downtown Holiday Inn on December 3—and it drew flies. None of the city's three daily newspapers sent a reporter, and there were no TV cameras present. In fact, the only media representatives on hand to sample the elaborate spread of canapés and pasta casseroles were Brian Williams from the Canadian Broadcasting Corporation, a kid from the weekly *Mississauga News* and a guy from CJBC, the French-language CBC radio station.

The promoters were crestfallen about the sparse attendance . . . and I was none too thrilled, either. Granted, I'd been out of the ring for more than three years, and Felstein, whom I could've knocked out in my sleep, wasn't even a household name in his own household. Still, his pedestrian record of 16–12–1 was good enough for the CBF to rank him the No. 1 challenger for the "vacant" title, so who was I to argue? Perhaps it was naive, but I thought the novelty factor alone might generate some media attention. I was wrong—but that only made me more determined to ensure it didn't happen again.

When I began training for Felstein, my weight was up around 270 pounds. My goal was to get down to 230, so I had my work cut out for me. Teddy set a pretty rigid schedule for workouts and sparring at the Lansdowne gym and I put myself on a strict diet, but taking off the weight was a long, arduous process.

When Gemini Promotions called another press conference a couple of weeks before the fight, I decided to help spice things up by creating a little bad blood. I phoned Felstein and told him that when he got up to speak, he should insult me. "I don't care what you say, just make it good . . . nothing is off-limits," I said. "Then I'll pretend to get mad and we can take a couple of pokes at each other. We'll play it by ear and see what happens, okay?" Bobby readily agreed.

This time the conference was held at the Westbury Hotel, and there was a strong media turnout. When it was Felstein's turn to speak, he came through like a champ. Pointing at my rather ample girth, he declared that he would have no trouble whatsoever "laying a licking on washed-up Georgie Jell-O."

Georgie Jell-O?? Not bad at all!

I responded by leaping out of my chair in mock anger, but then as I started to approach him, Bobby turned and bolted for the door! It was priceless. He was running like hell, but just as I started to chase him, my lawyer stopped me so I could sign some mortgage papers. It was like a wacky cartoon.

With the writers and photographers scrambling to keep up and TV crews bringing up the rear, I ran out to the parking lot to find Felstein frantically trying to start his car. I ran up to it and started kicking the door, the fenders . . . anything I could put a boot on. The media guys loved it.

Unfortunately for Bobby (and unbeknownst to me), the car wasn't his; it was a loaner from the shop where his vehicle was being repaired. I never asked him how he explained the caved-in door and dented fenders when he returned it, but I'm sure he was quick to put the blame squarely on the shoulders of one "Georgie Jell-O."

The fight wasn't nearly as entertaining as that press conference—but more than 5,000 fans jammed the joint to watch it. I came in at 249 pounds and wore velvet powder-blue trunks to try to hide my gut (it didn't work). Felstein was 220, but his lanky 6-foot-4 frame made our weight disparity look even worse.

From the opening bell, Bobby's fight plan was simple: hold when he could and run when he couldn't. He might as well have brought along a pen and offered to sign a non-aggression pact. I was more than miffed, because some genuine animosity had built up between us over the past couple of months, and his all-talk-and-no-show tactics made me want to tear his head off.

We were both huffing and puffing after three rounds, and on more than one occasion I growled, "C'mon and fight, you bastard!" The referee, Harry Davis, earned his pay by repeatedly prying Bobby's arms apart when he grabbed me, but it still took longer than I expected to find my punching rhythm.

As it turned out, I was the one who eventually got up on my toes (at 249 pounds!) and started firing the jab. I finally dropped Felstein with a left hook about 30 seconds into the ninth round. He regained his feet as Davis tolled eight, but there was blood pouring from Bobby's mouth and he wore a frightened look that told me he was ready to go. I knew I had him. A right uppercut to the jaw, followed by a left to the ribs and another right to the head floored him again, and this time Davis didn't bother to count. "Sorry, Bobby," he said. "That's all."

I felt euphoric afterward. It was nice to hear the cheers again, but what really made it special for me was that I'd shown up the Canadian Boxing Federation for what they were: a bunch of spineless twerps who never should have taken away my title in the first place.

But the CBF was nothing if not mulish. Nine months later we went through the same ridiculous bullshit when the federation ordered me to defend the championship against yet another No. 1–ranked pretender: "Cowboy" Earl McLeay of Calgary, Alberta.

Unlike Felstein, McLeay at least had some pedigree. A former national amateur champ, he turned pro with a 31-second KO of Jerry Nolan in 1971, then won seven of his next eight—all by knockout—before moving to California and signing on as regular sparring partner for Ken Norton. Fighting at home for the first time in five years, McLeay won a 12-round decision over George Jerome at the Alsan Convention Centre in Calgary on February 27, 1977, to claim the bogus Western Canada heavyweight crown and elevate himself to the top of the CBF's short list of challengers for my title.

We met eight months later, on December 8 at the CNE Coliseum in Toronto. I think I trained for about 20 minutes—which is 18 minutes longer than the fight lasted. The Canadian Press described it as "the most mismatched title bout in Canadian boxing history."

I hurt McLeay with the first punch I landed: a short right hook to the head, just seconds after the opening bell. A minute later I backed him into his corner and threw a five-punch flurry that dropped him to his knees. He beat the count (barely), but was wobbling badly as I drove him back across the ring with left hooks. The last one, a right uppercut, dumped him between the bottom two ropes, where he teetered for a couple of seconds before dropping completely out of the ring and landing on the press table. He ended up on the floor, then got to his feet and started walking away from the ring in a northwesterly direction. I remember thinking it was like he was headed to the airport. It was all over at 2:24 of Round 1.

PART
FOUR

POST-

FIGHT

AS I STATED AT THE BEGINNING OF THIS BOOK, what's happened to my family and me since I left boxing has been a personal holocaust. Add up every punch I ever took, multiply the total by 10,000 and it wouldn't come close to equaling the pain of losing Jesse, Georgie Lee, Stevie and Lynne to drugs and suicide.

Physical pain is one thing; you suck it up, you endure, you heal. Emotional pain is something entirely different. I don't think anything compares to being beaten down emotionally, because being punched in the heart and soul is a thousand times worse than being punched in the head.

Even though nearly 30 years have passed since the nightmare started, in my heart it feels like yesterday. I'm constantly reminded of that.

Jesse's drug problem started after he had a dirt bike accident in May of 1984, just a few weeks after his 20th birthday. He wiped out while braking the wrong way, and the crash tore off his left kneecap. The complicated surgery to reattach it involved removing a piece of muscle from his left thigh and reconnecting the tendons and ligaments, after which his doctor prescribed Demerol for the pain. But a week later the same doctor (our next-door neighbor) took Jesse off the powerful painkiller. I didn't know it at the time, but Lynne asked for the prescription to be canceled because she was afraid Demerol was too addictive. My son was then put on Tylenol 3 for a few weeks, but it didn't help. I remember seeing him sitting on his bed, rocking back and forth with both hands cupped over his knee. Even though I had no idea how much he was hurting, I thought he'd be okay.

Not long after his surgery, Jesse went to a party in Toronto's east end. He complained to someone about the pain in his knee, and that someone replied that he had something that would help. That was my son's introduction to heroin.

Four months later, before I fully realized that I had one heroin addict under my roof, I had three of them. Georgie Lee and Steven were hooked, too. *Bing, bing, bing* . . . just like that. But I was oblivious. My life was very chaotic at the time because Lynne and I had separated. When that happens, when you don't have somebody to talk to about problems with your kids, sometimes you don't see the red flags. For the most part I was walking around like I was deaf, dumb and blind. I had no idea they were routinely shooting up in the basement of our house.

Jesse took his mother's absence extra hard because he believed it was his fault that she left. It wasn't. Lynne had had issues—mostly with Georgie Lee—for a long time before that, but never with Jesse. Everything came to a head the night she kicked Georgie Lee out of the house shortly after he came home from another stint in prison. He was drinking heavily again, and she wouldn't stand for it. The only problem was that Lynne had the same affliction. With all due respect, she needed help every bit as much as Georgie Lee did. "Do as I say and not as I do." That was her inflexible stance. I told her that she and Georgie Lee should go to Alcoholics Anonymous meetings together. She didn't like that. She promptly kicked him out of the house and I just as quickly let him back. But it was the lull before the storm.

The very next day, Saturday around noon, as I recall, Lynne announced that lunch was ready. As I left the kitchen to walk into the dining room, I looked up to my left and saw a 6-foot oar in flight with the sharp side of the blade headed towards the top part of my unprotected skull. Crack! Twin rivulets of blood seeped into my eye sockets, as I searched for a towel to staunch the flow of claret.

And in order to maintain a sense of calm and order while under extreme duress, I waved a castigating finger in my wife's face. With the panache of Paul Newman playing Cool Hand Luke, all the while resisting the temptation to knock her for a loop, I proudly announced, "Now Lynne . . . that wasn't nice!"

That same day, I gave her 14 grand to rent a townhouse nearby so she could stay with our daughter, our granddaughter Rachel and our daughter-in-law Jackie for a year in an all-female home. She moved out the next day.

I didn't realize how much Jesse misunderstood the situation until one evening when I woke up close to midnight. As I looked up at the hallway window, I saw a sliver of light that looked like it was coming from the garage. I was curious, so I went out and opened the door. What I saw froze my blood: Jesse was standing on a chair, trying to throw a noose over a beam.

"What the hell are you doing? Are you crazy?" I shouted. I remember feeling like my heart was pounding so loudly that I had to really yell, thinking I was only seconds away from seeing my son die right in front of me. Jesse looked scared and confused, but eventually we both calmed down enough that he was able to tell me how upset he was about his mother leaving.

My youngest son's sensitivity was evident from the time he was a little kid. I remember when he was about five years old, I took him fishing at a stocked pond in the town of Orangeville, just north of Toronto. The first time Jesse hooked one, he excitedly ran around the pond with a huge grin on his face. That was the start of his lifelong love affair with fishing and the outdoors. Years later, when other kids his age were more enamored with *Playboy*, Jesse's preferred reading material was *Field & Stream* and *Outdoor Life*.

Jesse got into trouble a few times and went to jail as a young offender for something he didn't do. Regardless of the circumstances, he always seemed to be on the wrong side of the law—a pattern that was set the first time he got arrested.

It started one afternoon when Steven, who was 16 at the time, was out walking with his girlfriend, not far from the house. Jesse, who was 12, was kind of tagging along behind. The three of them were minding their own business when another kid, about Stevie's age, started hassling the girl about tossing a pop bottle on the grass. Bottles on the boulevard were a common sight in the neighborhood, so Stevie told the guy he was wrong, that his girlfriend wasn't responsible.

Well, the argument escalated to the point where the two of them started to wrestle. When they fell backwards on the pavement, Stevie hit his head so hard that he was groggy and couldn't defend himself. When the other kid grabbed Stevie by the hair and started pounding his head on the pavement,

Jesse screamed at him to stop. When he didn't, Jesse smashed a bottle and threw it at him.

The throw was accurate enough that the bottle cut the kid's face. He immediately released his grip on Stevie and took off, howling in pain. Meanwhile, someone had called an ambulance for Stevie, who was unconscious. He was taken to Etobicoke General Hospital, while the other kid went to Humber Memorial to get his face patched up.

A short while later, after a couple of police officers interviewed the kid, they showed up at the house, demanding to talk to Jesse. He wasn't home, so I told them to come back the following afternoon. I also informed them that Stevie was still at Etobicoke General if they wanted to get his side of the story.

When the same two cops returned the next afternoon, I let them in and told them I'd get Jesse, who was downstairs. Instead of waiting, they handed me a pink slip of paper: a notice that 12-year-old Jesse Miles Chuvalo was formally charged with assault. I was dumbfounded. "You're charging my son based on what the other kid said?" All I got was a blank stare. "Did you speak to my other son, the one who's still in hospital after being knocked unconscious?"

"No," one of the officers replied. "We don't have to."

I went insane. There's no other word for it. We were standing in the kitchen, and I actually jumped up on the counter, which was about four feet high, and started screaming every obscenity in the book at the two cops. "Get the fuck out of here before I rip your fucking heads off." If they'd chosen to pull their guns, I would've been dead. Instead, they turned around and vamoosed out the front door.

Jesse and Georgie Lee applauded my stand—"Way to go,

Pops, way to go!"—but it marked the start of a very acrimonious relationship between my family and the Toronto police department that lasted for years. I got pulled over so often, you'd think I was Al Capone. The assumption was that if my kids were troublemakers, I was responsible. And it only got worse when Jesse's case went to court and the judge told the cops they'd arrested the wrong kid. It was one of the few times my son ever got off. (By the way, over the years my relationship with the police gradually improved, and I'm happy to be on very good terms with them today.)

About a year after that incident, Jesse had another serious scrape with the law following a fight with a 27-year-old who was 5 foot 10 and about 270 pounds. It started when Jesse and another kid, who was a few years older, got into a fight in the parking lot of a nearby apartment complex after the kid made a snide remark about my son's scarred mouth. Jesse was working him over pretty good when the big guy jumped in and clamped a headlock on him. The guy yelled, "Call the police, I'm making a citizen's arrest!" to a couple of girls who were standing nearby, but in the meantime he was squeezing Jesse's neck so tightly that my son started choking.

According to the girls and another eyewitness, Jesse pleaded for the guy to quit choking him. "If you don't stop squeezing, I'm going to stick you," he said. When the guy didn't stop, Jesse took a penknife out of his pocket and stuck him.

That did the trick. The guy released his grip and took off. He subsequently went to the hospital for repairs (the knife blade only went in about half an inch), and he gave a statement to the cops in which he described "a young assailant with a scarred mouth." Based on that description and the location of the fight, the police put two and two together. In short order, my son was arrested and taken into custody.

The case went to trial and I was livid when Jesse was sentenced to five years in a young offenders' detention center a hundred miles away in Bowmanville, Ontario, but I shouldn't have been too surprised. Just before court started, a French-Canadian security guard spoke to me to inform me that he had passed by the judge's chambers earlier and overheard the police talking about my son in a very negative fashion. In his strong accent, the guard said, "Your son—he go bye-bye!" He was right. My recently turned 13-year-old son was found guilty. To put it bluntly, the judge simply refused to consider testimony of eight eyewitnesses—seven girls and an impartial adult male, all of whom said that Jesse had only resorted to using his penknife after the beefy interloper ignored repeated pleas to stop choking him. "I choose not to believe them," the judge wrote in his ruling. "The victim was assaulted without provocation."

Jesse went into custody and was sent to Sick Kids hospital for a psychiatric assessment before sentencing, in accordance with the court ruling. I was asked to attend the interview but it didn't go as well as I might have hoped. In the psychiatrist's view, since my son was found guilty of assault without provocation, he was obviously looking for a sense of remorse but he wasn't getting any. Jesse still stuck to his story that he was being choked and he had to resort to stabbing the massive 270-pound complainant to save his own skin. Jesse basically told the psychiatrist that he wasn't guilty of assault without provocation; he was guilty of saving his own life. I bolstered my son's argument by totally agreeing with him. That proved to be the straw that broke the camel's back.

In his report filed to the court, the judge described me as an interfering parent supporting the outlaw stance of a threatening menace to society. He also recommended that I shouldn't be allowed to visit my son in jail for at least six months. Fortunately for me, the superintendent at the Bowmanville Training School saw things my way after a couple of aborted visits and I was allowed to visit Jesse on a regular weekly basis, much to my delight (and Jesse's). Although he'd fallen way behind in school (he told me the extent of "learning" at Bowmanville was discussing the previous night's hockey scores), he was determined to catch up. He went on to record the highest IQ of any student in the remedial high school diploma program he registered in, and after graduating he set his sights on going to college to fulfill his dream of becoming a game warden.

That dream died after Jesse's accident on the dirt bike.

Even after I found out he was using heroin, in a lot of ways I was still clueless. What did I know about kicking the stuff? I told myself my son was tough enough to quit, but when I think back, did I really believe he could accomplish that without help, without rehab, without really wanting to? I was so ignorant and stupid about not understanding how god-awful and all-powerful that drug is that I thought he could beat it without any real intervention on my part.

Once again, it was a case of me being oblivious to the obvious. From the outset, Lynne knew what we could be dealing with, going back to when she asked the doctor to take Jesse off Demerol because it was so addictive. But I never considered the awful progression as our son tried to cope with his pain. I never in a million years thought it would eventually lead him to heroin. And once he was hooked, it was just a matter of time before Georgie Lee and Steven followed. Jesse was the youngest of the three, but he had the strongest personality. In retrospect I can rationalize that it was pain that brought him to that horrible choice, but his brothers didn't have that excuse.

On February 18, 1985, Lynne and I took the family out for dinner at a neighborhood steak house. We'd recently started seeing more of each other, and it looked like we might be able to patch things up and get back together. Lynne was happy and relaxed, and I remember feeling good about having everyone together again. Well, almost everyone. Mitch was in Guelph, going to school, and Jesse said he wanted to stay home. It was still a crowded table, with Vanessa, Georgie Lee, Stevie, his wife, Jackie, and their daughter, Rachel, and we spent a nice evening catching up with what was happening in each other's lives. When it was time to say goodnight, Lynne and the girls went back to her place and Georgie Lee and Stevie went home with me.

What happened next changed my life—and the lives of every member of my family—forever. Georgie Lee was the first one in the house, and in a matter of seconds I heard him shouting, "Pops! Pops! Something's wrong! Jesse's sleeping, but he's making funny noises. He's on the floor."

When I ran into the bedroom I saw a .22-caliber rifle lying near Jesse and a pool of blood on the floor. He was making a noise like he was snoring.

In my ignorance about what to do, I grabbed the phone and called for an ambulance. Then I called the doctor who lived next door. He refused to come over because of the gun. And it took 45 minutes for the ambulance to arrive! My son never had a chance. He might have still been alive when I made those calls, but in the meantime his lungs filled with blood.

Jesse was dead on arrival at Humber Memorial Hospital—the same hospital we had driven to after Lynne gave birth to him on the front seat of the car 20 years earlier. Our son was too early to be born there and too late to die there. The attending physician walked up to me and said, "He's gone."

It was like a bolt out of the blue. The ache and the overwhelming sense of loss that crushed my heart at that moment will always be with me. I lost my son in the cruelest way possible, and like anyone else who has ever gone through such a horrible ordeal I couldn't help feeling that I failed him. I knew Jesse was an addict, but in my stupid, naive way, it never occurred to me that he would die. Somehow, I felt he would be okay—but he wasn't. The unimaginable despair of being an addict made him lodge that rifle barrel against the roof of his mouth and pull the trigger. And when Jesse died, I knew my other two addicts would die one day, too. It was just a question of time.

It's been nearly three decades, but not a day goes by that I don't think of Jesse. Ever since he died, I can't go to sleep without having a light on. Darkness concentrates my misery, like I'm suffocating.

Other reminders of who he was and what he meant to those who knew and loved him sometimes come from the most unexpected sources.

In the fall of 2008, my pal Chuck "Spider" Jones was working out at a Toronto gym when a stranger approached and asked if he could get a message to me. After introducing himself as Paul Allman, the guy handed over a book, a note and a photograph. The items ended up in Spider's desk for a couple of years, but in the fall of 2010, at a press conference for a boxing event in Mississauga, he took me aside and gave them to me.

The book was *And No Birds Sang* by Canadian author Farley Mowat. The photo was of Jesse, taken decades earlier on a school field trip to Arizona and New Mexico. In the note, Allman wrote that he and Jesse had been friends since they were 14.

"One day at school, between classes, Jesse was reading a book that looked interesting and I wanted to read it as well," Allman wrote. "I asked if I could borrow it when he completed it. Jesse agreed, but cautioned me that it was a gift from his grandparents and I better not lose it. Well, after all these years, here it is. Please cherish this book as I have. Not a day goes by without a thought for Jesse. The picture is how I remember my friend."

I was stunned. I think the photo was taken around 1980. Jesse looks about 16—and happy. During that particular field trip, after getting into some kind of tiff with one of the adult chaperones, he took off from the group. Angry and upset as he was, he still somehow remembered that former light heavyweight champ Bob Foster was a sheriff in Albuquerque. Bob had fought on the undercard of my third bout with Robert Cleroux in Montreal on August 8, 1961, but as much as I admired his talent over the years, he was never more than a casual acquaintance. Still, Jesse had heard me say many times that Bob was one of the greatest light heavyweights in boxing history—and a nice guy, too.

I was really surprised that Jesse had the wherewithal to contact Foster. Thankfully, Bob smoothed things over with the chaperone and talked my son into rejoining the class. Years later, after Jesse died, I got a chance to thank Bob in person when we ran into each other at the International Boxing Hall of Fame in Canastota, New York.

I still choke up when I look at that photo, but I feel blessed to have it. I just regret that I've never been able to track down

Paul Allman to thank him for his kind gesture. I'd like him to know how grateful I am.

❖   ❖   ❖

IF Georgie Lee and Steven weren't full-blown addicts before Jesse's death, it didn't take them long afterward. They'd both already spent a lot of time behind bars for robbing drugstores to get the pills they craved when they couldn't buy heroin, and after their brother died, their quest for smack became all-consuming.

When they had money my sons would hook up with a dealer in the bar of what was then the Parkdale Hotel, a skid row dive near where I once trained at the Toronto Athletic Club. Stevie later told me that as soon as the guy showed them the white stuff in the palm of his hand, just looking at it, in the flash of one single second he and his brother would both crap their pants. With feces running down their legs, my sons would hand over their dough and amble into the bathroom. Once inside, they'd roll up their shirtsleeves, heat up the white stuff in a teaspoon, suck it up in a syringe and shoot it into a waiting vein. Only then would my handsome sons clean themselves off.

I get sick to my stomach every time I tell that story to young people in my presentations at schools, because I realize all of them (and now everyone reading this book) will harbor images of my sons shooting heroin into their veins with excrement still lumped in their pants. It's very painful for me to talk about Steven and Georgie Lee that way, but if it helps deglamorize drug use, it's worth it. In the minds of some kids, the drug-induced deaths of rock stars and actors like John Belushi, River

Phoenix, Janis Joplin and Jimi Hendrix are cool. In movies like *Pulp Fiction* and *Scarface*, the drug lifestyle is portrayed as sexy and cool. I call it a seduction of imagery, because the movies never show addicts crapping their pants.

My sons bought into that seduction—and that's why I think they would want me to talk about it truthfully. In the beginning, they didn't know they would start shaking and sweating at the anticipation of another hit, or that they would get so excited at the sight of heroin that they would soil themselves; nobody does. I don't think anyone who's not an addict can imagine what it would be like to covet something so strongly that when you see the object of your desire, you lose total control of your bodily functions. Only drugs can make you do that.

Both of my sons overdosed again and again, but during the two-month stretch from mid-December 1986 to February 12, 1987, Stevie OD'd 15 times—including once at a police station. Can you imagine? By definition an overdose is when you ingest enough drugs either orally or intravenously that you'll die without proper medical intervention, so it's a miracle he didn't kill himself long before it actually happened.

Fifteen minutes before midnight on New Year's Eve, 1986, I was streaking across Toronto with Steven overdosing on the front seat beside me. We were headed to the Addiction Research Foundation (ARF), a renowned drug treatment facility with an infirmary. When I burst through the front door with him slung over my shoulder, the first person I saw was the attending night nurse, Joanne O'Hara. She had previously worked with Lynne at Northwestern Hospital and had sought solace from my wife after losing a daughter to sudden infant death syndrome.

Joanne told me to carry Stevie to the infirmary, where she stripped off his clothes, put him on a cot and covered him with a sheet. A minute or two later a doctor showed up, but his prognosis wasn't very hopeful: "Mr. Chuvalo, we will work on your son and try to revive him," he said. "If we are successful, we'll either keep him here or move him to a hospital downtown. Come back in 30 minutes."

When I returned half an hour later, Joanne was waiting in the foyer.

"How's Steven?" I asked.

"He's not here," she said.

"What are you talking about?"

"We revived him and propped him up on the edge of the bed. All of a sudden he punched the doctor and knocked him down, then he grabbed some clothes, got half-dressed and took off."

What she was telling me didn't seem possible; there was a foot of snow outside and it was 20 degrees below freezing. I went to the infirmary to see what my son had left behind: a pair of work boots, one sock, undershorts, undershirt, a heavy bomber jacket, gloves, a toque and a scarf. That meant that all he had on was one sock, a pair of jeans and a short-sleeved nylon shirt. And I knew he'd be on the hunt for more drugs—if he didn't freeze to death first.

I went to every hellhole I could think of downtown, but there was no sign of Stevie. After a couple of hours, I gave up and dejectedly went home. That's where I found him. He was unconscious, stretched out face-first on the floor. At the tip of his outstretched fingers was a half-empty bottle of Valium. Another OD.

This time I took him to Humber Memorial, and they revived him. A couple of days later Stevie told me that when they first revived him at ARF, all he could think about when he saw the doctor was how to get the drugs he'd stashed at home from a previous heist. That's how powerful his craving was. After he knocked the doctor down and made his escape, my son walked and ran 17 miles in 20-below zero temperatures just to get those pills—all the while passing people who thought he was just another drunken New Year's celebrant.

Two and a half weeks later, on January 17 (Muhammad Ali's 45th birthday), at four o'clock in the morning, I found Stevie on top of a snowbank just a block from the house. A couple of hours earlier, my daughter-in-law Jackie called to say that he had taken off in the middle of the night, so once again I went into search mode. By this time, me bursting through the emergency entrance at Etobicoke General shouting, "Overdose! Overdose!" had become a common occurrence, but on this occasion my son's exposure to the elements made it more serious. After seeing his ashen face, the nurses immediately started cutting off his soaking-wet clothes with razor blades. As they placed him naked on a stretcher and wheeled him into the ER, I started to pray.

After a few minutes one of the nurses came out and told me that Stevie's body temperature was so low that if it dropped just one more degree, he would die. I braced myself for the worst . . . and kept praying. After what seemed like an eternity, his body temperature started to rise and he pulled out of danger.

The last of Stevie's 15 overdoses in that two-month period happened on February 12, 1987. I'd made the 45-minute drive to Hamilton early that morning to do a real estate transaction, and on my way home I was listening to the one-o'clock news on the car radio when I heard my name in the lead story: "The sons of former Canadian heavyweight boxing champion George Chuvalo—George Lee Chuvalo and Steven Chuvalo—were apprehended and arrested this morning for robbing Armour Chemists, a drugstore at the corner of 401 Highway and Islington Avenue . . ."

In retrospect, I should never have left Steven and Georgie Lee home alone. When I left the house that morning, they were wired, badly in need of heroin. Not having any money, they opted for their second choice: prescription drugs like Valium, Seconal and Fiorinal. They put a hatchet and a butcher knife in a gym bag and walked two miles to the store. When they stormed in, brandishing their weapons, the terrified druggist fled to the back of the shop while a female clerk calmly stood her ground as my sons filled the gym bag with jars of pills from the shelves.

By the time the police arrived on the scene, Stevie and Georgie Lee had already fled down an embankment and followed the meandering course of the Humber River for a couple of miles to make their escape—all the while dipping into the bag and swallowing handfuls of pills. They finally made their way to a bus stop but had no money for tickets. After selling some pills to a guy at the stop, they bought some bottled water, got on the bus . . . and started swilling down more pills. Ten minutes—and three stops—later, they stepped off and promptly collapsed on the sidewalk, one brother neatly stacked on top of the other. It would have been cartoonish, like something out of Laurel and Hardy or the Keystone Kops, if it wasn't so pathetic.

That stunt earned Stevie and Georgie Lee sentences of two years less a day at the Ontario Correctional Institute in

Brampton. In a way it was a relief, because OCI had a very good reputation for rehab, and I thought they would really get some help kicking their habit. The two of them had been incarcerated so many times (the total eventually reached 23 different facilities), but they'd never made a serious effort at rehab before. I thought this might be the time.

One morning seven months after my sons robbed Armour Chemists, Lynne got a telephone call from a sergeant with the Toronto police department. He called her at Northwestern Hospital, where she was an electrocardiogram technician.

"Your son George left his wallet here at the station a few months ago, Mrs. Chuvalo. Would you like to come down and pick it up?" After Lynne said she would come during lunchtime, the sergeant said, "No, no . . . come after four." My wife thought that was a little odd, but said she would be there.

When Lynne showed up and asked for the sergeant by name, he greeted her with: "Mrs. Chuvalo, do you have $300?"

"No, why?"

"For outstanding traffic tickets," said the cop. "You are now under arrest."

It was pretty obvious why my wife had been instructed not to come to the station until after four o'clock: in those days all the banks were closed by that time, and ATMs weren't around yet. If being placed under arrest wasn't humiliating enough, Lynne was told she would have to submit to a full body search. She started screaming and hollering, thinking about how Stevie and Georgie Lee had been in that same station, and now she was there too, being horribly mistreated. She was locked in a cell, but before anything worse could happen, a younger cop saw what was going on and intervened.

The whole episode was my fault. I was the one who got the tickets, but the car was registered in Lynne's name. After she used her one phone call to tell me what happened, I contacted my lawyer, who had enough cash on him to get her released a few hours later.

Georgie Lee came out of jail for the last time on October 27, 1993. It was three weeks shy of his 31st birthday, and he'd already spent almost a third of his life behind bars. Since Jesse's death, Georgie Lee had often talked about overdosing so that he could be with his brother in heaven, and he'd once even slashed his wrists, but on that day, when he came home from Warkworth Institution, a medium-security facility near Campbellford, Ontario, he looked and sounded better than he had in years. While he'd never been overly devoted to exercise on the outside, my son worked out constantly in the joint. He was solid and muscular, thanks to lifting weights and hitting the heavy bag, and his demeanor gave Lynne and me renewed hope that he'd finally cleaned up his act. I remember his mother prepared some delicious homemade soup on the day Georgie Lee came home. He was happy and smiling as she hugged and hovered over him.

That's my last recollection of my son alive, eating that soup.

Three nights later, Georgie Lee was in a Parkdale flophouse with another guy and a girl who, like him, had both been in and out of jail multiple times. Georgie Lee overdosed, but when the paramedics showed up, he said, "Fuck off!" He'd rented the room for just one night, and the front desk called at 11:30 the following morning to tell him to get out. By 11:45, he was dead. They found him seated in a chair, wearing only a pair of under-shorts, with a syringe sticking out of his left arm. (My son died on Halloween, October 31, 1993, the same day as actor River

Phoenix, who collapsed from drug-induced heart failure outside a West Hollywood nightclub.)

When I got the call to go to the morgue, I was in a daze. And when I got down there and they pulled Georgie Lee out of a filing cabinet for corpses and then put him on the slab, it caught me off guard. I was angry, upset and crying, all at the same time. When they pulled him out like that, it was as if he was some sort of meaningless commodity, like he had no value. It hit me like a ton of bricks.

When I got back to the house, Lynne was beside herself with grief. In a barely audible voice, she said, "Phone my mother." I dialed the number, and when my mother-in-law answered, I told her, "Lynne wants to speak to you." My wife broke the news that Georgie Lee had passed away, then all of sudden she stopped talking and hung up.

"What's the matter?" I asked.

Lynne answered like she was in a trance. "My mother said she won't come to see me now . . . she'll see me at the funeral."

At that moment I thought to myself, "What mother in the world would do that? What mother in the world wouldn't walk a hundred miles over broken glass to comfort her daughter over the loss of a second son?"

My wife had had issues with her mother for years—something that was probably at least partially responsible for Lynne becoming a heavy drinker by the time she was in her early 20s.

I remember one day when our sons were just little guys, everything was perfectly normal and we were all just enjoying being together. Then all of a sudden Lynne smashed her back up against the wall in the hallway, crying uncontrollably. When I asked what was wrong, she replied, "My mother doesn't love me." Then she started pouring out her heart: "Look where my mother lives, about a mile away. She hardly ever comes to see us, yet she'll take a 90-minute bus ride to go see Patsy [Lynne's sister] and then stay with her for the weekend."

I'd never considered that. But when I called my mother-in-law to express my concern, she said, "Oh, I love both my daughters the same. Lynne is just imagining that."

"Maybe that's so," I told her, "but actions speak louder than words. You're never here and you never want to spend time with her. How is she supposed to know that you love her?"

I remember replaying that conversation in my head after Georgie Lee's funeral, when Lynne's mother didn't come back to our house. When I called her to ask why she didn't come to our house, she simply said, "I went to Patsy's to comfort her." Unbelievable.

It was so hard to be with Lynne after Georgie Lee died because every time we started to talk, we'd start to cry. We were on automatic. As a result of our being so upset in each other's company, we literally couldn't look at each other. At night, I slept in our bedroom while she slept across the hall in Jesse's room . . . in the same room and the same bed where he'd shot himself eight years earlier.

In the wee hours of the morning on November 4, four days after Georgie Lee died, Lynne came into our bedroom to forage through her hope chest. We didn't say anything to each other. I didn't know it at the time, but she was looking for Fiorinal that our sons had stolen in a previous drugstore heist. Ironically, she'd saved the pills in the hope chest for the day she had no hope.

Before I left at 7:30 for an early appointment, I peeped

inside Jesse's room to see her lying on the bed in a burnt-orange tracksuit, with her backside facing me. "I'll see you later, doll," I said.

When I arrived back home at 1:47 p.m. (I remember looking at the clock as soon as I walked through the door of the house), she was on her back clutching the Holy Bible and the cremated remains of Jesse. A suicide note, written on the back of a grocery list, was on the table. She had written, "I looked for love and couldn't find any."

That was it—or so I thought. It wasn't until very recently—October 17, 2012, to be exact—that I suddenly remembered that Lynne had been lying on her back when I returned home that afternoon, which means she was probably still alive when I left in the morning.

"Steven, Mom's dead!" I yelled.

My son bolted from the kitchen through the long hallway we had in that house, smashing through the front door like a fullback busting through the line. Screaming his pain into the wind, he started kicking over garbage cans. I'll never forget that tormented scream, born from the realization of having to live with the pain and guilt of losing not only two brothers, but now his mother. It only plunged him deeper into the abyss. At Lynne's funeral three days later, Steven was stoned on heroin.

It's taken years for me to come to grips with my wife's suicide, and while I can't condone it, I can understand it. I think a woman feels pain differently than a man, and I think a mother feels pain differently than a father. A woman has a nine-month head start on loving a child, so the relationship between a mother and child is fundamentally different than between a father and child. Feeling the pain that only a mother can feel, Lynne simply couldn't bear it any longer. First Jesse, now Georgie Lee. It was too much.

To be honest, at that moment I felt totally abandoned. Despite all our problems, despite the turmoil and the separations, I loved Lynne and I know that she loved me. When she died, I lost my best friend.

The deaths of Georgie Lee and Lynne four days apart put me in the lowest point of my life. I was walking around like I was in a coma. Stevie told me later that I was in bed for a month and a half, but I don't remember. Friends apparently came around to visit, and I must have gotten out of bed once in a while to eat and go to the bathroom, but for the most part that period is a total blank.

What I do remember is seeing Joanne O'Hara at Lynne's funeral. My wife had been a comfort to Joanne after she lost her 10-week-old daughter to sudden infant death syndrome, and Lynne had introduced us at work some 15 years earlier. Shortly before Christmas, when I was back on my feet again, I happened to run into Joanne on the street and she asked if it would be all right if she and her kids—11-year-old Jesse and four-year-old Ruby—dropped by the house for coffee on the day after Christmas. It turned out to be a very nice visit, after which I asked if she would mind driving me to the homes of a couple of buddies, since I didn't have a license at the time.

We had coffee the next few mornings, and before long I realized that Joanne was making me feel alive again. Still, I felt uneasy because Lynne had been dead just eight weeks. I thought to myself, "You're not supposed to be feeling like this." I was debating the situation with myself like I was two different people. But there was no denying I liked being with

Joanne. She knew the pain of losing a child, and as an RN she was used to helping calm down people who might otherwise go off the deep end. At the time, she seemed like the only person in the world that could do that for me.

Joanne and I eloped on January 27, 1994, in Wilson, New York. We didn't tell anybody. There was absolutely nothing going on between us before Lynne died, but in the weeks that followed, Joanne's kindness, empathy and love saved my life. It was as simple as that. If people take issue, I can't help it—but I understand. I couldn't help marrying her; Joanne was my pillar of strength, the anchor I needed when nothing else in my life was making sense.

I was 56 when I got married for the second time. Who the hell falls in love at 56? That's the age when you're just supposed to be looking for a companion, but until you've been in my shoes, you can't really understand. After all that I'd lost, I needed something strong and positive to hold on to. Joanne was like my *Celestine Prophecy*, which is a beautiful book by James Redfield about spiritual awakening and the people you meet for a reason.

Exactly one year later to the day, we got married for the second time in a Catholic ceremony in Toronto. To be honest, I felt guilty that our elopement happened so quickly after Lynne's death, but I never for a second doubted that it was the right decision. I knew that most people—especially Mitchell and Vanessa—wouldn't understand (they still don't), but if it wasn't for Joanne, I would not have survived. And you know what? I know in my heart that Lynne would have been okay with it, too. She would have understood.

To be honest, my decision to marry Joanne came down to

a choice between perhaps killing myself sometime later in the '90s, or being the way I am now: living and being as happy and as normal as I could hope to be. Nobody can accuse her of being a gold digger, either, because just before we were married, I lost my house and we had to move in with her mother. I was totally broke when the Croatian Credit Union foreclosed on my mortgage after I'd missed a couple payments and they hadn't given me enough time to find a new lender. It only added insult to injury when my furniture ended up being piled on the front lawn for everyone to see. Financially, I was down and nearly out, but that was the least of my worries. Joanne's love and support brought me back to the land of the living.

Meanwhile, with Stevie back behind bars at OCI for yet another drugstore robbery, I once again held out hope that this might be the time he'd get himself straight. Part of me still believed that was possible—but only by him being locked up and getting treatment. We'd been down this road before when I'd gotten Georgie Lee into rehab, but it only lasted a couple of weeks; he couldn't stick it out. Still, Steven did pretty well at Ontario Correctional Institute. He looked healthy and happy, and for a time it seemed like he had a real shot at beating his addiction. He was doing so well, in fact, that in the fall of 1995 a camera crew from the Canadian Broadcasting Corporation's *The Fifth Estate* shot footage of me visiting him in jail as part of a documentary about the decimation of my family.

Today, nearly 20 years later, I still use that video to open the presentation I've made more than 1,500 times at schools, juvenile detention centers and other facilities all across Canada, parts of the U.S. and Europe on behalf of my Fight Against Drugs foundation.

The *Fifth Estate* segment first aired on December 5, and two days later I returned to OCI, where Stevie and I talked about touring the country together to tell our story after his release the following August. He wanted to talk about education, about self-esteem, about imagery. He wanted people to know that if he could have seen himself so out of control in the future, he would never have turned to drugs.

How out of control? Stevie once robbed three drugstores in 45 minutes. And when he wasn't breaking into pharmacies, he sought out alternatives. One night in Guelph, after he ran away from Mitchell's house, we found him lurking outside the animal hospital with a big rock in his hand. He said he wanted to bust in to steal the tranquilizer drugs they used on wild dogs, cats and raccoons.

When my son told me that, I could feel hot tears streaming down my cheeks.

When the kids see Steven up on the screen during my presentation, he doesn't fit their preconceived notion of an addict. He doesn't come across as a kid who'd crap his drawers at the very sight of heroin or a kid who'd been stabbed by another prisoner while doing hard time behind bars for robbing drugstores. He's handsome and articulate, and he speaks from the heart. "My father's never given up hope," he says. "When he says to me, 'You know, kid, I need you to be well, I need you to be okay so that I'm okay,' he's saying it with conviction, and he's always in tears when he says things like that. It hits home to me now, and I say to myself, 'Man, I've got to get better. I've got to be well for him and the rest of my family.'"

My son also talks about how he felt that he and Georgie Lee and Jesse all had a sense of worthlessness, and how he attributed that to a lack of education. A lot of that was my fault. Mitchell was an outstanding student and Vanessa was real good in school, too. Stevie did okay, but when he wanted to quit high school, I let him . . . because I thought he'd go right back. You know when he went back? When he was in jail. On the outside, he couldn't get it together. His marriage was through, he wasn't welcome back at his house, so it just got easier and easier for his addiction to win out. But behind bars, when he could concentrate on learning, Stevie did very well. He completed high school inside Collins Bay Penitentiary, and he was working on getting a BA in Russian Literature from Queen's University. It's hard to imagine my little drug addict son being so enthralled with such somber stuff from the likes of Dostoyevsky, Tolstoy and Solzhenitsyn, but he loved those guys.

I still have a hard time watching that video in its entirety. I usually just stick around for the first 30 seconds to make sure it's running properly, then I come back in the last minute or two when I see my son in jail. At that moment, I think about my young audience, and how they view the image up on the screen. My son looks like he could be in anyone's family. As they say in Spanish, he's *mui simpático*—very empathetic.

On August 17, 1996—exactly nine months and 15 days after the video was taped—I was in Albuquerque, New Mexico, working the corner for WBO super flyweight champion Johnny Tapia. He was making a title defense against Argentina's Hugo Soto, and the fight was going to be telecast on ABC's *Wide World of Sports* at 5 p.m. Eastern time.

Stevie was looking forward to watching it. Since being released on August 6, he'd been staying at Vanessa's apartment in downtown Toronto. At 1:30 on the day of the fight, Vanessa said she was going to visit some friends in Guelph, 45 minutes away, and that she would be staying overnight. Before she left, she gave her brother $100 and a pack of cigarettes. She took out three, leaving 17.

When Vanessa returned home with a couple of friends at 2:30 the following afternoon, she found a key in the lock of the apartment door. When she saw that, she kind of panicked. She turned the key and the door opened a few inches, but the inside chain was on. When she saw that, my daughter knew what was on the other side. She fled the building.

Two of Vanessa's friends went downstairs and got the superintendent. He came up to the 17th floor and after taking stock of the situation he called the police. Two officers showed up and cut the inside chain. They found Steven, clad in a pair of undershorts, sitting slumped over a desk. The dark indentation on the side of his neck from hitting the edge of the desk made it look almost like his throat was cut. There was a syringe sticking out of his left arm and an unlit cigarette between the first two fingers of his right hand. After he shot the heroin into his vein, before he could light his cigarette, he was dead.

I'm told it took about seven seconds.

After I got off the plane at Pearson International Airport at 4:30 that afternoon, I went through customs with my luggage and headed toward the sliding exit door. On the other side, I saw my driver, Marvin Elkind, alongside Joanne and her son Jesse, who was almost 14. Normally when I come home from a trip my wife is happy to see me, but this time I saw a look of dismay on her face.

"Joanne, what's the matter?" I said.

"We have to talk," she said quietly.

After I repeated the question and she gave the same response, I made it easy for her. I said, "Steven's dead, isn't he." It wasn't a question.

When she nodded her head, I started sobbing uncontrollably.

When you've already lost two sons to heroin, the prospect of losing a third is never that farfetched. During the course of Johnny Tapia's 12-round fight, I remember constantly thinking about Steven. How was he coping? Was he dead or alive? I seemed to ask myself that question 1,000 times over the course of the fight—three minutes a round, 36 minutes, 11 minutes between rounds. Thirty-six plus 11. During those 47 minutes, when I was getting paid to counsel, instruct and motivate Johnny Tapia, little did I know that before the broadcast had even started at five o'clock, my son had already passed away.

When the police checked Vanessa's apartment, they found the pack of cigarettes she'd given Stevie. There were 10 left. He'd started out with 17. That means he smoked six, with the seventh stuck between his fingers when he died. Vanessa gave them to him at 1:30, and I don't think it would have taken him more than a couple of hours to smoke six, so that means by 3:30—four at the latest—my son was already dead.

When I relate that story to my audiences, invariably there's an audible gasp. The kids don't expect that. They expect me to talk about Jesse and Georgie Lee and Lynne, but they don't expect another son—the one who's so alive and so hopeful on the video—to be gone.

When they see that, I hope the message sinks in. They're at the age when they're making some of the most important and monumental decisions of their lives, decisions that will shape their whole future. I talk about how they have to have their radar working, how they have to have their antennas working so they can tune in to what's going on and sort out the truth from all the bullcrap.

✧ ✧ ✧

TODAY, I'm still damaged goods. My remaining kids, Mitchell and Vanessa, are damaged goods. You can't lose a mother and three brothers and not be damaged.

When I wake up in the morning, I think about the kids I don't have anymore. Losing three sons and a wife is like having a wound that never heals. You take medication, try to keep it clean, free of infection . . . but it never gets better. It's always there. Little everyday things, like watching television or reading a book or speaking to an old acquaintance, can remind me of what I've lost, so there's a weird kind of dichotomy in my life.

I only know who I am and what I feel. I go through hell every day—but that doesn't mean I don't still enjoy my life. It doesn't mean I don't turn to mush when I see my grandchildren and they tell me they love me. They mean the world to me, and when I see them, I go nuts.

If I've learned one thing, it's that nobody can survive without love. I'm blessed to be surrounded by people who care about me, and that's what keeps me going. That's what keeps me motivated to do anything.

In my speeches, I always talk about what helps keep people alive, and how we need to have that connection tattooed on our psyche by hearing the words "I love you" from parents, siblings, spouses, our children and our grandchildren. I know it sounds corny, but I always tell kids they should kiss their parents every night before they go to sleep. It's a simple gesture, but it just kind of re-establishes and reconfirms the way we feel about each other. Young people ought to know that a parent or a grandparent really cares about them, and vice-versa.

When I talk about having that in our lives, some of the kids undoubtedly think, "Oh yeah, love—you're not going to bore me with that stuff, are you?" But what else is there? When you have to face adversity—and we all do, from time to time—you need to draw strength from the people that care most about you. And you have to feed off what you feel from others, too. Loving other people gives me strength, and other people loving me gives me strength. Otherwise I wouldn't be here.

And I know it works.

A couple of years ago, after I spoke at a junior high school in Barrie, Ontario, a young man wrote to tell me how he called the cops to report his own brother, who was planning to rob a drugstore to support his habit. The kid said that after hearing me speak he felt compelled to call the police—which is a pretty tough thing to do to your own flesh and blood. But he said he loved his brother and wanted him to live.

It had a happy ending: the kid got help and got off drugs.

It's that kind of feedback that keeps me fighting at 75—and I'm going to keep doing it until I run out of steam.

If I didn't keep fighting, it would be like my sons and my wife died in vain. And I don't ever want to feel that way.

CONTACT: www.fightagainstdrugs.ca

PART
FIVE

JABS

& HOOKS

APPEARING IN MOVIES IS A TIME-HONORED tradition for fighters, dating back to the silent-film era when James J. Corbett starred in *The Midnight Man* and Jess Willard rode shotgun in *The Challenge of Chance,* both of which were released in 1919. From all-time greats like Sugar Ray Robinson, Muhammad Ali and Mike Tyson to journeymen like Jack O'Halloran and Randall "Tex" Cobb, hundreds of pugs have taken the plunge—some more successfully than others.

For me, making movies seemed like a natural extension of being in the ring. When the lights go down and you know that thousands of fans are watching your every move, it's a rush; but at the same time, you have to take care of business to earn their respect and applause. I assume it's the same thing for movie stars.

My modest work on the big screen presented an opportunity to broaden the on-camera experience I'd picked up doing occasional TV appearances after becoming a member of ACTRA (the Alliance of Canadian Cinema, Television and

Radio Artists) at age 18, when I played a referee in a skit on *The Wayne and Shuster Show.*

One of my earliest TV roles was in an episode of *The New Avengers,* alongside dapper Patrick Macnee and the lovely Joanna Lumley. My character ("Huge Man" in the credits—how inspiring!) is killed in a hail of bullets in a Toronto vegetable market. In "The Fighter," an episode of the Canadian cop drama *Night Heat,* I played—surprise—a fighter. On *The Rez* I portrayed an aboriginal cop, while on *Counterstrike* (opposite Simon MacCorkindale and Christopher Plummer), I was again cast as a menacing bad guy. Those were just a few of my more memorable parts.

The TV acting was fun and interesting, but what I enjoyed more was making commercials. Over the years I knocked off several for the local Toronto market—everything from car lots to clothiers—but the real gravy was in national spots. Unlike series TV or movies, where it sometimes takes a day or two to set up a single scene, commercials often require only a few hours to shoot . . . and the checks keep coming as long as the spot is on the air.

I made my first national commercial in 1956, for Prestone antifreeze. I was 19 and didn't even own a car at the time, so it must've been a pretty good acting job! It was a little easier flogging Vicks cough drops (I'd actually used them), and the same held true when Kleenex came calling to feature my nose in testament to the tissue's "fluffy softness." A boxing ring in Winnipeg was the backdrop for my pitch for Sansui stereos, and I ventured into the U.S. market with a Miller Lite beer commercial that ended up paying me around $25,000—more than most of my fights!

My first movie role was pretty gruesome: as George Weiller, I bashed in Elke Sommer's head in the opening scene of *I Miss You, Hugs and Kisses* (1978).

The Weiller character was based on Joe Dinardo, a real-life acquaintance of mine. A former fighter, Dinardo made headlines across Canada during the sensational 1974 murder trial of a Toronto land developer whose wife was bludgeoned to death in the garage of their suburban home. Dinardo shocked the trial when he testified that the woman had offered him $10,000 to break her husband's arms and legs just a week before she was murdered. The husband was ultimately convicted of hiring a hit man to kill his wife and went to prison.

In the movie, the murder scene was shot in a genuine suburban garage, and Elke Sommer (a very nice lady) was the consummate professional, despite all the blood and gore. The "lead pipe" that I so gleefully used to whack her over the head was actually a cardboard tube filled with a mixture of thick red dye (blood) and tapioca (brain matter). It made a hell of a mess, so it's a good thing we managed to nail it on the first take. Other than a few flashback scenes, that was it for me. The rest of *I Miss You, Hugs and Kisses* (a.k.a. *Drop Dead Dearest* on video) is played out in courtroom action and recalls.

In 1979 I was cast in *Stone Cold Dead*, with Richard Crenna, Paul Williams and Winnipeg's Belinda J. Montgomery (fresh off her role as the scientist who saved and mentored merman Patrick Duffy on the TV series *Man from Atlantis*). Crenna portrays a lonely cop on the hunt for a mad sniper. After appearing in a gym scene together, we had a nice chat about boxing and life in general. He was a thoughtful, pleasant guy.

By far my most prominent movie role was as Marky, the barroom brute who arm-wrestles Dr. Seth Brundle (Jeff Goldblum) for the attentions of a hooker (Joy Boushel) in *The Fly* (1986). Director David Cronenberg called me out of the blue to offer the part in what turned out to be a very cool—and very successful—remake of the 1958 sci-fi classic.

Goldblum plays a brilliant but eccentric scientist who woos investigative journalist Veronica Quaife (played by Geena Davis, who would later become his real-life wife) by offering her the scoop on his research in the field of matter teleportation. When Brundle attempts to teleport himself, however, a fly gets trapped in the transmission booth with him and the good doctor eventually morphs into a horrific human/fly hybrid.

My scene with Goldblum was shot at Soupy Campbell's bar in Toronto's east end, and on the day we began filming, my daughter Vanessa and some of her Grade 8 classmates visited the set and met the cast and crew—all of whom were very accommodating.

If I were to critique my performance in *The Fly*, I'd have to say I'm not particularly pleased with it. For one thing, I don't think I sound tough enough or threatening enough in responding to Brundle's challenge. And physically, I probably could have been a little more intimidating—even though Goldblum, at about 6 foot 4, is pretty imposing in his own right.

Jeff was a quiet, studious guy who kept pretty much to himself and nibbled rice cakes between takes. Of course, with all that "fly power" pumping through his veins, his character was much more animated—as becomes obvious when we sit down to arm-wrestle.

It took a week or so for the prop people to manufacture my

prosthetic right "arm," which had phony skin stretched over my real skin from knuckles to wrist. There were translucent tubes with tiny holes attached to my arm under the phony skin, which was perforated to allow fake sweat and blood to seep through as Goldblum's character tightens his grip on my hand.

The scene ends with him twisting my arm so violently that it snaps almost in half. With the bone grotesquely protruding and blood gushing out like a fire hydrant (there was a guy off-camera, frantically working a pump that kept the red stuff flowing), I cut loose with what I shamelessly submit is one of the better bad-guy screams in movie history. Two thumbs up!

For my next few roles—in *Circle Man* (1987), *Prom Night III: The Last Kiss* (1990) and *The Return of Eliot Ness* (1991)—I tried to improve on my performance in *The Fly*.

In *Circle Man* (a.k.a. *Last Man Standing*), I play Maxx, an enforcer/bodyguard for a guy named Napoleon (Michael Copeman) who organizes bare-knuckle cage fights. Besides a few choice bits of dialog, I get to throw my weight around a little. With a great cast featuring Vernon Wells (*The Road Warrior*), William Sanderson (*Newhart*) and former Mr. Universe bodybuilding champ Franco Columbu, it's an engaging movie that's become something of a cult classic. And if you look closely at the crowd milling around the cage for the big finale, you'll spot my buddies Marvin "The Weasel" Elkind and Baldy Chard, a couple of Toronto "collectors" (extortionists is too harsh a term) who were hired as extras.

In *Prom Night III: The Last Kiss*, I'm Mr. Walker, a high school teacher. It was a cute role. In the opening scene, I'm scoffing down a huge sandwich while my students are supposed to be writing an exam. The character is a real jerk, so I yell a lot ("Shut up, asshole!") and whack my desk with a pointer. Later on, I get killed . . . but then come back as a ghoul after punching my way out of a grave. That scene was filmed at one o'clock on a cold, rainy morning in Toronto, and I caught a pretty nasty cold waiting in a sod-covered hole for the director to yell "Action!"

The Return of Eliot Ness was a made-for-TV production starring Robert Stack in a reprise of his long-running role on the classic series *The Untouchables*. The story is set in 1947—15 years after the original—and the plot involves Ness returning to Chicago for the funeral of a former colleague who was murdered after apparently being exposed as corrupt. In real life, Stack was just like the character he made so famous: unflappable, very straight, a little bit stiff . . . but very likable. He told me his father had been a boxing commissioner in California in the 1930s.

With so much else happening in my life, it was another seven years before I had another movie role: a cameo as a ring announcer in *Dirty Work* (1998), a farcical romp about two goofballs (played by Norm Macdonald and Artie Lange) who open a "revenge for hire" business. Directed by Bob Saget (*America's Funniest Home Videos*), it features a star-studded cast that includes Jack Warden, Don Rickles and Chevy Chase. The list of other names making cameo appearances is equally impressive: Chris Farley, John Goodman, Adam Sandler (as Satan), Gary Coleman, Ken Norton . . . and my buddy Mike Anscombe, portraying himself as a news anchor.

That's pretty much it for movie work that I can brag a little about. If anyone remembers the last two films I was in—*In the Dead of Space* (1999) and *Lee's Offering* (2005)—it's only because they're so awful.

In the Dead of Space (the video version is called *Space Fury*) is so bad that my role as Marshall Popov is one of the film's best—and I'm only on screen for about five minutes! In what's probably the best action scene of the whole movie, I ride around on a tank while dodging bullets during a violent skirmish. All the while, I'm puffing on a big cigar and barking out cheesy dialog ("Shoot! Shoot! . . . My men will charge in and destroy you!") in a not-so-convincing Russian accent. Talk about command presence!

As bad as that one was, I thought *Lee's Offering* was worse—although some people have told me it's brilliant *film noir*, whatever that means. All I can say is that I and my buddy, Chuck "Spider" Jones, are the two best actors in the thing, so what does that tell you? At the Toronto premiere, I was so embarrassed that I slunk out before it ended, and the few reviews I read only confirmed that it was a real stinker.

Other than *The Fly*, my movie roles were pretty obscure, so it always amazes me when fans want an autograph on a poster or picture from any of those other films. In fact, I usually ask them for a copy!

On a related note, interviewers sometimes ask me what it's like to be part of pop culture more than four decades after my last fight, and the answer is always the same: great! I'm flattered that a stylized image of my fist crashing into Floyd Patterson's face was used on the covers of a couple of record albums released almost 30 years apart—*Exile on Main Street* by the Rolling Stones (1972) and *Greatest Hits* by Alice in Chains (2001)—and an artistic rendition of that photo was also featured in *Mad* magazine. Speaking of records, my mug graces the CD cover of *Curve,* released by Our Lady Peace in

2012 (I also do a voiceover on the final track), and songs about me are on albums by Colin Linden (*Raised by Wolves*, 1997) and The Lollipop People (*We Need a New F-Word*, 2006).

Another nice tribute came in 2008, when goalie Ray Emery of the National Hockey League's Ottawa Senators had my portrait painted on his mask. Emery's attitude impressed me, too; he didn't take any crap. When guys tried to crash his crease, he'd haul off and belt them. I liked that. I must have autographed a couple dozen replicas of his mask for fans over the next few months.

Whether it is on a goalie mask, a boxing glove or any of the thousand and one other things that people ask to get signed, I inevitably get comments about my signature, which I've been told is one of the more—ahem—*stylish* among fighters. Truth is, I always try to write it with a little flourish: a big G and a big C, with smaller middle letters and a long, curling L that trails down to form the O. Lots of people tell me it reminds them of a speed bag, but that's not something I was consciously aiming for when I came up with it. The "Keep punchin'" inscription that I often include comes from Rocky Marciano. I always thought the way he wrote it looked pretty cool, so I started using it, too.

To be honest, if you'd told me in 1978 that I would still be signing autographs on a daily basis 35 years later, I'd have said you were nuts—but I'm happy to report that it never gets old. It's humbling to be remembered by folks who want that little keepsake, and I would never think of not signing, no matter what.

The only time the autograph thing gets a little taxing is during induction weekend at the International Boxing Hall of Fame in Canastota, New York. Between the new inductees and the regular roster of old-timers who show up each year, the event is a magnet for fight fans and memorabilia collectors from all over the world. I'm invited down every June and I usually bring along my buddies Stevie Graley, Edwin Morales and Murray Greig to help keep track of all the photos and memorabilia thrust my way to be signed, but after three solid days of writing my name over and over again, I can barely grip a pen.

Those marathon autograph sessions also give fans an up-close-and-personal opportunity to snap photos and ask questions. Here are my answers to some of the more common queries, along with some thoughts on other topics that often come up when I'm interviewed:

THE BEST I FACED

FIGHTER: MUHAMMAD ALI

Most people think he was the greatest heavyweight champion of all time, and I wouldn't disagree. Muhammad was the whole package, and he could fight you any and every way. I think if you took every champ from John L. Sullivan right up to the Klitschko brothers and threw them all into a round-robin tournament, Ali would come out the winner. When Muhammad was at his best, none of those other guys could touch him.

BOXER: ALI

He had the quickest hands and quickest feet, which made him very adept at avoiding punches. But as far as power goes, Muhammad's was only so-so. Against guys like Zora Folley and Cleveland Williams he proved he could punch pretty hard if he was properly set, but he never really got set with me.

STRONGEST: GEORGE FOREMAN

I remember getting on the inside against him early in our 1970 fight, and he just shoved me back. Nobody ever did that, before or since. If you stayed close to George you could do okay, but if he made himself some room to pull the trigger, it was usually a short night.

DEFENSE: JOE FRAZIER

He was an expert at bobbing and weaving, and he slipped and countered very well, too, especially in the early part of his career. He moved his head extremely well left to right coming at you, fighting out of a crouch. It's very tough to land a clean shot on a guy who can do that as well as Joe did.

CHIN: ALI

Angelo Dundee told me that I had Muhammad hurt and ready to go in the fifth round of our second fight (1972), in Vancouver. I nailed him right on the point of the chin and he wobbled . . . but I thought he was fooling around. Usually when I hit a guy on the button, something happened. But Ali was able to suck it up and recover.

WHO HIT THE HARDEST?

1) MIKE DEJOHN AND GEORGE FOREMAN (TIE)

DeJohn set a record on the old *Friday Night Fights* with a one-punch KO of Charley Powell in just 47 seconds. Mike was a real sharp banger with a great uppercut and a real good hook. I don't remember a thing about getting hit by his right uppercut early in our 1963 fight, but later, when I watched the film, I saw my knees buckle ever so slightly for a split second. I dropped him three times after that and went on to win a majority decision.

Foreman? Like I always tell people, imagine getting hit by a Mack truck at 50 miles an hour. And that was just his jab!

2) LYNNE CHUVALO

No question, my first wife was the pound-for-pound champ when it came to dishing out big hits. Like all married couples, Lynne and I had our fair share of fights, but most of them never went beyond the yelling stage. I say "most," because on three memorable occasions, she cracked me over the head with—in chronological order—a glass pitcher, a frying pan and . . . an oar!

All of those things hurt, but getting thumped by a heavy glass pitcher was the worst.

It was November 1959, shortly after my bout with Yvon Durelle, and my buddy Chuck Scriver and his girlfriend, Betty, were over at my apartment for a spaghetti and meatball supper. Lynne and I were back together after a short split up, which was mostly my fault—excuse me, entirely my fault. And she wasn't too pleased about a couple of indiscretions that had occurred during our recent separation, either. Anyway, I was happy to have Chuck and his lady over for a nice, quiet dinner with my wife and my first-born son, Mitchell, who was still in diapers.

Lynne put out a lovely spread of heaping plates of spaghetti and meatballs, and when I asked where the utensils were, she told me to go get them myself. I went to the drawers, intent on pulling out knives, forks and tablespoons, but before I could assemble them properly, I got suckered from behind—thump—

a crushing blow on my once-again unprotected skull. She gave me a throbbing, pulsating goose egg, two inches high and still rising. I felt like Deputy Dog in the movie cartoons when he got whomped with a club by an ill-tempered Mrs. Deputy Dog. He'd sport a high-rise reddish goose egg with seven or eight hairs widely spaced out over a stretched lump of scalp.

I turned around, and Lynne just stood there with a look that said, "What? You're still standing?"

In the meantime, Chuck and Betty scurried out the door. (And I never saw Betty again until 2011, some 52 years later, when she and Chuck reunited.)

Fellow tenants would have heard the pandemonium of screaming and yelling, and I knew the boys in blue would be coming soon. The police showed up after I left and questioned Lynne about what had happened. She told them that there had been just a noisy misunderstanding and that we had patched up our differences. And in a way she was right. Not long after, we made a commitment to stay together because we had a young son and he needed both of us in his life.

3) MEL TURNBOW

I remember thinking to myself, "Oooooh, that was a good one!" after Turnbow cracked me with a big right hand at Montreal's Paul Sauve Arena in 1966.

MY FAVORITE MEMORY OF TEDDY McWHORTER

His pure, unadulterated joy after I knocked out Jerry Quarry in 1969. The fight was all but lost, but then I landed the big left hook that snatched victory from the jaws of defeat. When

Quarry was counted out, Teddy started jumping up and down in the corner, yelping and howling with unbridled emotion. It was like we'd reached our pinnacle. I remember thinking about how in the early days we'd sit in Glen's Pharmacy next door to the gym in Detroit and play "Our Day Will Come" by Ruby and the Romantics on the jukebox. It was like our theme song.

Teddy's two big dreams were for me to win the world championship and for him to open a hot dog stand (he claimed to have a secret recipe that would make him a millionaire). He died in 2003 at the age of 89, and I still miss him.

FANTASY FIGHTS I WOULD PAY TO SEE

JOE LOUIS VS. MUHAMMED ALI

Guys who stood in front of Joe and didn't move too much were in a lot of trouble, but he always had problems with stick-and-move guys—just look at his fights with Billy Conn and Jersey Joe Walcott. Ali was a lot bigger and punched much quicker than either Conn or Walcott—and he moved like a gazelle. I don't think Muhammed would have had any problem handling the Brown Bomber, either by late stoppage or unanimous decision.

SONNY LISTON VS. GEORGE FOREMAN

Explosive punching power puts both these guys on my list of the all-time top-10 heavyweights. They worked as sparring partners and were very familiar with each other's style, but in a real fight I'd give a slight edge to Liston—at least against the young version of Foreman. But in the incredible comeback George put together to regain the title after a 10-year layoff, he became a far more patient puncher while still being deadly accurate. It's conceivable that an older George could handle Sonny. Either way, a KO would end it.

SUGAR RAY ROBINSON VS. SUGAR RAY LEONARD AT WELTERWEIGHT

As great as Leonard was, I can't see this fight being more than mildly competitive. At his peak, Robinson was the greatest pound-for-pound boxer who ever lived—and he could beat you any way you wanted to fight. Nobody was slicker or quicker, but he could also stand his ground and brawl with the best of them. Leonard was a brilliant tactician and no slouch in the speed department, but I think he'd come up on the short end of a lopsided decision.

TONY ZALE VS. MARVIN HAGLER AT MIDDLEWEIGHT

The original Man of Steel versus The Marvelous One would be the ultimate war of attrition. Zale was a murderous body puncher who wore down his opponents before delivering the coup de grace, while Hagler ranks as one of the greatest southpaw punchers in any division. In my opinion, that would be the deciding factor. Marvin was a master at switching from southpaw to orthodox and back to southpaw without interrupting his punching rhythm, and that would be enough to eke out a narrow verdict.

Here are my all-time pick 'em bouts. On any given night either guy could win—and they'd all be entertaining as hell:

JACK DEMPSEY VS. MIKE TYSON

Dempsey wasn't big, but he was a relentless puncher, just like

Mike. With both guys firing their heavy artillery right from the opening bell, this one wouldn't last long. If I had to pick a winner, I'd go with Tyson because he was so good at overwhelming his opponents with non-stop pressure—especially early on.

IKE WILLIAMS VS. ROBERTO DURAN AT LIGHTWEIGHT

Williams's ferocious left hook vs. Duran's guile and iron will. What a matchup! This one would likely produce multiple knockdowns because neither guy would take a step backwards.

HENRY ARMSTRONG VS. MANNY PACQUIAO AT WELTERWEIGHT

Arguably the two greatest multidivision champions in boxing history. At a time when there were only eight universally recognized titles, Homicide Hank owned three of them, and Pac-Man has cemented his legacy by winning lineal world championships in four weight classes. If they fought 100 times, it would probably be close to an even split.

IF I HADN'T BEEN A FIGHTER . . .

I would've liked to become a criminal lawyer. I imagine that fighting to save people in court—even the guilty ones—must be pretty exhilarating. The only ex-fighter I know who became a criminal lawyer is Willie de Wit, who won a silver medal at the 1984 Los Angeles Olympics and went on to become Canadian heavyweight champion as a pro. He practices law in Calgary, Alberta, and says there are a lot of similarities between fighting in the ring and fighting in the courtroom.

Being a surgeon would be very rewarding, too. Only God is more powerful than a surgeon.

FAVORITE BOOKS

I've always appreciated the written word, and I still try to spend at least part of every day reading, whether it's a newspaper, a magazine or a good book (mostly nonfiction). Some of my favorites over the years have been *The Prophet*, by Khalil Gibran; *The True Believer*, by Eric Hoffer; and *The Presidential Papers*, by Norman Mailer.

FAVORITE MOVIES

A FACE IN THE CROWD (1959)

In his first big-screen appearance, Andy Griffith is sensational as an Arkansas hobo who's transformed into an overnight media sensation by Patricia Neal.

REQUIEM FOR A HEAVYWEIGHT (1962)

You knew there had to be a boxing movie on my list! This one kind of combines the sagas of Primo Carnera and Luis Firpo, and the all-star cast, led by Jackie Gleason, Mickey Rooney and Anthony Quinn, includes cameo appearances by a couple of guys I fought: a very young Cassius Clay (in the opening scene) and South American champ Alex Miteff.

RETURN TO PARADISE (1998)

Starring Vince Vaughn, Anne Heche and Joaquin Phoenix, this tale of friendship against the backdrop of the Malaysian drug trade really hits home.

FAVORITE MUSIC

I love the blues and country. I'm especially partial to Waylon Jennings, Merle Haggard, Willie Nelson, Muddy Waters, John Lee Hooker and Ray Charles. I loved Elvis when I was a kid, too. As for a memorable song, I think I'd go with "Seven Spanish Angels," a 1984 release by Ray Charles and Willie Nelson that briefly went to No. 1 on the country charts. I really liked it when it came out, and years later, when I heard it again just before I went to Albuquerque, New Mexico, to work with Johnny Tapia in 1996, I remember thinking it was a premonition that my son Stevie was going to die.

MY CULINARY EXPERTISE

I love to cook. I can make stuffed peppers, cabbage rolls, all kinds of stews and sauces, all kinds of fish. I like experimenting with different cuisines: Jamaican, Thai, Greek. A little bit of everything. But I'm no good at cleaning up afterward. I'd like to be a little less messy, because it drives my wife nuts.

THE BEST PLACES I'VE VISITED

Thailand and Bosnia-Herzegovina. The scenery, food and overall friendliness of the people make Thailand one of my favorite destinations. Bosnia-Herzegovina is my ancestral homeland, so it's always special to be so warmly welcomed by relatives and old family friends.

FIGHTERS I FOLLOWED AS A KID

Joe Louis, Sugar Ray Robinson and Willie Pep were three of the best in the business, so I watched them pretty closely. Two other guys I admired were Vince Foster and Eduardo Lausse. Foster was a hard-punching welterweight contender from Chicago who died in a car crash in 1949. Lausse, an Argentinean middleweight, had a murderous left hook and went 75–10–2 from 1947–60. Heavyweight Bob Satterfield was another big puncher I really liked to watch. He had a weird pigeon-toed stance, but he could knock anybody out with either hand.

REGRETS IN THE RING

It hurt seeing Ernie Terrell get the decision in our WBA title fight in 1965 because I know in my heart that I won. But balanced against the knowledge that my manager, referee Sammy Luftspring and the judges were muscled and threatened beforehand, I can understand it. If they truly believed they would be roughed up, what other result could I expect?

The most lingering regret from my career is not getting a shot at the British Commonwealth championship. When I think about how long the Brits rebuffed me—more than 15 years—and how the spineless Canadian Boxing Federation didn't lift a finger in protest or in any way support my efforts to secure a title shot, it still hurts. Hey, it might even have robbed me of a knighthood!

MEETING A PRINCE AND A PRESIDENT

As a Member of the Order of Canada (the country's highest civilian honor), I was invited, along with my second wife, Joanne, to a reception for Queen Elizabeth and Prince Philip in Ottawa in 2002. I'd been briefly introduced to the royal couple back in 1968, but this time I got a chance to speak to the prince as he made his way down the receiving line. I thought he looked pretty good for being 80—like an old movie star. As we shook hands, I said, "Prince, I met an old friend of yours a couple of months ago."

"Who's that, George?"

"Sir Henry Cooper."

When he asked if we ever fought each other, I related the story of Cooper's manager, Jim Wicks, telling me, "Henry doesn't even want to meet you socially." The prince responded with a clipped "Ha...ha...ha," then moved on down the line.

Back in 1971, the Yugoslavian consulate invited Lynne and me to meet President Josip Broz Tito and his wife, Jovanka, in Ottawa. Prominent Canadian athletes, politicians and business people of Yugoslavian descent were invited, including hockey stars Frank and Peter Mahovlich. The reception was originally planned for Toronto, but after *The Globe and Mail* ran some stories about possible assassination threats, it was moved to Ottawa. When Lynne and I were introduced, Tito asked where we lived.

"Toronto," I replied.

The president's people obviously kept him up to speed on what had been happening, because be responded by idly twisting a cigarette holder between his thumb and forefinger as he stared up at the chandelier and muttered, "Toronto . . . Toronto . . . *Guzva! Guzva!* [Turmoil! Turmoil!]"

Tito's reaction was so unexpected—and so comical—that I actually started to snicker. If his bodyguards from the Yugoslavian secret police noticed my little indiscretion, they didn't let on.

TRAINING AND PROMOTING

The first fighter I trained and managed after my retirement was Donnie "El Toro" Poole, a pretty good welterweight from Scarborough, Ontario. He was originally managed by my pal Ron DesRoches, who asked me to take a look at the kid. After turning pro in 1980, Poole reeled off a string of quick KOs and looked to be on the verge of going places when he all of a sudden got a big head and wanted out of his contract. To complicate the situation, I never had complete reins on him as far as training, so before long he was gone. Poole eventually signed with Dave Wolf (the guy who later turned Winnipeg's Don Lalonde into a world champ), but his career went south pretty fast.

Jimmy Gradson and Razor Ruddock were two other guys I was involved with. Gradson was tough as nails and could really punch, but he was also lazy and couldn't manage his weight properly. The first fight I ever promoted was between him and crosstown rival Eddie Melo, at 175 pounds. They really didn't like each other, and the CNE Coliseum was packed when they squared off on May 4, 1982. When Jimmy won on a last-round KO, it was like he was world champion; but he became so enamored with being king of his home turf—Queen and Bathurst—he forgot to train.

Shortly afterward, Gradson blew a $75,000 payday for a fight on CBS television because he couldn't make 160 pounds. Then I got a call for him to fight light heavyweight Donny Lalonde in Winnipeg after Lalonde's scheduled opponent pulled out at the last minute. I didn't want to take it because Jimmy was 208 pounds and the fight was in eight days, but he assured me he would KO Lalonde. Gradson trained himself down to 183 two days before the fight, but at the weigh-in, after being in a steam bath all night, he looked like a boiled chicken. Lalonde stopped him in 90 seconds.

I started working with Ruddock in 1985 when Ronnie DesRoches was his manager, and right away I could tell Razor had all the tools to be a world-class heavyweight. Before he beat former champ Mike Weaver in a 10-round decision in 1986, I took Ruddock down to Miami to spar with Larry Holmes, who was training for his title rematch with Michael Spinks. After three days, Larry's brother gave us our walking papers ("You gotta go") because Razor kept beating Holmes to the jab—outjabbing reputedly heavyweight boxing's greatest jabber.

Before the Weaver fight, Ruddock had nine months to go on his contract (I had 10 per cent of it), but even then I was telling his manager he should extend the deal. We had a good thing going, and I really believed Ruddock could become a world champion. But people get funny sometimes when it comes to success and loyalty. After Razor beat Weaver, he thought he could knock everybody out, so he just walked away and waited for the contract to expire. He ended up losing back-to-back fights against Mike Tyson five years later, but in my opinion he never came close to realizing his full potential.

What I went through with Ruddock pretty much soured me on training, and other than joining Murray Greig to work the corner for Canadian light heavyweight champ Danny Stonewalker in his 1990 WBO title bout with Michael Moorer and a later stint with WBO super flyweight champ Johnny Tapia, I never went back to it.

MISSING MEMORABILIA

In recent years I've gotten several requests to autograph and/or authenticate a lot of oddball memorabilia from my career—stuff like my old New York State boxing licenses, contracts for some of my bouts in the '60s, fight-worn gloves . . . even the boots that I supposedly wore while training for my second fight with Ali.

It didn't take a rocket scientist to figure out where the stuff was coming from: Irving Ungerman.

Soon after he became my manager in 1964, Irving and I agreed that Irving would save the gloves, robes, posters and other memorabilia from my fights because one day they might make nice keepsakes for my kids and future grandchildren. He said he'd take care of it, and from then on he scooped up whatever he could and put it away in storage. This was long before sports memorabilia became a huge industry, so I never gave it a second thought; it was enough to know that we had a verbal understanding that my stuff would be there when I asked for it.

In the years following my retirement I periodically asked Ungerman for the things he'd put away for me, but he always had some lame excuse about why he couldn't produce them. We were both leading busy lives, so I just let it slide—but I never forgot about the stuff. Then, one day in 2008, a guy called out of the blue and told me Irving's nephew—who may or may not have known the history—had been selling off my gloves, contracts and other items, including a large cache to Elite Sports Marketing, a well-known memorabilia outfit in Florida. I ended up paying them a visit in Tampa, and the owner showed me a canceled check for $45,000 that he'd given Ungerman—and that was just one payment!

I called Irving right away and told him I'd seen the check. "You told me you'd keep those things for my grandchildren," I said. "Even if they didn't want them, they could use the money to help with their education." He responded with: "What about my grandchildren? Don't they deserve something?"

What kind of twisted logic is that? No member of the Ungerman family ever traded punches with Muhammad Ali or Joe Frazier or George Foreman. There was no Ungerman DNA on those gloves and equipment. Yet here was this miserly multimillionaire trying to squeeze one last payday from stuff he had no right to sell.

In a 2010 interview with the *Toronto Sun*, Ungerman said he was "shocked and saddened" that I'd gone public with my bitterness over his memorabilia sell-off. He denied there was ever an agreement between us that the stuff still belonged to me. "I gave George plenty over the years, including helping him set up his Fight Against Drugs foundation," he told reporter Steve Buffery. I would love to hear how he helped me with the "Fight Against Drugs." What a load of crap!

But I must admit that my good friend Steve Stavro led a group of donors including the Greek–Macedonian community and Irving, who had been prodded to cough up at least a couple of grand on his part. This was to make a healthy down payment for a condo, after the Croation credit union had unceremoniously dumped my furniture and other belongings on my front lawn. The credit union closed on my mortgage after I'd missed a couple of payments and had not given me enough time to find a new lender.

MY "COMEBACK"

In the fall of 2010 I laced up the gloves for a three-round charity exhibition with comedian Rick Mercer, host of the CBC's hit series *The Rick Mercer Report*. Sponsored by the Alcohol and Gaming Commission of Ontario, proceeds went to the United Way and my Fight Against Drugs foundation. The ring was set up in the atrium of an office building in downtown Toronto, and an overflow crowd showed up to watch Mercer collapse like he'd been shot after I gave him a little tap.

That went a lot more smoothly than in 1996, when I was the cornerman for a boxing match between Owen Hart and Raymond Rougeau on the first World Wrestling Federation card ever held at Montreal's Molson Centre. The script called for Owen to get mad at me after the bout and push me out of the ring. At that point, I was supposed to pretend to punch him.

Well, things got a little carried away. With all that adrenaline pumping, Hart really gave me a good shove, and I reacted instinctively by throwing a left hook that laid him out cold! I felt terrible for the kid; I was 57 years old and hadn't thrown a real punch for years, but I just forgot to pull it.

PROFESSIONAL RECORD OF GEORGE CHUVALO

1956

April 23	Gordon Baldwin	Win: KO 2	Toronto
April 23	Jim Leonard	Win: KO 2	Toronto
April 23	Ross Gregory	Win: KO 1	Toronto
April 23	Ed McGhee	Win: KO 1	Toronto
June 11	Johnny Arthur	Win: UD 8	Toronto
Sept. 10	Joe Evans	Win: KO 1	Toronto
Oct. 22	Howard King	Loss: SD 8	Toronto
Nov. 19	Bob Biehler	Win: UD 8	Toronto

1957

Jan. 14	Sid Russell	Win: KO 1	Toronto
March 4	Walter Hafer	Win: KO 3	Toronto
March 25	Moses Graham	Win: KO 1	Toronto
April 22	Emil Brtko	Win: TKO 2	Toronto
June 6	Joe Schmolze	Win: KO 4	Fort William, Ont.
Sept. 9	Bob Baker	Loss: UD 10	Toronto

1958

Jan. 27	Julio Medeiros	Win: UD 10	Toronto
April 21	Howard King	Win: KO 2	Toronto
June 16	Alex Miteff	Draw: 10	Toronto
Sept. 15	James J. Parker	Win: KO 1	Toronto (Canadian title)
Oct. 17	Pat McMurtry	Loss: UD 10	New York

1959

| Sept. 14 | Frankie Daniels | Win: TKO 7 | Toronto |
| Nov. 17 | Yvon Durelle | Win: KO 12 | Toronto (Canadian title) |

1960

July 19	Pete Rademacher	Loss: UD 10	Toronto
Aug. 17	Bob Cleroux	Loss: SD 12	Montreal (Canadian title)
Nov. 23	Bob Cleroux	Win: UD 12	Montreal (Canadian title)

1961

March 27	Alex Miteff	Win: SD 10	Toronto
June 27	Willie Besmanoff	Win: KO 4	Toronto
Aug. 8	Bob Cleroux	Loss: SD 12	Montreal (Canadian title)
Oct. 2	Joe Erskine	Loss: DQ 5	Toronto

1962

Inactive

1963

March 15	Rico Brooks	Win: KO 2	Detroit
April 22	James Wakefield	Win: TKO 2	Windsor, Ont.
April 29	Chico Gardner	Win: KO 4	London, Ont.
May 18	Lloyd Washington	Win: KO 2	Battle Creek, Mich.
Sept. 27	Mike DeJohn	Win: MD 10	Louisville, Ky.
Nov. 8	Tony Alongi	Draw: 10	Miami Beach, Fla.

1964

Jan. 17	Zora Folley	Loss: UD 10	Cleveland
March 18	Hugh Mercier	Win: KO 1	Regina (Canadian title)
July 27	Don Prout	Win: TKO 3	New Bedford, Mass.
Oct. 2	Doug Jones	Win: TKO 11	New York
Nov. 10	Calvin Butler	Win: KO 3	Hull, Que.

1965

Feb. 1	Floyd Patterson	Loss: UD 12	New York
April 19	Bill Nielsen	Win: TKO 8	Toronto
June 7	Sonny Andrews	Win: KO 1	Saint John, N.B.
June 30	Dave Bailey	Win: KO 3	Regina
Aug. 17	Orvin Veazey	Win: KO 3	Regina
Nov. 1	Ernie Terrell	Loss: UD 15	Toronto (WBA world title)
Dec. 7	Joe Bygraves	Win: Pts. 10	London, England

1966

Jan. 25	Eduardo Corletti	Loss: Pts. 10	London, England
March 29	Muhammad Ali	Loss: UD 15	Toronto
May 14	Levi Forte	Win: TKO 2,	Glace Bay, N.S.
June 23	Oscar Bonavena	Loss: MD 10	New York
Aug. 16	Mel Turnbow	Win: KO 7	Montreal
Sept. 15	Bob Avery	Win: KO 2	Edmonton
Oct. 12	Dick Wipperman	Win: TKO 5	Montreal
Nov. 21	Boston Jacobs	Win: KO 3	Detroit
Nov. 28	Dave Russell	Win: KO 2	Saint John, N.B.
Dec. 16	Willie McCormick	Win: KO 3	Labrador City, Nfld.

1967

Jan. 16	Vic Brown	Win: KO 4	Walpole, Mass.
Feb. 22	Dick Wipperman	Win: KO 3	Akron, Ohio
March 20	Buddy Moore	Win: KO 2	Walpole, Mass.
April 4	Willie Besmanoff	Win: KO 3	Miami Beach, Fla.
May 27	Willie Besmanoff	Win: KO 2	Cocoa, Fla.
June 22	Archie Ray	Win: KO 2	Missoula, Mont.
July 19	Joe Frazier	Loss: TKO 4	New York

1968

June 5	Jean-Claude Roy	Win: UD 12	Regina (Canadian title)
June 30	Johnny Featherman	Win: KO 1	Penticton, B.C.
Sept. 3	Levi Forte	Win: KO 2	Miami Beach, Fla.
Sept. 17	Vic Brown	Win: TKO 3	Toronto
Sept. 26	Manuel Ramos	Win: KO 5	New York
Nov. 12	Dante Cane	Win: KO 7	Toronto

1969

Feb. 3	Buster Mathis	Loss: UD 12	New York
Sept. 8	Stamford Harris	Win: KO 2	Lethbridge, Alta.
Nov. 16	Leslie Borden	Win: KO 3	Kimberley, B.C.
Dec. 12	Jerry Quarry	Win: KO 7	New York

1970

May 1	Billy Tiger	Win: KO 10	Detroit
May 10	Gino Ricci	Win: KO 1	Kimberley, B.C.
June 30	Charlie Reno	Win: KO 3	Seattle
Aug. 4	George Foreman	Loss: TKO 3	New York
Aug. 15	Mike Bruce	Win: KO 2	Sarajevo, Bosnia-Herzegovina
Oct. 24	Tommy Burns	Win: KO 1	Hamilton, Ont.
Nov. 5	Tony Ventura	Win: TKO 4	Montreal
Dec. 11	Charles Couture	Win: KO 2	Youngstown, Ohio

1971

May 10	Jimmy Ellis	Loss: UD 10	Toronto
Nov. 17	Cleveland Williams	Win: UD 10	Houston

1972

Jan. 28	Charley Chase	Win: TKO 6	Vancouver (Canadian title)
Feb. 21	Jimmy Christopher	Win: KO 2	Winnipeg
May 1	Muhammad Ali	Loss: UD 12	Vancouver (NABF title)
Aug. 10	Tommy Burns	Win: KO 1	Nelson, B.C.
Sept. 5	Charlie Boston	Win: KO 2	Port-au-Prince, Haiti

1973

Sept. 25	Tony Ventura	Win: TKO 3	Cheektowaga, N.Y.
Oct. 30	Mike Boswell	Win: KO 7	Cheektowaga, N.Y.

1977

March 7	Bobby Felstein	Win: KO 9	Toronto (Canadian title)
Dec. 8	Earl McLeay	Win: KO 1	Toronto (Canadian title)

1978

Dec. 11	George Jerome	Win: KO 3	Toronto (Canadian title)

TOTAL BOUTS: 93 ✧ WINS: 73 ✧ LOSSES: 18 ✧ DRAWS: 2 ✧ KOS: 64

✧ Inducted into Canada's Sports Hall of Fame (Toronto), 1990
✧ Inducted into the World Boxing Hall of Fame (Los Angeles), 1997
✧ Named a Member of the Order of Canada (Ottawa), 1998
✧ Awarded a star on Canada's Walk of Fame (Toronto), 2005
✧ Invited to Ljubuski, Bosnia-Herzegovina, for the unveiling of a life-size bronze and granite statue of George Chuvalo, 2011

ACKNOWLEDGMENTS

IT'S impossible to condense a lifetime's worth of gratitude into a few sentences, but here goes. Most of all, I want to thank my wife, Joanne, for the love and support that's helped me want to stay alive, and Murray Greig, my longtime friend and confidant, for his perseverance on this project. My boxing career would not have been possible without Teddy McWhorter and all my sparring partners and opponents over the years, and, of course, thanks to my friends and fans across Canada and around the world who have always been in my corner.

—GC

THANKS to George for his years of friendship, trust and sensational lamb spaghetti; to Joanne for her patience and understanding; and to all the sportswriters who kept boxing in the spotlight during the golden era of the 1950s and '60s. Many historical blanks were filled in by gleaning old newspaper accounts on microfiche and reviewing yellowed copies of *The Ring* and *Boxing Illustrated*.

—MG

INDEX

and the media, 106–7, 150, 173, 179
  as trainer, 74, 97, 174, 248
Dundee, Chris, 106–7, 164
Dunlop, Bob, 251
Dunn, Richard, 255
Dunphy, Don, 57, 108, 109, 225, 269,
  282
Duran, Roberto, 71, 343
Durelle, Yvon, 75, 76–77, 87, 120, 204,
  339, 353
Durham, Yank, 191
Duvalier, François, 276
Duvalier, Jean-Claude, 276

E

Eagleson, Alan, 247
Earlscourt Boxing Club, 33, 38, 41
East, Packy, 148
East York Arena, 34
Eaton's, 29
Eddie (cousin), 180
Edmonton, 8, 117, 118, 165
Edmonton Sun, 119
Ed Sullivan Show, The, 139
education, 320
Edwards, Ronnie, 275, 276, 278
Elbaum, Don, 280, 281
Elite Sports Marketing, 351
Elizabeth II, 347
Elkind, Marvin, 154, 321, 333
Elliot Lake, 258
Ellis, Jimmy, 197, 198, 199, 223, 224,
  230, 248, 281, 356
El Rancho Motel, 218
Emery, Ray, 336
Enberg, Dick, 282
Erskine, Joe, 82–83, 90, 147, 160, 354
Eskin, Lew, 54–55, 183, 228
Espinoza, Gabe, 219
Etobicoke General Hospital, 299, 309
Evans, Benny, 269
Evans, Bob, 99
Evans, Joe, 49, 73, 353
Ewald, Ted, 88

Exile on Main Street, 335
Expo 67, 165

F

Face in the Crowd, A, 344
Famous Knockouts, 102, 284
fantasy fights, 341–43
Fariello, Joe, 216
Farley, Chris, 334
Fear Strikes Out, 145
Featherman, Johnny, 204, 356
Felstein, Bobby, 287, 288–90, 357
Felt Forum, 268
Ferguson, John, 243–44
Fernandez, Florentino, 230
Ferndale, MI, 89
Field & Stream, 298
5th Street Gym, 105, 106–7, 230
Fifth Dimension, The, 235
Fifth Estate, The, 10, 318–19, 320
Fight Against Drugs Foundation, 196,
  318, 324, 351–52
Fight of the Year, 145, 218
Firpo, Luis, 344
first night, 22
Fitzsimmons, Bob, 5
Fleischer, Nat, 148, 169, 175
Flores, Johnny, 223
Florio, Dan, 136–37
Fly, The, 332–33, 335
Foley, Vic, 48
Folley, Zora, 112, 113, 130, 181, 191, 211,
  281, 337, 354
football, 35
Foote, Arnold, 286–87
Foreman, George, 5, 219, 232, 233–34,
  281
  comeback, 239
  technique, 236, 262, 338, 339
  vs. Ali, 238, 266
  vs. Chuvalo, 4, 74, 92, 98, 175,
    236–37, 240, 356
  vs. Liston, 341–42
  as world champion, 261

Louis, Joe, 5, 86–87, 138, 141, 204, 269, 346
    on Chuvalo, 179
    as "special adviser," 154–55, 171
    on trading cards, 24, 29
    vs. Ali, 259, 341
    vs. Conn, 26
Louisville, KY, 101, 165
Louisville Courier, 101
love, 323–24
Lovett, Bunny, 108–9
Lucas, Richie, 25
Luftspring, Sammy, 56, 83, 156, 175, 346
Lujubuski, 243
Lumley, Joanne, 330
Lyle, Ron, 207, 229, 281

M

MacCorkindale, Simon, 330
Macdonald, Norm, 334
Machen, Eddie, 126, 130, 142, 152–53, 189, 205, 223
Macnee, Patrick, 330
Madden, Owney "The Killer," 59–60
Madison Square Garden, 93, 130, 136, 140, 199
    Chuvalo at, 4, 8, 56–57, 193, 205–6, 236, 268
Mad magazine, 335
mafia. *See* organized crime
Mahovlich, Frank, 347
Mahovlich, Peter, 347
Mailer, Norman, 344
Main Bout Inc., 163, 165, 166, 167
Maine, 198
Malden, Karl, 145
Malitz, Mike, 163, 164
Maloney, Arthur, 67–68
management, 47, 74
Man from Atlantis, 331
Manitoba Boxing and Wrestling Commission, 253–54
Maple Leaf Gardens, 38, 48–49, 141, 207–8, 210, 248

and the Ali-Terrell fight, 164, 165, 166–67, 179
Maravilla, Roque, 55
Marciano, Rocky, 5, 42, 49, 50, 126, 138, 141, 181, 200, 336
    contract offer from, 124
    death, 218
    as "special adviser," 154–55, 171
Marie (cousin), 68
Marquart, Billy, 206
Marquess of Queensberry rules, 52, 72, 98, 106
Martin, Leotis, 186, 191, 197
Massachusetts, 198
Masteghin, Giorgio, 161
Mathis, Buster, 133, 184, 188, 191, 206, 211–12, 218, 224, 248
    vs. Chuvalo, 214–17, 284, 356
Mavrovic, Zeljko, 243
Maynard, Bob, 212
McAlinden, Danny, 7
McBeigh, Tommy, 84, 86
    as manager, 75–76
    as trainer, 52, 55, 60, 61, 71–72, 73
McCauley, Dave, 130
McCauley, J.D., 245
McCormick, Willie, 184, 355
McCrory, Andy, 275
McDonald, Mickey, 30, 31
McGhee, Ed, 41, 353
McGrandle, Billy, 219
McKenzie, Merv, 167, 168, 169
McLeay, Earl, 214, 290–91, 357
McMurtry, Pat, 56–58, 59, 70, 81, 130, 210, 232, 353
McNeeley, Tom, 83, 126, 142, 147, 204
McWhorter, Teddy, 128, 137, 171, 253, 262
    appearance and background, 86–87
    character, 74, 341
    contracts, 125
    at fights, 97, 99, 100, 127, 131, 220, 227, 242, 250, 251, 262, 340–41
    as friend, 89, 101, 107, 109, 110, 217, 218, 341

McWhorter, Teddy (*cont.*)
  in Haiti, 275, 278
  as interim manager, 103
  in Paris, 160–61
  as trainer, 88, 94, 155, 173, 190, 199,
    230, 234, 288
  training methods, 91–92, 129–30,
    192
Medeiros, Julio, 50, 51–52, 138, 353
media
  Canadian, 7, 168–69
  race in, 139–40, 157–58
Mehmedbasic, Hajrudin, 241
Melo, Eddie, 348
memorabilia, 350–51
Mercante, Arthur, 131, 183, 236, 237, 238
Mercer, Rick, 352
Mercier, Hugh, 113, 114, 116–17, 119,
  219, 354
Merritt, Jeff, 206, 251
Mexico, 207
Miami, 7, 109–10
Miami Beach, 107
Miami Beach Boxing Commission, 109
Miami Herald, The, 107
Midnight Man, The, 329
Mignacca, Mrs., 28
Mignacca, Rollie, 28
Mildenberger, Karl, 197, 198
Milice de Volontaires de la Sécurité
  Nationale, 276–77
Milkovich, Johnny, 36, 67
Miller, Art, 230
Miller Lite, 330
Millie (cousin's wife), 180
Mississauga News, 288
Missoula, MT, 189
Miteff, Alex, 52–56, 55, 81, 94, 96, 106,
  223, 344, 353, 354
Moll, Dick, 189
Montgomery, Belinda J., 331
Monticello, NY, 136
Montreal, 79–80, 165
Montreal Canadiens, 244

Moore, Archie, 37, 42, 75, 103, 115,
  179, 232
Moore, Buddy, 186, 355
Moore, King George, 60, 72, 130
Moorer, Michael, 88, 239, 350
Morales, Edwin, 337
Morgan, Brian, 283
Mount Sinai Hospital, 199
movies
  Ali appears in, 56, 239, 344
  choice of, 74, 344–45
  Chuvalo appears in, 209, 329,
    331–35
Mowat, Farley, 305
Mowat, Glen, 34, 37, 38
Muhammad, Herbert, 163, 166
Murray, Jim, 169, 223
Myrtle Beach, 187

N

National Film Board of Canada (NFB),
  150
National Hockey League (NHL),
  243–44
National Hockey League Players'
  Association, 247
Nation of Islam, 115, 126, 149–50,
  150–51, 162, 163, 166, 171
NBC, 282
Neal, Patricia, 344
Nelson, BC, 272–73
Nelson, Willie, 345
Nesterenko, Eric, 244
Neuhaus, Heinz, 42
New Avengers, The, 330
Newman, Mel, 125
New York City, 7, 57, 132, 139, 206
New York Herald Tribune, 178
New York Post, 216
New York State Athletic Commission,
  142, 165, 191, 198–99, 216, 226,
  282
New York Times, The, 144, 145, 167,
  178, 195

statue, 243, 357
Stavro, Steve, 352
Steele, Richard, 204–5
Steward, Emanuel, 87–88
St. George's Day, 41
St. Mary's Roman Catholic Church
    boxing gym, 30, 31, 32
St. Michael's College, 35–36
Stone, Sammy, 230
Stone Cold Dead, 331
Stonewalker, Danny, 350
St. Rita's school, 23
Sullivan, Ed, 139, 141
Sullivan, John L., 60, 337
Sully's Toronto Athletic Club, 85, 245,
    284
Summerfield, Tracey, 251
Summerlin, Johnny, 87
Summit Series, 277
Sun, The, 160
SunPac, 287
Sylvio Cator Stadium, 277

T

T, Mr., 283
Tampa, FL, 22, 351
Tapia, Johnny, 320, 322, 345, 350
Telemedia radio, 282
    television, 26
    boxing on, 34, 119
    Chuvalo appears on, 40, 57–58, 102,
        139, 260, 268, 329–31, 352
    closed-circuit, 247
Terrell, Ernie, 94, 102, 112, 126, 205
    management, 153–54
    technique, 155
    vs. Ali, 163, 164, 166, 268
    vs. Chuvalo, 72, 156–57, 172, 175, 184,
        346, 355
    and world championship, 135,
        152–53, 197
    world ranking, 134
Texas, 134, 198
Thailand, 345–46

Thomas, Willie, 230
Thomson, Sonny, 37, 41, 71, 72
"Thrilla in Manila," 266–67
Tiger, Billy, 230, 356
Title Shot, 31
Tito, Josip Broz, 241, 347–48
Tomic, Fabijan, 243
Tom Rank, 263
Tonton Macoute, 276–77
Toronto, 30, 82, 147, 165, 207–8, 347–48
    media in, 7, 144, 168, 169
Toronto Argonauts, 267
Toronto Police, 299–300, 311
Toronto Star, 78–79, 167, 169, 179, 285
Toronto Sun, 351
Toronto Telegram, 54, 170, 208–9, 244
Toronto Western Hospital, 194
Torres, Jose, 235
Townsend, Billy, 48
track and field, 35
trading cards, 24, 29, 71, 172
trainers, 74, 192
Trojack, Steve, 252
Trotter, Ed, 93–94, 97, 103, 104, 107
True Believer, The, 344
TSN, 202
Tunney, Frank, 41, 48
Tunney, Gene, 57
Turman, Buddy, 140
Turnbow, Mel, 175, 183–84, 189, 215,
    340, 355
Turofsky, Lou, 54
Twentieth Century Fox Studios, 263
Tyson, Mike, 5, 53, 329, 343, 349

U

UFO sighting, 180
Ungerman, Irving, 136, 253
    background and character, 18, 74,
        125–26, 165, 166, 186–87, 233–34
    contracts and payments, 125, 188,
        247, 262
    and Fight Against Drugs Foundation,
        351–52

fight arrangements by, 157, 163, 164, 211, 217, 234, 247–48, 254
at fights, 132, 220, 227, 285–86
as investor, 200
as manager, 8, 120–21, 127, 128–29, 154–56, 190, 191, 192, 195, 208, 212, 216, 261
and the media, 139, 171, 195
and memorabilia, 350–51
as promoter, 179–80
Ungerman, Karl, 125
United Press International, 54, 209
United Way, 352
University of Toronto Schools, 63
Untouchables, The, 334
U.S. Supreme Court, 228

V

Valan, Harold, 215, 216, 217
Valdes, Nino, 42, 52, 78
Vancouver, 119, 165, 257, 258
Vancouver Sun, 266
Vaughn, Vince, 344
Veazey, Orvin, 148, 355
Ventura, Tony, 245, 284, 356, 357
Verdun, QC, 165
Vicks, 330
Vietnam War, 165, 166, 167, 169, 170
Villemain, Robert, 278

W

Wakefield, James, 92, 354
Walcott, Jersey Joe, 80, 148, 176, 341
Waldheim, Don, 206
Walker, Billy, 147, 161
Walker, Don, 134
Walls, Earl, 33, 42, 48
Ward, Forest, 206
Warden, Jack, 334
Warkworth Institution, 312
Warner, Don, 107
Washington, Lloyd, 93, 354
Wasser, Moe, 125
Waters, Muddy, 345

Wayne, Johnny, 40
Wayne and Shuster Show, The, 40, 330
Weaver, Mike, 349
weightlifting, 33
Welch, Raquel, 151, 164
Wells, Vernon, 333
We Need a New F-Word, 336
Wepner, Chuck, 206, 207, 209, 212
Western Canada heavyweight title, 291
Western Technical-Commercial School, 62, 63
Westphal, Albert, 159
Wicks, Jim, 159–60, 347
Wide World of Sports, 260, 268, 320
Willard, Jess, 329
Williams, Brian, 288
Williams, Cleveland, 60, 133, 134–35, 149, 184, 337, 356
vs. Chuvalo, 248, 249–50, 261
Williams, Dave "Tiger," 245
Williams, Ike, 343
Williams, James, 229
Williams, Paul, 331
Winnipeg Free Press, 254
Wipperman, Dick, 184–86, 189, 212, 213, 215, 245, 355
Wolf, Dave, 348
Woody, James J., 205, 206, 215
World Boxing Association (WBA), 152
and Ali's title, 125–26, 135, 153, 169
heavyweight elimination tournament, 191, 197–98, 199
rankings, 83, 135, 211
World Boxing Council, 126
World Boxing Hall of Fame, 5, 133, 205, 229, 357
world championship, 6, 152–53, 191, 197–99
Ali's title, 114–15, 125–26, 168
See also under World Boxing Association (WBA)
world heavyweight championship, 78
World-Telegram, 185
World Wrestling Federation, 352